Paul, Apostle of Weakness

Paul, Apostle of Weakness

Astheneia and its Cognates in the Pauline Literature

REVISED EDITION

DAVID ALAN BLACK

Foreword by
JAN LAMBRECHT

☙PICKWICK *Publications* · Eugene, Oregon

PAUL, APOSTLE OF WEAKNESS
Astheneia and its Cognates in the Pauline Literature, Revised Edition

Copyright © 2012 David Alan Black. All rights reserved. Except for brief quotations in critical publications or reviews, no part of this book may be reproduced in any manner without prior written permission from the publisher. Write: Permissions, Wipf and Stock Publishers, 199 W. 8th Ave., Suite 3, Eugene, OR 97401.

Pickwick Publications
An Imprint of Wipf and Stock Publishers
199 W. 8th Ave., Suite 3
Eugene, OR 97401

www.wipfandstock.com

ISBN 13: 978-1-61097-603-9

Cataloging-in-Publication data:

Black, David Alan.

    Paul, apostle of weakness : astheneia and its cognates in the Pauline literature / David Alan Black — Rev. ed.

    xx + 194 p. ; 23 cm. Includes bibliographical references and index.

    ISBN 13: 978-1-61097-603-9

    1. Astheneia—Biblical teaching. 2. Astheneia (The Greek word). 3. Bible. N.T. Epistles of Paul—Criticism, interpretation, etc. I. Title.

BS2655 A67 B58 2012

Manufactured in the U.S.A.

I dedicate this book to my wife of 35 years. It has been my honor and privilege to share her cancer journey for the past three years. Together Becky and I are rediscovering the secret of Paul's life: "For to me to go on living is Christ, and to die is gain."

Contents

Foreword by Jan Lambrecht | ix
Preface to Second Edition | xi
Abbreviations | xiii
Introduction | xv

1 Overview of the Pre-Pauline Development | 1
2 1 Thessalonians and Galatians | 9
3 The Corinthian Correspondence | 53
4 Romans, Philippians, and 1 and 2 Timothy | 112
5 The Pauline Concept of Weakness in General | 147

Bibliography | 167
Author Index | 181
Scripture Index | 185

Foreword

IT IS LAUDABLE THAT David Alan Black, after more than 25 years, provides a second edition of his Basel doctoral thesis *Paul, Apostle of Weakness*. This worthwhile second edition, with almost completely the same text as the first xerographic copy, is now printed properly and with footnotes instead of endnotes. Some of these notes are new, a few others expanded. The bibliography, however, is seriously updated.

The readers of this book will admire its simple but quite elegant style as well as Black's careful way of approach and balanced presentation of Paul's remarkably different ideas on weakness—anthropological, christological, and ethical. Moreover, Black brings all of us deeply to reflect upon our own finitude and limits, our sufferings and often powerlessness, and, mercifully, also upon the weakness of fellow companions. Paul's problems are acute especially in 1 and 2 Corinthians. His language can be paradoxical and provocative indeed: "Whenever I am weak, then I am strong" (2 Cor 12:10b). The new publication of Black's work continues to offer stimulating reading.

Jan Lambrecht
Professor Emeritus of New Testament and Greek at the Catholic University of Leuven, Belgium.

Preface to Second Edition

THIS BOOK WAS ORIGINALLY conceived in Basel, Switzerland, where I was enrolled as a student from 1980 to 1983. I wrote this book as my doctoral dissertation. I had no idea, when I first wrote it, the difference it would make in my life. Since its original publication in 1984, my life has undergone several severe tests. This was not completely unexpected. The problem of pain is as old as the human race. But until it becomes personal, until our own lives or homes or friends are hurting, it remains a purely theoretical matter. Each problem I've faced since writing this book has been a challenge for me. Yet at the same time I can honestly say that every challenge has been more than matched by God's power-in-weakness. *How odd*, I sometimes think to myself. *I spent a year writing a dissertation. I spent the past 27 years learning what it meant.*

The apostle Paul was no stranger to difficulty. He felt himself to be severely handicapped. He referred to his "thorn in the flesh" ("thorn" is possibly an under-translation). Whatever it was, it constantly tormented him. He felt like it was a stake upon which he had been impaled. Who among us does not have his or her thorn? Who has never felt hindered from fully serving the Lord because of some disability? But God has a way of using our thorns for his purposes. The great Baptist preacher Charles Spurgeon once said, "Grace grows best in winter." As I look back over the seasons in my own life I see that I've been forced to learn the lesson of my dissertation over and over again: The thorn may not be removed, but the grace is always sufficient.

In this second edition of *Paul, Apostle of Weakness* I have not produced a total rewrite of the book. Instead I have sought to update the discussion (and bibliography) and to more vigorously express my thoughts in language that is understandable to educated church people and not just to

Preface to Second Edition

scholars. Greek and Hebrew words have been transliterated and printed in italics, with an eye on readers who may not be familiar with the biblical languages. And I have used inclusive language in this edition, not because of any requirement of the publisher, but because it is the right thing to do.

Many have helped me with this revision, and I acknowledge their assistance with gratitude. Special mention must be made of my personal assistant, Mr. Andrew Bowden, who has helped me in innumerable ways; to the librarians at Southeastern Seminary, who were eager to help with biblical resources; to my faculty colleagues, whose encouragement was invaluable; and to my wife Becky, whose faith has inspired me almost daily to pursue a closer walk with Christ. To all these I am deeply grateful. I save one person for special mention. He is the one who heard Paul's thrice-repeated prayer that his "thorn" might be removed and who said, "I won't do it because I want you to learn that my grace is enough." For readers of this book, my simple prayer is: "May his grace be enough for you too."

Abbreviations

AB	Anchor Bible
AnBib	Analecta Biblica
BEC	Baker Exegetical Commentary on the New Testament
BHT	Beiträge zur historischen Theologie
Bib	*Biblica*
BibInt	*Biblical Interpretation*
BJRL	*Bulletin of the John Rylands University Library of Manchester*
BNTC	Black's New Testament Commentaries
BSac	*Bibliotheca Sacra*
BT	*The Bible Translator*
BZNW	Beihefte zur Zeitschrift für die neutestamentliche Wissenschaft
CBQ	*Catholic Biblical Quarterly*
CTR	*Criswell Theological Review*
FNeot	*Filologia Neotestamentaria*
GTJ	*Grace Theological Journal*
HNTC	Harper's New Testament Commentaries
HTKNK	Herders Theologischer Kommentar zum Neuen Testament
HTR	*Harvard Theological Review*
ICC	International Critical Commentary
Int	*Interpretation*
JBL	*Journal of Biblical Literature*
JETS	*Journal of the Evangelical Theological Society*

Abbreviations

JSNT	*Journal for the Study of the New Testament*
JSNTSup	Journal for the Study of the New Testament: Supplement
KEK	Kritisch-exegetischer Kommentar über das Neue Testament
Neot	*Neotestamentica*
NICNT	New International Commentary on the New Testament
NIGTC	New International Greek Testament Commentary
NTS	*New Testament Studies*
NovT	*Novum Testamentum*
ResQ	*Restoration Quarterly*
RevExp	*Review and Expositor*
SBLDS	Society of Biblical Literature Dissertation Series
SNT	Studien zum Neuen Testament
SNTSMS	Society for New Testament Studies Monograph Series
ST	*Studia Theologica*
THNT	Theologischer Handkommentar zum Neuen Testament
TNTC	Tyndale NT Commentaries
TWNT	*Theologisches Wörterbuch zum Neuen Testament*
TZ	*Theologische Zeitschrift*
WBC	Word Biblical Commentary
WMANT	Wissenschaftliche Monographien zum Alten und Neuen Testament
WUNT	Wissenschaftliche Untersuchungen zum Neuen Testament
ZNW	*Zeitschrift für die neutestamentliche Wissenschaft und die Kunde der älteren Kirche*
ZTK	*Zeitschrift für Theologie und Kirche*

Introduction

THE FOLLOWING STUDY IS an examination of every occurrence of *astheneia* and its cognates[1] in the Pauline epistles, both in their immediate contexts and in their relation to Pauline thought as a whole. The basic conviction upon which our study builds is that the concept of weakness, like other significant expressions in the anthropological sphere, is of profound importance in the religious terminology of the apostle Paul. It is obvious merely from a count of the occurrences of *astheneia*, etc. in the different books of the NT how predominately it is a Pauline word. It is missing altogether from 2 Peter, Jude, the epistles of John, and Revelation. In James and 1 Peter it occurs once only, and in Mark but twice. In all the non-Pauline writings the root appears only 39 times, and of these occurrences the great majority are in the Gospels, where it has the simple meaning of illness. In contrast to this, 44 instances of it occur in the Pauline corpus of letters, more than all the rest of the NT writings combined, and in much smaller compass, being limited primarily to his chief epistles, Romans and 1 and 2 Corinthians.

Numbers alone prove that *astheneia* must be regarded as a characteristic Pauline word, but over and above the significance of quantity is the special meaning the word comes to bear in his letters. Paul has made the word-group the vehicle of a profoundly important element in his teaching and parenesis. Indeed, one may even speak of Paul as the "Apostle of Weakness." The title is justified inasmuch as Paul has given a sharper theological definition to the word-family than is evident elsewhere, so that we may with some justification regard him as the creator of the "doctrine" of weakness. Not only is every essential point of the NT concept of weakness reproduced in the apostle's writings, but also Paul takes us a stage further by

1. *Asthenein, asthenēma, asthenēs.*

Introduction

his explicit identification of Christ and weakness, which gives to the primitive Christian motif a distinct Christological meaning. This development of the *theology* of weakness, if one can call it that, is characteristically Pauline. Only the author of Hebrews, who himself may have been a Paulinist, can be said to approximate the depth and meaning of the Pauline usage.

Not surprisingly, therefore, the Pauline concept and understanding of weakness is most extensively developed in his three longest doctrinal letters: Romans and 1 and 2 Corinthians. These epistles from the middle period of Paul's apostolic career have an unquestioned authenticity and chronological relationship firmly established by internal references to the collection for the poor. Within these writings Paul's thinking seems to have evolved in direct relationship to historical events. Of the major events in Paul's career, certainly the opposition of his enemies (whoever they may have been) played a sizeable role in this evolution. Especially 1 and 2 Corinthians suggest the supposition that only when Paul's active career brought him into contact with these opponents did he demonstrate with any specificity his understanding of weakness. Thereby the idea moved from the circumference to the center of his thinking, a phenomenon which is most clearly seen in the "Narrenrede" of 2 Corinthians 10–13, where from a purely lexical view we have the most frequent occurrence of the terms for weakness in the NT. This fertile soil of knowledge concerning the apostle's unique perception of weakness and its implications for Christian living is supplemented further by scattered occurrences of the words in Paul's other letters, which constitute an additional, and equally valuable, source for our understanding of the motif.

It is therefore all the more surprising that the Pauline weakness vocabulary has received virtually no intensive or comprehensive study. The brief article by Stählin in the *Theologisches Wörterbuch zum Neuen Testament*,[2] which first appeared in 1933, is already out of date and in need of supplementation. The discussion of "Schwachheit" by Link in the *Theologisches Begriffslexikon zum Neuen Testament*[3] treats the Greek terms, but only briefly examines the NT passages in which they appear. With reference to the distinctively Pauline usage, Link devotes only two pages to that discussion. The interpretation of the Pauline use of our words has until now centered almost exclusively on "problem" passages such a 1 Corinthians 8, 2 Corinthians 12, or Romans 14. The most important studies of the mean-

---

2. Stählin, "*asthenēs*, ktl," 488–92.
3. Link, "Schwachheit," 1101–05.

Introduction

ing of *astheneia*, etc. in specific contexts are those of Rauer,[4] Theissen,[5] and Güttgemanns.[6] The most thorough and complete investigations of the words at the height of their development (2 Corinthians 10–13) are by Käsemann,[7] Fuchs,[8] and Cambier.[9] These last three studies are especially noteworthy, albeit brief, attempts to explore the question. Special notes have been devoted to the word-group in various commentaries, but on a limited scale, and nowhere is the concept of weakness in Pauline thought examined in its totality. Therefore, this dissertation is an attempt to make at least a beginning in investigating comprehensively the fascinating subject of weakness language in Paul. The ground is not well trodden, and we hope therefore to make fresh observations.

METHODOLOGY

The method of word study proposed here is that outlined by James Barr[10] and modified by David Hill.[11] These authors emphasize the importance of the immediate context in which the words appear for the proper understanding of their meaning.[12] The basic principle is that the terms used by the biblical writers take their meaning primarily in relation to the context and the historical setting in which they are found. Receiving special emphasis is what Luther called the *sensus grammaticalis*: the plain and obvious significance of the words as their author intended them to be understood with reference to the contemporary situation. All application must be rooted in *this* meaning.[13] This exegetical-contextual interpretation of *astheneia* and

---

4. Rauer, *Die 'Schwachen' in Korinth und Rom*.

5. Theissen, "Starken und Schwachen," 155–72.

6. Güttgemanns, *Leidende Apostel*, 142–70. See also the Salzburg Diplom-Arbeit of Kitzberger, entitled "Die 'Starken' und 'Schwachen.'"

7. Käsemann, *Legitimität des Apostels*, 37–43.

8. Fuchs, "La faiblesse," 231–53.

9. Cambier, "Le critère paulinien," 481–518. We might also mention the recent popular work concerning the physically disabled in the Bible, edited by Schmidt and entitled, *In der Schwäche*. In the section on Paul (pp. 147–53), Lorch observes, "Doch in den Begriff 'astheneia' lässt sich alles das einbeziehen, was wir unter Behinderung verstehen" (p. 147).

10. *The Semantics of Biblical Language*.

11. *Greek Words*, 6–22, 294–300.

12. See Hill, *Greek Words*, 18.

13. For a brief explanation of this principle, see Blackman, "The Task of Exegesis," 6–7.

Introduction

its cognates then becomes the basis upon which the subsequent theological interpretation builds, thus making it possible to avoid forcing the terms into the investigator's own preconceived framework.

With this in mind, we may now indicate the exegetical procedures we will seek to follow in the subsequent study. First, a necessary preliminary to the study of *astheneia* and related words in Paul is their usage in both secular and Septuagintal Greek as well as in the non-Pauline writings of the NT. Although Paul gave the words a characteristic content, he inherited terms that had a previous history and that already possessed certain generally accepted meanings. We will therefore devote chapter 1 to the examination of the *astheneia*-termini in Classical Greek, the Greek LXX (including an overview of the relevant Hebrew equivalents), and the rest of the NT. This will enable us to determine the possible influence of those writings upon the language of Paul, and later to note points of similarity and contrast between the Pauline and the pre-Pauline usage as well as that of the other NT authors.

The second step, and according to the methodology proposed above an extremely important one, is to define the *astheneia*-termini from letter to letter and from context to context. Therefore all the passages in the Pauline literature where the words appear must undergo a detailed exegetical examination, thereby allowing the context to have its rightful place in investigation. This we hope to accomplish in chapters 2–4. Specifically, this stage of research involves the following three procedures. (1) First, the historical circumstances of each writing must be adequately accounted for. The letters of Paul that contain a weakness word are therefore arranged chronologically and discussed in light of their historical situation, and any problems that directly bear upon the study of the word (such as the identity of Paul's Corinthian opponents) are treated. The chronological study helps us to determine whether the words are used differently in the earliest and latest Pauline writings, while the historical study aids in the proper determination of the setting of the words (e.g., parenetic, didactic, apologetic, etc.). (2) Next, the terms must be subjected to a strict contextual analysis, including matters of textual criticism (where necessary), vocabulary, style, and syntax. (3) Third, the words must be analyzed in terms of the role they play in Paul's overall argument in the particular epistle under consideration.

Finally, it is necessary to investigate the relation of the motif of weakness to Paul's thought in general and thus to determine its function in Pauline theology. Therefore in chapter 5 we will seek to allow the terms, as illuminated and defined by their contexts, to delineate the role they played in the theological vocabulary of Paul. We hope thereby to make a helpful contribution to Pauline theology in particular and to NT theology in general. In the conclusion we will attempt to review the salient issues and to summarize the major results of our study of the Pauline weakness motif.

The major burden of this dissertation, therefore, may be simply summarized as follows: to define *astheneia* and its cognates from context to context as they appear in the letters of Paul and to reconstruct from this data the Pauline concept of weakness. The primary focus is upon the historical-literary context; the secondary focus is upon the relation of the words to their wider significance in Pauline thought. Such an investigation of Paul's weakness terminology, first in the immediate setting, and then in the broad, can lead to results that otherwise are too easily overlooked. *A priori* judgments about the meaning of the terms hinder rather than help the exegetical task and thus are to be avoided. Only when the historical situation and literary context are understood is the motif of weakness related to Paul's theology.

It should be acknowledged from the outset that our study is necessitated, as well as complicated, by the fact that the terms as employed by Paul are never explained or explicitly defined. Therefore, although we are treating a definite Pauline concept, we are not dealing with a specifically defined motif. Paul reveals no persistent tendency to express his ideas on weakness in a set phrase or even in similar phrases; instead, he employs a wide variety of formulations, each unique to its own setting. Nevertheless, we believe that our concern is with a fundamental, and partially unified, concept of Paul, not with a mere peripheral one. Paul is the first NT writer to use the words; he does so more often than all other NT writers combined; he builds most upon the concept of weakness. It is this unique "Pauline" use of the vocabulary of weakness that makes an investigation of this nature possible.

Perhaps at this point a word concerning Pauline authorship is in order. In this study we will examine all the NT epistles written under Paul's name that include *astheneia* or one of its cognates. Two short references to this word-group appear in epistles generally considered to be deutero-Pauline: 1 and 2 Timothy. While this is not the place to discuss the thorny questions of authorship, it may be said here that the problem of the Pastorals is not so acute in the case of *astheneia* and its cognates. The passages involved reveal no significant theological development and represent the common technical use of the root for physical illness. Nevertheless, for the sake of completeness, these passages must be considered.

Introduction

Finally, a study of this kind necessitates the use of a large number of general books on Pauline theology as well as the major commentaries on the Pauline epistles. The extent to which the writer is under obligation to these excellent aids will become obvious in the body and notes of this writing. While this monograph makes no pretense of supplanting the commentaries or other independent investigations of the words, it may serve to bring out in a more integrated manner the basic literary unity and theological perspective of the motif in Paul. At the very least, it will attempt to open up some new possibilities of interpretation which the reader may then assimilate into his or her own study of the terms.

1

Overview of the Pre-Pauline Development

It is not within the scope of the present study to pursue in any great detail the usage of *astheneia* and its cognates outside of Paul. But an assessment of the idea in the Pauline literature would be incomplete without at least a brief survey of the evidence provided by authors other than Paul. Our survey begins with a discussion of the etymology of the words, followed by an examination of the usage of the terms in Classical Greek, the Greek OT, the NT Gospels, and the non-Pauline epistles and Acts. Succeeding this is a brief introduction to the Pauline usage.

ETYMOLOGY

Words deriving from the *asthen*-root all have the basic meaning of "weakness," "impotence," "powerlessness," in contrast to the opposite notion contained in *dyna*-, which stresses capacity or ability. The word-group is formed with *a privativum* from *sthenos*, which means "Stärke, Kraft, Vermögen, Macht."[1] The combination *a-sthenēs*, therefore, means "ohne Stärke, kraftlos."[2] Chantraine unhappily admits that *sthenos* is a "terme archaïque sans étymologie."[3] The problem of recovering the etymology of *sthenēs* cen-

---

1. Frisk, *Wörterbuch*, 2.698.
2. Ibid.
3. Chantraine, *Dictionnaire Étymologique*, 1000.

ters on the suffix *-nos*, *-enos*, as well as the fact that *sthenos* is the only word in Greek with initial *sth*. Buck,[4] however, speculates that *sthenos* ("strength") derives from the weak grade of the Sanskrit root *sagh*, "be a match for," and this appears to be as good a suggestion as any. "Weak," being the opposite of "strong," is thus often expressed in the Indo-European languages with the negative compound "not-strong," the Germanic family being the only notable exception to this.

In Greek *sthenos* may be compounded with *dori-*, *empedo-*, *eury-*, *eu-*, *mega-*, *megalo-*, and *a-*. Several Greek names are formed by composition with *sthenos*, including *Agasthenēs*, *Dēmosthenēs*, *Eurysthenēs*, *Sthenelaos*, *Sthenelos*, *Stheneus*, and *Sthenios* (*-ias*), the latter name being used to designate Zeus and Athena. Names in composition attest the antiquity of the stem *sthen*, as Chantraine notes: "L'importance dans l'onomastique des composés en *-sthenēs* dénonce le caractère archaïque de *sthenos*, concurrencé ensuite notamment par *dynamis*. Mais *asthenēs* est courant."[5] Constructions from the root *asthen* appearing in the NT are *asthenēs*, *astheneia*, *asthenein*, and *asthenēma*. The latter term, while current in Hellenism, is found only once in the Greek Bible (Rom 15:1).

THE CLASSICAL USAGE

The terms for weakness have the advantage of being familiar to students of Classical Greek, where they were commonly used to express the idea of bodily weakness, i.e., illness. The three most widely used terms are *asthenein*, *astheneia*, and *asthenēs*. An example of this usage is Herod. 4:135: *hoi de anthrōpoi astheneias men eineken kataleiponto* ("the people are being left behind because of their imperfect health"). Thucydides (7:47) refers to a season in which humans are most liable to illness: *tēs hōras en hē asthenousin anthrōpoi malista*, while Euripides makes Orestes complain, *anarthros eimi kasthenō melē* (*Or* 228). The terms are also frequently used as antonyms for *dynamis*, *ischyros*, or *hikanos*. As early as Thucydides, *asthenēs* becomes appropriate to indicate such a contrast: *kai houtoi ouk astheneis, all hikanoi blapsai* ("These [enemies] are not weak, but able to injure," 1:35). Failure to make an alliance in preparation for war is evidence to Thucydides of a lack of wisdom and a weakness (*aboulia kai astheneia phainomenē*, 1:32). Aeschylus refers to one's "paltry wisdom" (*asthenei sophismati*, Pr: 1011),

---

4. Buck, *Selected Synonyms*, 296.
5. Chantraine, *Dictionnaire Étymologique*, 1000.

and Herodotus chides the Greeks for overestimating their own strength: *epistametha de tēn dynamin eousan asthenea* ("We know their strength is weak," 7:9a). In this same line of thought, old age is described by Antiphon as *astheneia gērōs* (4:3). In all these occurrences, the connotation that is suggested by the etymology of the words is never wholly absent.

Throughout Classical Greek the terms are applicable not only to physical weakness or impotence but also to economic matters. Herodotus refers to *hoi chrēmasin asthenesteroi* (2:88), while Aristophanes speaks of those who are "poor and famished, lacking all home supplies" (*tous penētas asthenountas kaporountas, Peace* 636). It is in the philosophical prose writers of the 5th century BC, however, that we find the most highly developed usage. Plato, for example, sees *astheneia* as a negative quality of the human soul, referring to *tēn tēs anthrōpinēs physeōs astheneian* (*Laws* 854). In the *Rhetoric* (1419a, 18), Aristotle describes the *astheneia tou akroatou* as an *astheneia charaktēros*, an "ethical weakness." This philosophical usage is, however, more the exception than the rule among the Classical authors.

These examples show that the Greek writers are often highly individualistic in their use of the words, so much so that it is impossible to detect a normal association that may have had an influence upon writers of the NT. It does seem clear, however, that the dominant sense of *astheneia* and its cognates in Classical Greek is non-ethical, the words being used primarily in terms of their physical or social connotations, while at the same time being capable of denoting the inward nature of humans.[6] Therefore, in summary we may say that the *asthen-*root in the earliest phases and down through the Classical period meant broadly "powerless," and thus was capable of taking on a wide variety of specific meanings as it was used in different contexts.

THE USAGE OF THE SEPTUAGINT

There appears to be much flexibility in the use of the word-complex in the LXX, which may be the reason for the confusingly large number of Hebrew equivalents. In all, the words occur eighty-three times in the Greek OT (outside of the Apocrypha, where the words are not of importance), approximating the total found in the NT. The Pentateuch and the historical

---

6. Cf. Chantraine (*Dictionnaire Étymologique*, 1000): "*asthenēs* 'sans forte' est un terme important; courant en prose, il présente un sens général, peut s'appliquer à la pauvreté, à l'insignifance, mais finalement est utilisé (par euphémisme) pour les malades."

books attest this group of words infrequently, the great majority of instances being found in the poetic and prophetic literature, in which both *asthenein* and *asthenēs* figure prominently. The sense of sickness is not attested in the LXX, unless one understands certain statements of the psalmist, as for instance his cry, *eleēson me Kyrie, hoti asthenēs eimi* (Ps 6:3), to refer to bodily weakness, i.e., disease.[7] The words are often used in the general sense of weakness, when, for example, in Gen 29:17 Leah's eyes are described as weak, and when in 2 Sam 3:1 the ruling power of Saul is spoken of as having grown weak (*ho oikos Saoul . . . ēsthenei*), in contrast to David's, which had grown stronger (*ekrataiouto*). The general weakness of humanity is the subject of the narrative concerning Samson, who correctly predicted of himself, "My strength shall depart from me, and I shall be weak (*asthenēsō*)" (Jud 16:17). Also included in this category is the reference in 2 Kgs 19:26 to those "weak in hand" (*ēsthenēsan tē cheiri*), and in Ezek 17:14 to a weak kingdom (*basileian asthenē*).

In the poetic and prophetic writings of Israel, the words are used in the great majority of cases in the specific sense of "stumble" or "fall," a notion practically foreign to the profane Greek understanding of *asthenein*. In a large number of instances *asthenein* represents the verbal forms of the root *kśl*, "stumble," "stagger," while *astheneia* often corresponds to the noun *mkśwl*, a "hindrance," or "stumbling block" (cf. Gk. *proskomma*).[8] This meaning is attested chiefly in prophecies announcing the judgment of God upon those who have rebelled against Yahweh and who, therefore, will "stumble and fall." One striking feature of these judgmental pronouncements is the recurrence of the third person future of *asthenein* to denote this stumbling. Indeed, the expression "the ungodly shall fall" (*asthenēsousin hoi asebeis*) in Zeph 1:3 is a convenient designation of the entire OT conception of spiritual judgment (cf. Prov 24:16; Jer 6:21; 18:15; Dan 11:14, 19, 33, 35 [Theodotion]). The Greeks possessed nothing that corresponded exactly to this Hebrew conception of *asthenein*. Ordinary Greek usage, as we have seen, normally understood the word in terms of natural weakness, without any further connotations of divine judgment.

---

7. Interestingly, in his prophecy against the "shepherds" (i.e., leaders) of Israel (Ezek 34:4), Ezekiel distinguishes between the "weak" sheep (*to ēsthenēkos*) and the "sick" one (*to kakōs echon*).

8. On the relation of *asthenein* to the Hebrew root *kśl*, see Barré, "Paul as 'Eschatological Person,'" 509–14.

Overview of the Pre-Pauline Development

THE NEW TESTAMENT GOSPELS

Apart from Jesus' statement on Mount Olivet that the flesh is *asthenēs* in contrast to the spirit that is *prothumon* (not *dynatē*) in Mark 14:38 (=Matt 26:41),[9] the terms are generally used as the most common NT expressions for illness, or bodily weakness. In the Synoptic Gospels, "weakness" is characteristically a Lukan term, though Matthew is not far behind. Mark uses the verb and the adjective once each. John, however, says there is an *astheneia pros thanaton* (John 11:4), language that bears a resemblance (perhaps only superficially) to his pronouncement in 1 John 5:16 that there is a *hamartia pros thanaton*. In John 6:2 the healing miracles of Jesus over the sick (*epi tōn asthenountōn*) are said to attest his Messianic power and to fulfill the prophecy of Isaiah: *autos tas astheneias hēmōn elaben* (Isa 53:4). This latter significance is present also in the Synoptists. Thus it is only with some reservation that one can speak of a theological usage of the words in the Gospels, though it does exist.

A survey of the material both in the Synoptists and John's Gospel reveals that the terms for weakness are most commonly used absolutely without the addition of *sarx* or *nosos* for sickness. The more significant references in the Evangelists can be conveniently arranged into three main categories:

1. Occurrences in the so-called "Sammlungberichten"—short passages that summarize Jesus' activity. An example of this is John 6:2: *etheōroun ta sēmeia ha epoiei epi tōn asthenountōn* (cf. John 2:23; 6:14). The use of the imperfect tense denotes the continuous nature of the action: the multitudes "were continually seeing" the signs he "habitually did" for the sick. This characteristic usage of "signs" (*sēmeia*) is significant, because it is the equivalent of the favorite word for the miracles of Christ in the Synoptic Gospels, *dynamis*.[10]

2. Occurrences in the commission accounts (the sending out of the apostles) in Matt 10:8 and in Luke 9:2; 10:9. In Luke 9:2, for example, the twelve disciples are commanded not only to preach the spiritual message (*tēn basileian tou theou*) but also to heal the sick: *kai iasthai tous astheneis* (=*asthenountas* in CKW Byz). The performance of such miracles

---

9. Hill correctly sees no foundation for the Pauline doctrine in this saying of Jesus, since in Mark *sarx* normally refers to the frailty of humanity, not to "life in opposition to God and the Spirit" (*Greek Words*, 242).

10. On John's preference for *sēmeion* see Morris, *Gospel of John*, 684–85.

serves to reveal the reality of the spiritual power and authority (v. 1) of the preachers. This juxtaposition of *dynamis* and *asthenēs* can hardly be coincidental (cf. Luke 10:9: "Heal those ... who are sick [*tous ... astheneis*], and say to them, 'The kingdom of God has come near to you.'").

3. Accounts that report specific healings. For instance, the healing of the nobleman's son in John 4:46–54, a case of healing at a distance, is a "sign" (*sēmeion*) of the power of Christ over our helplessness and disease (cf. v. 46, *ēsthenei*). The account exposes not only one's need but also Jesus' all-sufficiency. The women who followed Jesus, ministering with much faithfulness and devotion, are said to have "been healed of evil spirits and infirmities" (*apo pneumatōn ponērōn kai astheneiōn*), touched by the divine power of the Messiah (Luke 8:2). See also Luke 13:11, 12; John 5:3–7; and esp. John 11:1–6, the narrative of the raising of Lazarus, where the weakness-termini appear four times.

THE NON-PAULINE EPISTLES AND ACTS

The verb *asthenein* appears once in James 5:14 and three times in Acts (9:37; 19:12; 20:35), while the adjective *asthenēs* occurs in 1 Pet 3:7, Heb 7:18, and three times in Acts (4:9; 5:15, 16). There remain the four occurrences of the noun *astheneia* in Hebrews (4:15; 5:2; 7:28; 11:34) and its sole appearance in Acts (28:9). The impotence of the law as means of salvation is in view in Heb 7:18, while Peter speaks of the woman as the "weaker sex" (*hōs asthenesterō skeue*). The author of Hebrews infuses the noun with theological significance when he writes in 4:15 that Christ is able to sympathize with our weaknesses: *dynamenon sympathēsai tais astheneiais hēmōn* (cf. 5:2: *epei kai autos perikeitai astheneias*). The heroes of faith *edynamōthēsan* (11:34), a magnificent summary of the writer's concept of faith as that which overcomes and is always driving forward, never retreating (Paul ascribes as much to Abraham in Rom 4:19). Elsewhere, the word-group expresses weakness in the purely physical sense (cf. James 5:14; Acts 4:9; 5:15, 16; 9:37; 19:12; 28:9).

Overview of the Pre-Pauline Development

INTRODUCTION TO THE PAULINE USAGE

The root *asthen* appears in the writings of the NT eighty-three times and in the Pauline Epistles forty-four times, or 53 percent of the total.[11] The following table provides us with an overview of its distribution in Paul:

	Rom	1 Cor	2 Cor	Gal	Eph	Phil	Col	1 Thes	2 Thes	1 Tim	2 Tim	Tit	Phlm	Total
astheneia	2	2	6	1						1				12
asthenein	4	2	7			2					1			16
asthenēma	1													1
asthenēs	1	11	1	1			1							15
Totals	8	15	14	2		2	1			1	1			44

Based upon this table, the following observations can be made concerning the Pauline use of *astheneia* and its cognates. The first and most striking matter is their uneven distribution. The words are found most often in Romans, 1 Corinthians, and 2 Corinthians. In these three letters alone they appear thirty-seven times, or 84 percent of the total in Paul. On the other hand, the words are lacking altogether in Ephesians, Colossians, 2 Thessalonians, Titus, and Philemon. They are found infrequently in Galatians, Philippians, 1 Thessalonians, and 1 and 2 Timothy. The motif is most extensively developed in 2 Corinthians 10–13, in which the words appear fourteen times, the total for this letter. The second largest complex of the termini is 1 Corinthians (fifteen times), and the third largest is Romans (eight times). In other instances the terms occur only once or twice, sometimes with different connotations even within the same literary context (e.g., Gal 4:9, 13).

It is apparent at once that the major Pauline use of *astheneia* and cognate words is in those letters usually designated as "doctrinal" epistles (viz., Romans, 1 and 2 Corinthians). Furthermore, uneven distribution of the terms throughout the Pauline letters suggests a development. In view of the words' distribution in the letters to Corinth, it would appear that this evolution of thought took place in the Corinthian setting, for Paul uses the words far more frequently in 1 and 2 Corinthians than in any other of his letters. If figures can prove anything, these figures would seem to suggest that it was primarily in the Corinthian correspondence that the Pauline

---

11. Cf. Morgenthaler, *Statistik*, 79.

idea of weakness developed. However, it is enough to observe here that the words appear to play an important role in Paul's theological epistles; how great a role and what kind remain to be determined.

We now proceed to an examination of the Pauline use of *astheneia* and its cognates. Although there is every reason to think that Paul describes weakness in cases where he does not use the words, we have deliberately limited ourselves to the exegesis of passages where the words are actually found. While the terms are colored to a degree by the literary and popular, the Hebrew and Septuagintal usages, none of these usages can define what *Paul* meant by the terms and for which purposes he employed them. Therefore, while the study of the usage of the words in the pre-Pauline literature may be a necessary preliminary task, the meaning of *astheneia* and its cognates in Paul can be discovered only when we turn to the writings of Paul himself and let the apostle be his own interpreter. This appears to be not only the best method of investigation, but also the only valid one.

2

1 Thessalonians and Galatians

INTRODUCTION TO 1 THESSALONIANS

1 THESSALONIANS, WHICH CAN be dated fairly accurately in AD 52, was written soon after Paul's departure from Thessalonica, either during his brief stay in Athens or (more probably) shortly after arriving in Corinth. Paul writes the letter partly out of joy at the good report recently brought to him by Timothy, and partly to address a series of questions raised by the Thessalonian community. The epistle should be viewed against a background of eschatological excitement. Paul had instructed his converts in Thessalonica about the last things (1 Thess 1:9–10; 2 Thess 2:5), but because of Jewish opposition was forced to leave the city hurriedly, evidently without completing his instruction concerning the parousia. This led to a number of problems, not the least of which were the bewilderment in the community when several of their number died before the coming of Jesus (1 Thess 4:13–18) and the mistaken belief by some that the day of the Lord had already come (2 Thess 2:1–2).

Unprepared for the death of fellow Christians and uncertain as to the time of the promised parousia, the Thessalonians began to question whether or not they could trust Paul's word, and began looking anxiously for a definite sign of the Lord's coming (1 Thess 5:1–11). Thinking perhaps that their departed loved ones were unworthy of the parousia, they grew increasingly concerned about their own salvation. These doubts were fed by the intense persecution they faced at the hands of their fellow citizens (1 Thess 2:14–16). With problems like these, the danger of returning to their old life was very real (1 Thess 4:5–8). Moreover, some of the Thessalonians, preoccupied with the coming of Christ, neglected their daily responsibilities, refusing to work and relying on others for support (1 Thess 4:11–12; 2 Thess 3:1–15). Perhaps this attitude also involved sexual laxness (1 Thess 4:3–8) and disrespect for the leaders of the church (1 Thess 5:12–13).

Thus in spite of the overall healthy condition of the church (1 Thess 3:6; 4:1), needs still existed among the believers in Thessalonica. After a word of thanks and an explanation of his activities (1 Thess 1:2—3:13), Paul takes up the concrete problems that the community was facing and treats them in turn. The parenetic portion of the letter (4:1—5:22) can be divided as follows:

a) 4:1–8 regarding sexual purity;

b) 4:9–12 regarding brotherly love;

c) 4:13–18 regarding the parousia;

d) 5:1–11 regarding watchfulness; and

e) 5:12–22 regarding church life.

The epistle concludes with a benediction (5:23–24, 28) and final instructions (5:25–27).

EXEGESIS OF THE TEXT

The first[1] instance of the *astheneia* word-group in Paul's correspondence occurs in 1 Thess 5:14, where the apostle commands the Thessalonian

---

1. While recognizing the uncertainty of the chronology, both relative and absolute, of Paul's literary remains, we propose to examine his letters that contain an *astheneia*-word in the following order: 1 Thessalonians, Galatians, 1 Corinthians, 2 Corinthians, Romans, Philippians, 1 Timothy, and 2 Timothy. Though the question of dating is not without significance in a study that attempts to trace the development of Pauline thought, we cannot discuss here at length the reasons that lie behind our decision to arrange the letters in this order. Suffice it to say that there is general agreement on the order 1 Corinthians–2 Corinthians–Romans; see the introductory sections on these letters in Guthrie, *Introduction*; Harrison, *Introduction*; and Hiebert, *Introduction*, Vol 2. It is our position, in basic agreement with Harrison and Hiebert, that both 1 Thessalonians and Galatians were composed prior to the Corinthian epistles and that 1 Thessalonians is

Christians to "help the weak" (*antechesthe tōn asthenōn*). This clause is part of a larger series of admonitions recorded in 5:12–22, and together with the preceding and following exhortations and commands summarizes Paul's thoughts as he closes his first letter to a Macedonian church. In light of the obvious triadic arrangement in v. 12 and in vv. 16–18, it is tempting to arrange all of the exhortations into five groups of three main exhortations each. We may thus subdivide the injunctions in 5:12–22 as follows:[2]

Now we ask you, brothers and sisters,
- (1) to respect those who labor among you, and
   - who care for you in the Lord, and
   - who admonish you, and
- to hold them in the highest regard in love for their work's sake.
- Live in peace with each other.

Now we urge you, brothers and sisters,
- (2) warn the idle,
   - encourage the faint-hearted,
   - help the weak.
- (3) Be patient with all people.
   - Make sure that nobody pays back wrong for wrong, but
   - always try to be good to each other and to all people.
- (4) Always rejoice,
   - continually pray,
   - in everything give thanks; for this is God's will for you in Christ Jesus.
- (5) Do not quench the Spirit.
   - Do not despise prophecies. But
   - put all things to the test: hold on to the good,
      - abstain from every kind of evil.

---

the earlier writing; that Philippians was written during Paul's Roman imprisonment (*ca.* AD 60–62); and that the Pastorals, if Pauline, were written toward the end of Paul's life, sometime between the apostle's first arrival in Rome and his execution.

2. This series of triplets that to the present writer seems so obvious has escaped the notice of most commentators. Frame (*Thessalonians*, 192) alone approximates our arrangement. More recently, Wanamaker (*Thessalonians*, 190–92) seems to adopt our arrangement.

Paul, Apostle of Weakness

The triadic[3] structure of these exhortations reveals that Paul is taking up and treating in turn five principle subjects in the span of ten short verses:

(1) The church's responsibility to its spiritual leaders (12–13)

(2) The church's responsibility to its needy members (14a–c)

(3) The church's responsibility to all people (14d–15)

(4) The church's spiritual privileges (16–18)

(5) The church's spiritual responsibilities (gifts) (19–22)

Out of this extended passage several questions arise that bear upon our study of the Pauline weakness terminology. The first question, of course, concerns the exact definition of the words *tōn asthenōn*: what does Paul mean by "the weak"? The Greek words, taken by themselves, yield little help in answering the question. Therefore we are forced to broaden our investigation to include the context in which the words are found (vv. 12–22). One is immediately curious as to why the command to help the weak is included at this point, and in what connection it stands in relation to the other formulas that immediately precede and follow. It is obvious that before we can answer the question of the specific meaning of *tōn asthenōn*, a beginning at least must be made in ascertaining the position of the words within the context of vv. 12–22. Finally, there remains the broader question of the position of these verses within the argument of the epistle as a whole. Thus the difficulty of ascertaining the exact identity of "the weak" in 5:14 is compounded by other questions regarding the context, both near and remote, in which the words appear. These are difficult questions, but an answer to each can at least be suggested. It will be helpful if we discuss these questions in the following order (working from the general to the specific):

(a) the place of 5:12–22 within the letter;

(b) the relation of 5:14 to its immediate context; and

(c) the meaning of the adjective *asthenēs* within the context of 5:14.

---

3. The triadic arrangement of words, phrases, and clauses is remarkably frequent in 1 Thessalonians. In addition to the more obvious examples of triadic structure (e.g., 1:3 faith, love, hope; 2:10 holy, righteous, blameless; 2:19 our hope, our joy, our crown of glory; 5:8 faith, love, hope; 5:23 spirit, soul, body; as well as these triplets in 5:12–22), triplets may be discerned in 1:5, 8; 2:3, 6, 12, 15; 4:11, 16.

1 Thessalonians and Galatians

The place of 5:12–22 within 1 Thessalonians.

The first question we must raise is that of the relation of the injunctions in 5:12–22 to the rest of the letter. Are these various phrases a cluster of unrelated ethical exhortations, or do these exhortations and commands have immediate relevance to the specific situation in Thessalonica? In view of their wide applicability, many scholars view these various phrases as simple, general exhortations. Thus these admonitions are described as "general principles of Christian ethics,"[4] or "eine Reihe allgemeiner Ermahnungen,"[5] or simply as "Selbstverständlichkeiten."[6] One author gives the division 5:12–22 the heading: "Shotgun Paraenesis (Random Instructions),"[7] while another emphasizes its "general character."[8] E. Lohse no doubt summarizes the thinking of many when he writes (referring to the exhortations in 1 Thess 4:1–12; 5:13–22; and Romans 12–13): "In diesen Abschnitten werden nicht Weisungen erteilt, die durch bestimmte Vorfälle oder Anfragen der Gemeinde ausgelöst sind, sondern es wird traditionelles Gut entfaltet, um der Gemeinde zu zeigen, was ständig gilt und wie sie sich verhalten hat."[9] If this is true, then these verses contain only "general truths," and as such have little or no direct applicability to the Thessalonian community. Support for this view is adduced both from the catechetical nature of these admonitions as well as the similarity between these verses and the broad, comprehensive exhortations found in the parenetic portion of the letter to the Romans (esp. chap. 12).

However, while it *may* be true that these verses contain only "general exhortations," perhaps Paul is less arbitrary at this point than most scholars will allow. Paul's usual concern in his ethical teaching is to be both concrete and specific. V. P. Furnish, referring to such Pauline admonitions as are found in 1 Thess 5:12–22, writes:

> There is a sense in which such exhortations may be classified as 'basic principles' or described as 'general truths,' but this does not mean that the Pauline ethic is devoid of specific content. On the

---

4. Bruce, "St. Paul in Macedonia," 335.
5. Marxsen, *Einleitung*, 33.
6. Marxsen, "1 Thess 4, 13–18," 25n. Indeed, Marxsen maintains that "erst im 2 Thess liegen konkrete Ermahnungen vor."
7. Roetzel, *The Letters of Paul*, 41.
8. Guthrie, *Introduction*, 580.
9. Lohse, *Die Entstehung*, 27.

one hand, these 'general' exhortations are themselves directed to concrete situations and problems in Christian congregations. And on the other hand, they stand side-by-side with other Pauline admonitions—which are quite specific.[10]

This means that, although parenetic sections in Paul can appear to lack specific relevance, general admonitions may be tailored by Paul to fit particular needs and thus may refer to specific and concrete situations. Admittedly, most of the exhortations in 1 Thessalonians are general enough to be applicable to all Christian communities. It is also true that Paul normally deals with the major, pressing needs of a congregation in greater detail. Thus "we cannot . . . draw a full portrait of life in the Thessalonian community"[11] from these phrases in 5:12–22. However, since many of these injunctions can easily be associated with particular situations within the community itself (see below), there is no reason not to seek to define these associations to the greatest degree possible. If this can be accomplished, it follows that their lack of relation to the rest of the letter is only apparent.

At this point, we may briefly consider the argument based upon the close similarity between this passage and parenetic sections in Romans, an affinity that is used to advocate that Paul intends in 1 Thess 5:12–22 only to pass on traditional matter. Best, for instance, notes the similarities between these verses and Rom 12:9–13 and seeks to draw a parallel between the (apparently) unrelated injunctions of Romans and the exhortations here.[12] However, despite the remarkable similarities between these two passages, does this fact necessitate the conclusion that Paul must have used unrelated tradition in 1 Thessalonians? The question must also be asked why he would have chosen this particular parenetic material and not another with which to admonish the Thessalonian congregation. Moreover, why are these injunctions included at this point in the letter—indeed, why are they included at all? Comparisons of these verses to Rom 12:9–13 actually prove nothing, for even if Paul wrote a series of unconnected exhortations in Romans[13] this is no argument that he must have done so here. And even if he

---

10. Furnish, *Theology and Ethics*, 72–73. Bultmann ("Allgemeine Wahrheiten," 253) agrees: "Es ist nach allem verständlich, dass allgemeine Wahrheiten, sofern sie in der konkreten Situation als Anrede begegnen, ihren notwendigen Platz . . . haben."

11. Best, *Thessalonians*, 237.

12. Ibid., 241–42.

13. That Paul's exhortations in Romans should be regarded as relating to particular issues in Rome is argued by Campbell, "Romans III as a Key," 22ff., esp. 37–40.

1 Thessalonians and Galatians

did employ traditional material in 1 Thessalonians it can still be maintained that he molds it to the epistolary situation and applies it to the addressees.

We conclude, then, that there are no *a priori* reasons why Paul could not have been addressing specific issues in 5:12–22. But are there any positive indications that the passage in fact is related to the rest of the letter? We suggest that one such indication is the concern of 5:12–13, which resembles the concern of 4:9–10. Another, and weightier, indication is the subject matter of 5:14. The first two groups mentioned, i.e., the idle (*tous ataktous*) and the faint-hearted (*tous oligopsychous*), can be identified with a good degree of certainty as belonging to the Thessalonian community. *Ataktous* can easily refer to the unemployed believers who are admonished in 4:11–12, while *oligopsychous* is a fitting description of the grieving saints in 4:13–18. Furthermore, the injunctions in 5:19–20 clearly refer to those in the church who despise prophecy and who seek to regulate or suppress the activity of the Holy Spirit. Thus there is ample material in the letter itself to justify this relationship. Taken together, these considerations suggest that the admonitions in 5:12–22 are to be understood in relation to the whole of the letter and especially in relation to the parenetic section that begins in 4:1. Therefore, in this study our working hypothesis will be that the statement "help the weak" should become understandable when proper attention is paid to the immediate background of the letter, and that the total sense of 5:14 is probably best explained as a resumption of what was discussed *in extenso* earlier in the epistle. If this is true, any interpretation that ignores the historical and local situation, and thus the intent of Paul in including these injunctions here, can automatically be excluded.

The relation of 5:14 to its context.

Granted that in these verses Paul may be referring to relevant issues within the Thessalonian community, it is now incumbent upon us to seek to define that relationship as specifically as possible. This section does not purport to be an exhaustive exegesis of 5:12–22, and we limit our discussion to those issues in these verses that are of crucial import to our understanding of *asthenēs* in 5:14. As mentioned earlier, the general flow of thought in 5:12–22 can be divided into five parts, which we now proceed to discuss in order.

Paul, Apostle of Weakness

(1) 5:12–13 The church's responsibility to its spiritual leaders.

Verses 12–13 refer to the responsible leaders of the congregation who oversee the church life in the Thessalonian community. They are those who labor (*kopian*) at a specific duty (*to ergon*). Members are requested to fulfill two obligations (*eidenai* and *hēgeisthai*) and are commanded to fulfill a third (*eirēneuete*) in relation to these leaders. This is to be carried out in an attitude of love (*en agapē*) and with the highest good of the church in mind.

One difficulty here is determining what type of ministry is in view. It would seem at this early stage in the development of the church that a semi-structured leadership as it is referred to later in the NT was unknown. However, Leon Morris[14] aptly notes that the first Christian communities were in all probability organized on the model of the Jewish synagogue; if so, this would imply that the church in Thessalonica had a group of elders who exercised a degree of oversight in the congregation. Furthermore, we know from the Lukan account of Paul's missionary activity that Paul appointed elders "in every church" (Acts 14:23). There is no reason to doubt that this practice existed from the very beginning and included the Christian communities in Macedonia.[15] Finally, from a purely practical point of view, it is hardly conceivable that a group of Christians who gathered regularly for public worship and service could continue for long without some type of leadership and structure, no matter how rudimentary. It is therefore, we think, incontestable that "there was from the beginning in Paul's churches as well as among his missionary colleagues, a class of persons who by virtue of their work were entitled to esteem, and some at least to financial support. Such a group must have been *ipso facto* visible and distinguishable from the congregation."[16] We may assume, then, that suitable members of the Thessalonian congregation had been appointed by Paul to exercise oversight in the church and to serve as spiritual guides and teachers. Thus in these verses the church is viewed as an *organization*,[17] no matter how loosely we may want to use the term in referring to the Thessalonian Christian community. In this light, the language of vv. 12–13 presents itself conveniently

---

14. *Thessalonians*, 164.

15. F. F. Bruce notes that, though often contrary to modern missionary methods, Paul's consciousness of the presence and power of the Holy Spirit in his ministry enabled him to appoint as elders those who had been only recently converted to Christianity (*Acts of Apostles*, 296).

16. Ellis, "Paul and Co-Workers," 444. Bruce, "St. Paul in Macedonia," 340, agrees.

17. The word is used by Hendriksen, *I and II Thessalonians*, 133.

as a description of the congregation's responsibility to those who were designated as its leaders.

These newly appointed leaders are described in v. 12 as *tous kopiōntas kai proistamenous kai nouthetountas*.[18] The Greek construction plainly indicates that this is one group of leaders that exercises a triple function, and not three different groups. These leaders are those who toil (*kopian*) continuously in the service of the church by exercising leadership (*proistenai*) in the practical affairs of the congregation and by admonishing (*nouthetein*) its members in the ways of the Lord.[19]

Not without significance for our study is the fact that these three designations are appropriate to the actual situation of the letter's recipients. The leaders are first designated as "the laborers" who have the responsibility of correcting "the idlers," an obvious reference to the discussion in 4:9-12. The fact that they are leaders "in the Lord" emphasizes that they act in the interest of Christ and for the good of the entire community, not for selfish gain (against the idlers' accusations to the contrary). That they can "warn" the church calls attention to the fact that these leaders have every right to admonish the idlers, and that the idlers in turn must heed their warnings. It is not necessary to assume that these leaders had exercised authority in a tactless or unloving manner;[20] Paul's exhortation in v. 14 to be long suffering toward all members of the congregation does not necessarily imply that

---

18. The verb *kopian* possibly emphasizes the spiritual nature of the service being rendered. Paul can use the word of his own occupation at tentmaking (e.g., 1 Cor 4:12), though he also employs it to refer to his apostolic activity (cf. 1 Cor 15:10; Gal 4:11; Phil 2:16), as well as the labor of others in the church (e.g., 1 Cor 16:16; Rom 16:12). The word *proistenai* is not at this stage a *terminus technicus* for ecclesiastical office, but rather serves as a fitting description of Christian leaders who "stand before" the congregation as spiritual guides. Though the term includes both the sense of "to lead" as well as "to care for," the latter meaning predominates in 1 Thess 5:12: "der Ton liegt nicht auf ihrem Vorrang oder ihrer Vollmacht, sondern auf ihren Bemühungen um das ewige Heil der Gläubigen" (Reicke, "*proistēmi*," *TWNT* 6:701-02). Only later was the term used for an official administrative *office*, as in *Herm.* 2, 4:3, *hoi presbyteroi hoi proistamenoi tēs ekklēsias* (cf. Prast, *Presbyter und Evangelium*, 366). The verb *nouthetein* emphasizes instruction that is directed toward the will rather than the mind, and that seeks to correct wrong behavior. See Behm, "*noeō, ktl.*," *TWNT* 4:1013-16.

19. With Frame (*Thessalonians*, 192), we take the participles *proistamenous* and *nouthetountas* to be further descriptions of the initial participle *kopiōntas*; cf. also Morris (*Thessalonians*, 166): "The labor in question is that of exercising leadership and admonition, though this should not be understood as defining it exhaustively." For a more recent discussion, see Wanamaker, *Thessalonians*, 192.

20. So Morris, *Thessalonians*, 164-65.

the elders needed to be faulted for any previous attitude of impatience. On the contrary, Paul must enjoin respect for the church's leaders.

This he does by beseeching the Thessalonians to respect (*eidenai*)[21] and to esteem highly (*hēgeisthai hyperekperissou*) their leaders, and by commanding them to seek peace among themselves (*eirēneuete en heautois*). This must be accompanied by Christian love (*en agapē*) so that the building up of the church is unhindered by a wrong spirit. Since disobedience to the leaders of the church is in reality disobedience to Christ, the head of the church, the Thessalonians are urged to hold their leaders in high regard. The last injunction, "be at peace," which may be an allusion to Jesus' teaching (cf. Mark 9:50), is shown by *heautois*[22] to be co-binding upon the members and leaders of the church, since *both* groups have the responsibility of seeking mutual harmony.

(2) 5:14a–c The church's responsibility to its needy members.

In this section we have three brief imperatives which represent the duty of the church in relation to the idle, the faint-hearted, and the weak in the community. The precise meaning of these three clauses will be discussed in detail after a look at the admonitions that follow them in 14d–22.

(3) 5:14d–15 The church's responsibility to all people.

It is difficult to decide whether the final clause of v. 14 belongs to the group of injunctions that precedes or follows it. The fact that the clause is included in v. 14 in our modern translations is not in itself an argument for the former view. While it is possible that the injunction can be regarded as a general summation of the three preceding commands,[23] in light of the triadic structure in this section the admonition probably belongs with the two following commands concerning (a) the amelioration of the *lex talionis* of the OT, and (b) the expression of Christian love in good behavior. Furthermore, these three injunctions are tied together internally by an emphasis in each upon all people (*pros pantas, tis . . . tini, eis pantas*). If this division

---

21. On this unusual meaning of *oida*, cf. 1 Cor 16:18, *epiginōskete oun tous toioutous*.

22. The variant *autois*, read by p30, ℵ, D, and others, is probably to be taken with the rough breathing, and is therefore the equivalent of the better-attested *heautois* (A, B, D2, K, L, and most others).

23. So e.g., Best, *Thessalonians*, 233.

is correct, it is easy to see the more general admonition ("be patient with all people") being defined explicitly by the admonitions that follow: long-suffering (*makrothymein*) involves (negatively) the refusal of paying back evil for evil, and (positively) the pursuit (*diōkein*) of goodness in all areas of life.

It is not hard to see the applicability of these admonitions to the community. With idle, faint-hearted, and weak Christians comprising a segment of the membership and with the oppression from without, it was only too easy for the Thessalonians to become impatient or to want to retaliate when wronged. It is especially in such circumstances that love and patience must be expressed, writes Paul, because only by restraint and persistent kindness can the peace of the community and an effective testimony to the world be maintained.

(4) and (5) 5:16–22 The church's spiritual privileges and responsibilities.

In 5:16 Paul turns without any formal transition from the specific needs of the church to the needs of the community as a whole, first in reference to the Christian life in general (vv. 16–18), then in reference to manifestations of the Spirit-filled life within the church (vv. 19–22). In every circumstance of life, including the troubling experiences within the church and the difficulties of persecution from non-Christians, the Thessalonians are enjoined to constant joy, prayer, and thanksgiving (vv. 16–18a). This proper inner attitude is fully in keeping with God's desire for the Christian as it is revealed in Christ (v. 18b).

In vv. 19–22 the reference shifts to the special *charismata* in the church—the gifts of the Holy Spirit. These four verses contain five short but incisive imperatives. The first two are directed toward those who may have tended to de-emphasize the use of certain gifts in the church, especially prophetic revelations or other particularly ecstatic gifts. The Spirit is conceived here metaphorically as a fire that is in danger of being put out by those who suppress the *pneumatica*. The church, says Paul, must stop trying to extinguish this flame (*mē sbennyte*), nor must it any longer despise or suppress (*mē exoutheneite*) activities of Christian prophets who bring the word of God.

The final three imperatives are given to counterbalance what Paul had just commanded. Because mere enthusiasm cannot necessarily be equated with genuine Spirit-worked activity, the Thessalonians are to test (*dokimazein*) all the *charismata* (here, especially prophecy), holding fast to that which is good (*to kalon*), while rejecting every kind of evil manifestation (*pantos eidous ponērou*). These last two commands are coordinate and define the positive and negative results of the testing of the *charismata*. With these injunctions Paul has completed his paraenesis and moves on to conclude the letter with a prayer (vv. 23–24), three requests (vv. 25–27), and a benediction (v. 28).

Three conclusions follow from the examination of the text of 1 Thess 5:12–22. First, the overall structure of the passage reveals that these seventeen brief exhortations are not as unrelated to each other or to the rest of the letter as a casual reading of the text might suggest. It is not difficult to regard vv. 12–22 as a resumption of the paraenesis that began in 4:1, nor is it difficult to envisage a development from the first series of injunctions in vv. 12–15, where Paul's concern is with Christian behavior, to the last series, vv. 16–22, where the inner life of the Christian is in view. Second, if our subdivision of these verses is correct, the clauses in 14a–c (of which *antechesthe tōn asthenōn* is one) can be understood as a bridge between the injunctions to the community concerning its leaders in vv. 12–13 and those regarding all people in vv. 14d–15. Thus the church is admonished first about its responsibilities as a Christian community, both to its leaders and to its needy members, before Paul brings up its responsibilities to those outside of the congregation. In this way we can account for not only the statement "help the weak," but also the two preceding admonitions to warn the idle and to encourage the faint-hearted.

Finally, it is evident that Paul's concern in these verses is not merely to list traditional parenetic material but to discuss (though briefly) serious matters that have come to his attention and that are directly relevant to the situation in Thessalonica. Though Paul's tone in this passage is one of gentle appeal rather than forceful command, we should not conclude from this that the apostle had nothing of a serious nature to impress upon his hearers. Paul's tone is brotherly, but it is also "big-brotherly," to borrow Morris' expression.[24] In light of the above discussion it is better to conclude that Paul considered a proper relationship to the idle, faint-hearted, and weak in the church of paramount importance for the overall health of the Thessalonian community. Consequently, the exhortations and commands given here are not merely general truths, but can be considered decisive

---

24. Morris, *Thessalonians*, 166.

1 Thessalonians and Galatians

reminders of central concerns that Paul occasionally alludes to or develops elsewhere in the letter, and as such have specific applicability.

The meaning of the adjective asthenēs within the context of 5:14.

No evaluation of *tōn asthenōn* in this passage would be adequate without a consideration of two preliminary matters. The first question concerns the identity of the *adelphoi* to whom these admonitions are being directed. Does the text imply that Paul at this juncture "vertit suum sermonem ad doctores" (Theod. Mops.), or does he address the entire congregation?

Some commentators (notably G. Friedrich and Masson) would prefer to extend the identification of the elders mentioned in vv. 12–13 into v. 14, except whereas in the preceding verses they are spoken *of*, here they are being spoken *to*. According to this interpretation, the verb *nouthetein*, which is found in both v. 12 and v. 14, is considered to be the sole responsibility of the leaders, who are described in v. 12 as *hoi nouthetountes*. Masson[25] says further that it hardly makes sense that the apostle, after calling the church to respect its leaders and their duties, should now turn to the entire congregation and tell them, "*You* do the work of the ministry." These scholars also point out that the entire passage seems to have a ring of authority to it such as only the church leaders are assumed to possess.

However, while it is true that the leaders of the church are described as "admonishers," in Pauline thought this fact in no way exempts the community as a whole from participating in mutual exhortation and admonition (cf. 5:11 *dio parakaleite allēlous kai oikodomeite eis ton hena, kathōs kai poieite*). Furthermore, the *adelphoi* who fulfill the duties of v. 14 can easily be said to *include* the leaders of the community. Perhaps the most forceful objection, though, is the repetition of *adelphoi* in v. 14. In the parenetic section of 1 Thessalonians (4:1—5:22), each time the term *adelphoi* is expressed (4:1, 10, 13; 5:1, 12, 25) the *entire* congregation is being addressed. The occurrence of *adelphoi* in 5:14 would be the only exception to this usage. In all probability, it is precisely *because* it appears that these injunctions were the responsibility of the leaders alone that *adelphoi* is repeated. The word serves to clarify that the following injunctions, like the preceding ones, are given to all and not only to the church elders. Their responsibilities include admonition, but not to the exclusion of the participation of others. The verdict therefore must be given with most commentators that

---

25. Masson, *Thessaloniciens*, 73.

these injunctions are being directed to all church members and not only to their leaders.[26]

The second question concerns the identification of the phrases "the idle" and "the faint-hearted" that precede the phrase "the weak." These three ascriptions can be considered as particular references to three sections in the Thessalonian church. The first two groups, as suggested earlier, can easily be identified with the unemployed and the disheartened who are addressed in 4:9–12 and 4:13–18 respectively. These groups are not to be considered "parties," and Paul makes no conscious attempt to distinguish them in his paraenesis from the *adelphoi*. However, since all the members of the church could hardly have been the type of people involved in idleness and disorderly conduct, or could have been inordinately anxious about the death of Christians, it is likely that we have to do with sections of the community, all three of which may have been sizable.

The first group, *hoi ataktoi*,[27] is the subject of Paul's admonitions in 4:9–12, where the theme is brotherly love.[28] Though Paul may have in mind only a few individuals who are idle, it is more likely in view of the attention they receive that he is here referring to a larger segment of the congregation. They are not only addressed as *adelphoi* (v. 10) and are large enough in number to bring disdain upon the entire church by a bad testimony to outsiders (v. 12), but are also in danger of disrupting the feeling of the community as a family (vv. 9–10). Waiting for the end, these Christians live in idleness and have abandoned their normal responsibilities. Ironically, it appears that the presumption of an imminent return of Christ, which Paul

---

26. *Modern* commentators, that is. The Greek fathers for the most part held to the other opinion; cf. Chrysostom: *"pros tous archontas dialegetai"* (cited by Eadie, *Thessalonians*, 201).

27. The adjective *ataktos* means not only "idle," but also "disorderly," and thus designates "den Menschen als den, der sich ausserhalb der notwendigen und gegebenen Ordnung stellt" (Delling, *"tassō, ktl.,"* TWNT 8:49). Spicq (*Notes de Lexicographie*, 1.159) makes a similar observation: "Les Thessaloniciens *ataktoi* s'émancipent à l'égard d'une règle de la vie communautaire." See also the extended note on *atakteō* and its cognates by Milligan, *Thessalonians*, 152–54.

28. In 1 Thess 4:9–5:11 we find a series of didactic sections each with the introductory formula "now concerning..." (*peri de* or *de . . . peri*, 4:9, 13; 5:1). This phenomenon, familiar to us from 1 Corinthians (e.g., 7:1, *peri de hōn egrapsate*), might suggest that Paul is replying to points raised in a letter from the Thessalonians. There is, however, no positive evidence for this, and it is just as possible that the questions raised at Thessalonica were communicated to Paul orally by Timothy; cf. Manson, *Studies*, 274–75.

1 Thessalonians and Galatians

himself believed and taught,[29] led to an unpauline eschatological "super-enthusiasm" resulting in the neglect of worldly duties.

Paul's reproof of these Christians is as interesting as it is instructive. Beginning with a word of praise for the brotherly love (*hē philadelphia*) of the Thessalonians, he moves almost imperceptibly from this general statement on love (vv. 9–10a) to its application in a particular situation (vv. 10b–12). True brotherly love, writes Paul, is seen on the one hand when believers work in order to support themselves and their dependents.[30] On the other hand, for believers to be guilty of idleness and sponging off their fellow Christians is an appalling denial of the *philadelphia* that should be mutually enjoyed in the community. Furthermore, Christians who are dependent on the support of others, yet who could support themselves, are a poor testimony of the gospel and bring dishonor upon the church. Thus Paul lays down a general principle of life that he then applies to a specific concern: love of the community involves responsible behavior, but a parasitic life only takes advantage of another's love and therefore is a scandal to Christianity. For this reason, the *ataktoi* must return to their occupations.

In the prolonged homily on the second advent in 4:13–18 the second group of Thessalonians, who may be described as *oligopsychoi*,[31] comes to the fore. In this passage Paul speaks of the events of the end time, when Jesus Christ will return, the dead shall rise, and the living shall be caught up to meet the Lord in the air. It is obvious that Paul's primary concern in these verses is not theological but practical, i.e., to deal with the anxiety of those Thessalonian Christians who have recently lost friends or loved ones. The theological content found here has the sole purpose of supporting the one end in view: *hina mē lypēsthe* (v. 13), "that you no longer grieve." Paul writes that those who are anxious over the question as to whether the Christian dead would experience the parousia can be comforted by the knowledge that the *first* thing to occur is the resurrection of those who sleep in Jesus.

---

29. Mearns ("Eschatological Development," 137–57, esp. 146–48), however, argues that the Thessalonians did *not* expect the second coming at the time of Paul's writing 1 Thessalonians, and thus that this could not have been their motive for giving up their work. According to Mearns, it was not until Paul had instructed them of the imminent return of Christ in 1 Thessalonians that he could accuse them of more than laziness (cf. 2 Thess 3:6–15). Mearns's suggestion is not plausible and made less so by the fact that the nearness of the parousia is already an assumption throughout the first letter (cf. esp. 1:10; 3:13; 5:1–11, 23).

30. Here Paul is possibly reminding the community both of his earlier oral instruction to work as well as his own incessant toil during his stay in Thessalonica (cf. 2:9).

31. See Dihle, "*psychē, ktl.*," *TWNT* 9:666–67.

No one can say with certainty why these Thessalonians believed the Christian dead were going to miss the parousia. Evidently Paul had not been able to instruct them earlier that the resurrection of the Christian would coincide with the return of Jesus. Perhaps too the dead were considered unworthy to participate in the parousia.[32] The Thessalonians may have regarded death as unnatural and due only to sin and disobedience. The severe punishment of Ananias and Sapphira (Acts 5:1–11), a story no doubt often recounted in the early church, only reinforced this view. Apparently the early Christians at first neither expected death for themselves nor accepted it as normal when it did occur among their number.[33] Paul deals with this problem in highly apocalyptic language in 4:13–18. He states that departed loved ones of those who sorrow are, in Christ, still worthy of the blessings of the End. In fact, they will even be allowed to precede the survivors to meet the Lord in the air. Then *all* Christians will participate in the eschatological life with Christ. Paul therefore closes this section by stating that this certainty is cause for mutual encouragement: those who through sorrow and doubting have become *oligopsychoi* can now find consolation at the thought of the resurrection of the dead at the parousia.

Having suggested plausible interpretations for "the idle" and "the fainthearted," we are now in a position to attempt an explanation of the significance of the words *tōn asthenōn*. From a purely linguistic point of view, the translation "the sick" is possible, but the meaning of physical weakness is rendered unlikely in a context that emphasizes only spiritual matters.[34] Many scholars have sought to interpret the terms in light of Paul's usage of *asthenēs* and cognate words in other letters. The most widely held view is that *tōn asthenōn* refers either to those who are hesitant about matters concerning the eating of food offered to idols (cf. 1 Corinthians 8) or to Christians who adhere to vegetarianism and the strict observance of a religious calendar (cf. Rom 14:1—15:6).[35] However, not only does this

---

32. Moore, *The Parousia*, 108–110.

33. Cf. Mearns, "Eschatological Development," 141.

34. But see Wanamaker (*Thessalonians*, 198): "Linguistically it [the term 'weak'] could also refer to the physically weak or to the economically needy. This latter deserves some consideration since *proistamenous* ('those who care for') from v. 12 might allude to caring for the needy."

35. Thus Best, *Thessalonians*, 231, and Stählin, "*asthenēs, ktl.*," *TWNT* 1:490. Wohlenberg (*Thessalonicherbrief*, 113) compares the expression with Romans 14 and 1 Corinthians 8, concluding that the weak are those "deren Glaube noch schwach war und deren Gewissen sich in die christliche Freiheit nur schwer zu finden wusste." He quotes

1 Thessalonians and Galatians

interpretation overlook the fact that 1 Thessalonians can provide the clue that makes the definition of *asthenēs* possible, the text itself speaks against this identification. Nothing in the letter suggests that the Thessalonians had such difficulties with diet or holy days as the "weak in faith" in Corinth and Rome faced.[36] Therefore we have to reject outright any interpretation that ignores the background and setting of 1 Thessalonians by jumping to (supposedly) parallel texts of Pauline letters.

Frame suggests a completely different solution to the problem.[37] He advocates that the weak are "those who are tempted to impurity," and that Paul treats this issue in detail in 4:3-8. However, while this view has the advantage of relating the designation in 5:14 to the broader context of the letter, its force is weakened by several difficulties. First, Frame's arrangement places Paul's discussion of "the weak" (4:3-8) *before* his treatment of "the idlers" (4:9-12) and "fainthearted" (4:13-18). This would suggest the order: weak, idlers, fainthearted. In 5:14, however, the appellation "the weak" is given the final position. If Paul were treating these subjects in order, it is more likely that he would have reiterated the terms in the same sequence. Another difficulty with the moral interpretation is that nowhere in Paul's discussion of 4:3-8 are the sexual offenders described, either explicitly or implicitly, as "weak." On the contrary they are portrayed as intentionally wronging and taking advantage of others (v. 6), burning with passionate, uncontrollable lust like the heathen (v. 5), and willfully rejecting divine counsel (v. 8). But perhaps the most forceful objection to Frame's position that may be offered is the word *antechesthai* itself. *Antechesthai* means essentially to "devote oneself to," to "cleave to," and thus comes to mean

---

with approval Grotius: "qui libertatem christianam nondum plane intelligunt." Friedrich (*Thessalonicher*, 248) takes basically the same position: "Wer die Schwachen sind, ist aus dem Text nicht zu entnehmen. Wahrscheinlich sind damit ganz allgemein die im Glauben Schwachen gemeint, die Paulus auch der Gemeinde in Rom ans Herz legt, damit sie sie in ihrer Gemeinschaft aufnimmt (Röm. 14, 1)." Dobschütz (*Thessalonicher Briefe*, 221) is less specific: "sittliche Schwäche," as is also Rigaux (*Saint Paul*, 584): "faible dans la foi." Masson (*Thessaloniciens*, 74) alone is hesitant to go beyond what is known of the believers in Thessalonica, designating the weak as "des members de 1' Eglise qui ne sont pas capables de marcher seuls et ont toujours besoin d' appui."

36. See Gaventa, *1 and 2 Thessalonian*, 82: "In 1 Corinthians Paul uses the term 'weak' of those Christians whose faith is not sufficiently strong to allow them to eat food that has been sacrificed to idols (see, for example, 1 Cor 8:7-14, and the similar discussion in Romans 14). First Thessalonians offers no evidence that such difficulties plagued the community at Thessalonica, and the term may generally apply to those who are vulnerable to pressure of various sorts."

37. *Thessalonians*, 198.

"help," "assist."³⁸ We would normally expect Paul's language to be stronger toward this group than the verb *antechesthai* allows. Paul's command to "abstain from immorality" (4:3) clearly implies antinomian conduct among this company of Thessalonians. The apostle makes it plain that Christian liberty does not permit believers to defraud their brothers and sisters. If, as we can easily infer from the text, these Christians were actually engaged in various forms of sexual sins, it hardly seems likely that Paul would sound so lenient in 5:14. Those who are disobedient to God in sexual matters are strongly reproved by Paul, as in 4:6-8, and in other contexts the apostle can command the church to excommunicate the offender (e.g., 1 Cor 5:1-5). Because sexual impurity corrupts the whole of the community, Paul is always firm to advocate strict separation of those unrepentant of extramarital relations from the rest of the church (cf. 1 Cor 5:6-12). Therefore, though one cannot be dogmatic on the point, it is nonetheless difficult to see Paul using a term like *antechesthai* to designate the attitude and action of the community toward the morally rebellious.³⁹

In our view, it seems more natural in terms of the context of 4:1—5:22 to interpret the words *tōn asthenōn* as referring to those Thessalonians who were worried about the delay of the parousia and who consequently were in danger of giving up hope. Paul deals with the question of these anxious Christians in the second half of his discussion of eschatological topics (4:13—5:11), that is, in 5:1-11. Whereas the problem in 4:13-18 concerned the fate of the dead, the topic of 5:1-11 is the concern of the Thessalonian Christians about the definite time of the promised arrival of Jesus. These believers are "weak" in that they have grown weary of waiting for the End and thus face the danger of being overcome by spiritual sleep.

This view commends itself for a number of reasons. First of all, it relieves us of the difficulty of trying to interpret the words *tōn asthenōn* apart from what is known of the local situation in Thessalonica. Second, it has the

---

38. Hanse, "*echō, ktl.*," *TWNT* 2:827; Thayer, *Lexicon*, 49. The verb (composed of *anti* "against" and *echesthai* "to hold oneself") is found only in the middle voice in the NT and means literally "to keep oneself directly opposite to anyone, hold firmly to, cleave to." The primary sense here is that of "keeping one's self directly opposite to another so as to sustain him" (Vincent, *Word Studies*, 4. 49).

39. It is instructive to note in passing that Paul bases his appeal in 1 Thessalonians against fornication not on the law, but on the assumption that if the Thessalonians recognize the presence of the Holy Spirit in them they will act accordingly: "Die eigentliche Begründung aber für das Verbot ist nicht gesetzlich, sondern echt paulinisch: Gott hat seinen Geist gegeben (v. 8). Dieser wohnt in den Gläubigen (1 Kor. 6, 19). *Darum* ist ein neues Leben gefordert" (Baltensweiler, "1 Thess. 4, 3-8," 12).

advantage of fitting in nicely with the general structure of the paraenesis running through 4:9–5:11, which is comprised of three sections, each of which deals with a particular subject: (a) 4:9-12, the necessity of work as an expression of brotherly love; (b) 4:13-18, the fate of the Christian dead at the time of Jesus' coming; and (c) 5:1-11, the necessity of watchfulness in view of the uncertainty of the parousia. Third, it is in keeping with the movement of thought that is marked by the use of *peri de* or *de . . . peri* ("now, about the subject of . . ."), found only at the beginning of each of these three sections. Thus in 4:9—5:11 Paul may well have had in mind three groups in the community who were in need of special attention and admonition, to whom he refers successively in 4:9-12, 13-18, and 5:1-11. Those who are idle (*tous ataktous*) Paul exhorts to go back to work and stop depending on the charity of fellow Christians. Those who are disheartened (*tous oligopsychous*) at the passing of loved ones Paul encourages with the news that the dead in Christ will precede the living into the heavenly kingdom. And those who have grown weary (*tōn asthenōn*) Paul admonishes to persevere in the faith and to prepare themselves for the imminent day of the Lord.

A number of exegetical and contextual points lends additional support to this interpretation, of which the following are the most important. First, the view is in keeping with the strongly eschatological tone of the letter: the community in Thessalonica was a church longing for the coming of the Lord. Perhaps this intense expectation of the parousia had led not only to idleness but also to a weakened, threatened faith. These newly converted Christians, expecting an immediate parousia issuing in sudden glory, were now faced with its delay, and even the most alert members were in danger of compromising their vigilance. Thus the expectation that the kingdom would soon break into the world may have left some unprepared to endure the severe adversity of the present life.

Second, the broader context of the letter itself lends to the words *tōn asthenōn* the sense of "weary," or "defeated." From what we know in the preceding chapters Paul had every reason to be anxious about the spiritual fortitude of the church in Thessalonica. Their faith was constantly undergoing great duress. They had given themselves without compromise to Christ, and immediately severe testing had come into their lives. It is even possible that some of the deceased for whom the Thessalonians were so anxious had fallen to the persecution at the hands of non-believers.[40] The stress of life in the midst of such suffering must have been tremendous. Little wonder, then, that there were "weak" Christians among the members of the community.

Throughout the letter Paul is anxious to point out that the persecution of the Thessalonians was not abnormal, but rather was to be expected as the credential that authenticated their reception of the word of God (2:13–16). They had turned to God from idols, and had consequently suffered for their faith (1:3, 9). Suffering is not an exception but the rule of Christian living (3:1–5). Paul had sent Timothy to strengthen their faith lest they become unsettled by undergoing severe trials (3:2). He acknowledges that their steadfastness is being tested by the Tempter who would thwart all of Paul's previous efforts on their behalf (3:5). For this reason Paul wants to return to Thessalonica to supply what is lacking in their faith (3:10). But since he cannot go, he prays for their inner strength (*eis to stērixai hymōn tas kardias*, 3:13) and exhorts them to a posture of alertness, like a soldier who dons defensive armor in preparation to receive an assault (5:8).

Thus it is not improbable that the weak in the community are singled out in 5:14 for mention (along with the idle and fainthearted) because the majority of the congregation (the strong), themselves able to withstand the battering to their faith, had refused to come to the aid of those who were growing weary. It was only too easy to lose patience with the infirm brothers and sisters and to give up on them. Paul, however, insists that the stronger in the community are to prove their strength by aiding and supporting the weaker members. In spite of their failings and weaknesses, they must be accepted, borne up, held fast, and nurtured (*antechesthai*).

Finally, it is not difficult to envisage Paul addressing these demoralized and distressed Christians in 5:1–11. These Thessalonians are overwhelmed by the prolonged persecution and the uncertainty caused by the delay of the parousia. The danger was very real of being overcome by spiritual sleep. Therefore Paul must enjoin the church to watchfulness, emphasizing that the parousia will come suddenly and that all must accordingly be alert. Believers can be ready for the day of the Lord, not by knowing when it will occur, but because they live "in the light" and stay awake. Thus it is

---

40. "Vielleicht sind einige der Verstorbenen, über deren Tod die Thessalonicher so betrübt sind (4, 13), sogar Märtyrer gewesen, die bei den Verfolgungen ihr Leben haben lassen müssen" (Friedrich, *Thessalonicher*, 205).

1 Thessalonians and Galatians

possible that these verses have reference primarily (though not exclusively) to the weaker members of the church. Because they have relevance to all members, they are addressed to the community as a whole (5:1, *adelphoi*).

Paul concerns himself with two major topics in this passage: (a) the time of the parousia (vv. 1–3), and (b) watchfulness (vv. 4–11). Paul's basic point is to remind these Christians both of the certainty and unexpectedness of the parousia. Though the Thessalonians were fully aware of the unpredictability of the End, they had in the meantime been reminded of their own *Sterblichkeit* and feared for their own position. There is irony in Paul's statement that they "know perfectly" (*akribōs oidate*) that the day is secret, for they not only appear confused about the subject, but Paul himself feels compelled to address the matter in the verses that follow. Paul therefore writes that the day of the Lord is certainly coming (*hēmera kyriou . . . erchetai*), but *when* it will come no one can know, for it will arrive like "a thief in the night," unexpectedly and suddenly. However, though the time of the parousia cannot be determined, it is as certain as giving birth is for a pregnant woman (v. 3).

In the next section (5:4–11) Paul warns the church that ignorance of the date of the parousia is no excuse for unrighteous behavior. He first reassures the Thessalonians that the day will not overtake (*katalambanein*) them, and as a result they have nothing to fear in the coming destruction of which Paul now writes (v. 4). This is because they are of a different character than the unbelievers as "children of light" and "children of day." This fact, however, entails the outworking of their character as believers in a life that conducts itself in accordance with the light and day (v. 6). Paul therefore enjoins them to wakefulness and sobriety. They must stay alert (*grēgorein*) by expressing the realities of their life in Christ by temperate behavior (*nēphein*).

That these Christians were weak and in need of strength and hope underlies the whole passage, but it comes to the surface most clearly in v. 8: "But since we belong to the day, let us be self-controlled, putting on faith and love as a breastplate, and the hope of salvation as a helmet." The Thessalonians, writes Paul, now must arm themselves with faith, love, and hope. Believers can be prepared for the arrival of the Lord by bearing the armor of God, which strengthens their inner person and focuses their hope upon the salvation to be revealed in Jesus Christ (v. 9), who died in their place (v. 10a). In the final analysis it is not of importance whether they presently are living or asleep, as it is the privilege of every believer to share in the life of the risen and returning Christ (v. 10b). Paul thus can close this section with an exhortation to mutual edification and encouragement (v. 11).

CONCLUSION: THE WEAK IN THESSALONICA

Any interpretation of 1 Thess 5:14 faces certain difficulties that make it impossible to do more than offer a hypothesis as to what Paul meant by *tous ataktous, tous oligopsychous,* and *tōn asthenōn*. If, however, the contextual arguments presented above are valid, the words are seen to fit neatly into a pattern. A good number of exegetical points lends support to the interpretation that these three designations refer to three specific sections in the church that are dealt with at length earlier in the letter. The idle and the fainthearted are relatively easy to identify with the unemployed and mourning within the community who are addressed in 4:9–12 and 4:13–18 respectively. The identification of the weak is more difficult, but we can suggest with a measure of plausibility that *tōn asthenōn* refers to those who are in need of perseverance in the midst of severe trials and who are exhorted to watchfulness in 5:1–11.

To many this will seem like reading a good deal into an otherwise simple expression. They have a point. All that can be said with certainty is there were apparently in the Thessalonian church some members whom Paul could describe as "weak" and who were in need of support and help by the other members. However, if we are to conjecture, it seems to us to be more in accordance with what we know of the community in Thessalonica to associate the weak with those who have become weary of waiting for the parousia. We can be certain that the delay of the End was a matter of concern within this early Christian community. We can also assume that as these Christians sought to live in accordance with what Paul had taught them, trials had entered their lives that incessantly wore on their endurance. It is certain too that some of the members, worried and anxious that the delay of the parousia meant perhaps their own death, were in immediate danger of giving up all hope. Therefore, it is altogether possible—if not probable—that Paul had these Christians in mind when he wrote 5:1–11 and when he later commanded the church to "help the weak."

INTRODUCTION TO GALATIANS

The occasion, purpose, and message of the letter to the Galatians are transparent. Not long after Paul left Galatia, certain "disturbers" (cf. 1:7, *hoi tarassontes*)—commonly identified as "Judaizers"—appeared there and demanded as signs of complete salvation circumcision and the works of the Mosaic Law. They claimed to represent the mother church in Jerusalem, a fact which no doubt influenced many of the fickle Galatians to receive their message.[41] The new missionaries had also attacked Paul personally, alleging that he was an impostor who acted without authority, and impugning the motives of his Galatian mission. This contradiction of his authority and gospel led the apostle to write at once, and with great passion, the rigorous polemic known as Galatians.

The letter is devoid of Paul's customary felicitations and thanksgivings. The apostle immediately takes up his defense against the false teachers by establishing his independence from the Jerusalem church and by defending the divine origin of the gospel that he preached (1:6—2:21). His primary purpose in this section is to show that the turning away in Galatia was a serious departure from the true gospel. The Galatians were to understand that they had received from the new missionaries a false account of Christianity (1:6, *heteron euangelion*), a "revised version of the Gospel."[42] This antithesis between the true and false evangel, seen as early as the introduction (1:1), dominates much of the letter to the Galatians.

In 3:1—5:1, having established the legitimacy of his apostleship and message, Paul proceeds to discuss the true meaning of the law, and shows by the illustration of Abraham that a person is saved on the basis of faith apart from works. In the section of the letter that specifically concerns our study (4:1–20), he proceeds from his negative polemic against the law to a positive statement of Christian liberty, and shows that Christians, as children and heirs, are no longer slaves to the elements of the world but are free to serve the true God. Circumcision, the observance of Jewish (or pagan) calendars, or any other ritual avails the believer in Christ nothing.

---

41. These "troublemakers" are usually identified with the emissaries of James (2:12), although it is also possible that there were enough native Jews in the Galatic territory to account for this enthusiasm for Jewish customs. If they were official representatives of the Jerusalem church to Galatia (cf. 2:4, 12; 5:12), Paul did not know them personally (cf. 5:10, *hostis ean ē*, "whoever he is"). Possibly they were also members of the zealot sect (cf. 1:14; 4:17); so Reicke, *Neutestamentliche Zeitgeschichte*, 165.

42. Manson, *Studies*, 170.

Therefore, since Christians are no longer slaves, it is foolish for them to turn back to the observance of such regulations.

In chapter 5 Paul recapitulates his main argument that believers are free from the law both by emphasizing the responsible use of freedom and by warning the Galatians against a false understanding of freedom that leads to libertinism. This brings him to write a series of practical exhortations (6:1–10) that are followed by the letter's conclusion (6:11–18).

EXEGESIS OF THE TEXTS

In the letter to the Galatians, weakness language occurs only twice but in two closely related places. The neuter plural adjective is found in the formulistic phrase *ta asthenē kai ptōcha stoicheia* ("the weak and beggarly elements") in 4:9, while *di astheneian tēs sarkos* ("on account of a weakness of the flesh"), a reference to the occasion of Paul's Galatian visit, appears in 4:13. Since both of these references are in highly polemical settings, it seems evident that each plays a vital role in Paul's argument against the legalistic threat to the Galatian churches. But because the terms are employed in two different paragraphs with differing themes and perspectives, each occurrence must be studied individually if we are to understand the specific role the motif plays in the argument of the author in Galatians.

Galatians 4:9

The first occurrence of *asthenēs* is in the section that comprises 4:8–11, where Paul begins a lengthy appeal to the Galatians based on his previous assertion that all Christians are sons and heirs of God and therefore free from the law. Although it would be a mistake to try to force logical cohesion all through this section—Galatians being an emotional *apologia pro vita sua*—we can reconstruct with some accuracy the apostle's train of thought in the broader context as follows: (a) in 4:1–7 he first illustrates the freedom of the Christian with an example from ordinary life concerning the legal status of a child; (b) in 4:8–11 he shows that the special observance of certain portions of the Jewish sacred calendar is a return to the "elements" from which the Galatians had been saved; and (c) in 4:12–20 Paul makes a personal appeal to the Galatians, based on his former relationship with them, to accept him and his message. The uniquely Pauline expression *ta asthenē kai ptōcha stoicheia* in 4:9, which is to be understood in conjunction with the parallel expression in 4:3, *ta stoicheia tou kosmou*, suggests a relationship of some sort between the first two of these paragraphs, i.e., between 4:1–7 and 4:8–11. This relationship is probably best understood in terms of Paul's concept of the status of Christians prior to the coming of faith. In 4:1–11 his main concern is to contrast the former condition of his readers with their new state after being converted. Since Paul views the human condition apart from Christ as servitude to "the elements of the world" (4:3), he is surprised to hear that the Galatians are ready to sacrifice all the privileges of their new religion by going back to their former state of slavery under these elements (4:9). Formerly the Galatians, mostly pagans, had been under bondage to heathenism, but have since "come to know God" (4:9). Do they now wish to enslave themselves again, this time to Judaism and its rituals?

Paul argues against returning to the elements first of all with an illustration of guardianship (4:1–7). The condition of humanity under the law is inferior, writes the apostle, because a person under law is like an heir who has been placed under a guardian and has no freedom of action. With this familiar custom the Galatians are to realize that, by returning to their former condition, they would be losing, not gaining, and would again become *nēpioi, douloi, hypo epitropous kai oikonomous* (4:1, 2). Next, Paul stresses that if the Gentile Galatians adopt Jewish practices, they will be returning to slavery from the glorious liberty enjoyed by the children of God in Christ Jesus (cf. 3:26). Therefore the apostle exhorts the Galatian Christians to leave behind religious ritualism lest they again become enslaved and forfeit their rights as heirs according to the promise (4:8–11).

In general, these verses are clear enough, but the passage is not without its problems. The main difficulty is the word *stoicheia* itself, which in 4:9 the KJV represents by "elements" and the RSV by "elemental spirits."[43] What exactly were these "weak" *stoicheia* to which the Galatians were in bondage (4:3) and under whose power they were in danger of returning (4:9)? A consultation of the lexicons reveals that the word is capable of an extraordinary range of meanings and its usage in Paul is by no means

---

43. Cf. NEB, "spirits of the elements"; NASB, "elemental things"; NIV, "principles."

settled.⁴⁴ Of all the interpretations advanced in the exegesis of this verse,⁴⁵ three possible meanings come into play.

First, *stoicheia* may be taken as referring to the law of Israel exclusively. Though this view is consistent with Paul's teaching on the Mosaic institution—that it enslaves people (3:23)—it is difficult to see its application to the Gentiles⁴⁶ who were never under the Mosaic system in their pre-Christian state. Nor does this view explain the additional phrase *tou kosmou* (4:3), which implies a non-divine origin of the *stoicheia*, in contrast to the Jewish emphasis on the other-worldly character of the commandments.

Second, the reference to the former bondage to the "elements" may be a description of enslavement to personal spiritual beings under whose power the Gentile Galatians had been held prior to their conversion.⁴⁷ The word *stoicheia* may come to mean "angels" or "spirits," and if this is Paul's meaning here, he will be referring to demonic bondage, which is the ul-

---

44. See esp. BDAG 946. *Stoicheia* is the neuter plural form of the adjective *stoicheios*, which means "standing in a row," "an element in a series." By metonomy, however, the word came to refer to the ultimate parts of anything. It is used in classical Greek to refer to the letters of the alphabet, from which came the meaning "rudiments," the "ABCs" of any subject. It can also refer to the component parts of physical bodies; in particular it was the Stoic term for the four elements: earth, water, air, and fire. In Christian writers from the middle of the second century A.D. the term is used in an astronomical sense to mean the heavenly bodies. In Hellenism the word came to include not only the physical elements but the spirits believed to be behind them, the "cosmic beings." These personified *stoicheia* came to be understood as the lords of the world, the final and most important principles of life, and as such were considered worthy of human worship.

The precise meaning of *stoicheia* is still a matter of debate, and the question must be left open until more evidence comes to light. For a detailed survey of the interpretations of the term in the pre-Christian, Christian, patristic, and modern eras, see Kurapati, *Spiritual Bondage*; cf. Bandstra, *Law and the Elements*, 5–30; Delling, "stoicheiō, ktl.," TWNT 7:670–82. On the meaning of *stoicheia* in Paul see esp. Bandstra, *Law and Elements*, 57–68; Delling, "stoicheiō, ktl.," TWNT 7:683–86; Mussner, *Galaterbrief*, 293–303; Burton, *Galatians*, 510–18.

45. In the commentaries the term is usually discussed under 4:3. However, by common consent the meaning of *stoicheia* is identical in both Gal 4:3 and 9, even though in the latter verse the expression *tou kosmou* is absent.

46. The context indicates that Paul wrote this section with the *Gentile* Galatians especially in mind: (a) they were previously idol worshippers (4:8), and (b) they had become Christians directly and not through Judaism as proselytes (3:1–6); cf. Burton, *Galatians*, 215.

47. So Boice, *Galatians*, 472, and many other commentators. The law and the *stoicheia* are so intimately related that some scholars see both Judaism and paganism among the personal spirits; cf. Reicke, "Law and World," 259–76, esp. 261–63, who identifies the "elements" with the good angels who ordained the law (cf. Gal 3:19).

1 Thessalonians and Galatians

timate contrast to freedom in Christ. The advantage of this view is that it agrees with the reference to the false gods (or demons) in 4:8 that the Galatians, as pagans, no doubt formerly worshipped. The disadvantage is that it is hard to see how Paul could include himself,[48] a Pharisee, among those who had been in bondage to weak and beggarly astral spirits who control the universe. Furthermore, this interpretation relies on literature somewhat late for the period in which Paul wrote his letters.[49]

Third, the word *stoicheia* may be taken as referring to the elemental stages of religious experience that are common to all people. According to this view, the expression "the elements of the world" indicates rudimentary teaching regarding rules, regulations, laws, and religious ordinances by means of which both Jews *and* Gentiles, each in their own way, tried to earn their salvation.[50] This meaning of *stoicheia*, or one closely related to it, is possibly involved also in Col 2:8 and 20.

Support for this latter viewpoint is, in our opinion, stronger than for the two former interpretations. Paul seems to apply his remarks in this chapter equally to the Jewish and Gentile worlds. Only this view allows for that fact. It is evident also that at least in one respect the *stoicheia* against which the apostle warns in Galatians involved Mosaic-Pharisaic ordinances. When Gal 4:10 is considered as an interpretation of 4:9, this verse indicates that the *stoicheia* can in a general way be considered merely as rudimentary religious observances, void of any authentic intrinsic meaning or worth. Elementary teachings regarding regulations such as these were employed by *both* Jews and Gentiles alike in their attempt to achieve redemption and salvation.[51] Jewish religion considered law-observance, as well as the keeping of the multitudinous rules added by religious leaders to those previously given at Sinai, as the way whereby salvation could be attained. The worshippers of pagan deities, on the other hand, sought to

---

48. Cf. 4:3: "So also when *we* were children, *we* were enslaved under *ta stoicheia tou kosmou*."

49. Cf. Delling, "*stoicheiō, ktl.*," *TWNT* 7:682–83 and Bandstra, *Law and the Elements*, 43–46 and 58. The meaning "spiritual power" for *stoicheion* is not attested before the *Testamentum Salomonis* dated to the 4th century A.D.

50. So, e.g., Hendriksen, *Galatians*, 157. Burton (*Galatians*, 518) defines *stoicheia* as "the rudimentary religious teachings possessed by the race."

51. The observance of "days, months, seasons, and years" (4:10) implies cultic activities known to both Judaism and paganism and which are probably to be regarded as *typical* religious behavior; so Betz, *Galatia*, 217. For the view that these activities are sacred *Jewish* seasons only, cf. Eadie, *Galatians*, 315–17; Hendriksen, *Galatians*, 165–66.

achieve salvation by their own rituals and in accordance with their own unregenerate nature, the *sarx*.[52] But both Jews and Gentiles in their pre-Christian state are in bondage to ordinances and regulations. Thus for the Gentile Galatians, under the influence of the false teachers, to turn again[53] to the *stoicheia* is in Paul's mind simply an exchange of one form of bondage (to heathenism) for another (to Judaism).

In the question in 4:9 begun by *pōs*—"How is it possible that you are returning again to the weak and beggarly *stoicheia*?"—Paul expresses his utter shock to learn that people who had been delivered from the enslaving teachings of paganism now wish to become enslaved all over again, this time by Jewish regulations. That they could consider a return to such bondage is especially incomprehensible in view of the fact that they had actually come to know God in a personal, genuine way.[54] Although the Galatians had not yet gone as far as the Judaizers had wanted them to go—they have not been circumcised (5:2)—Paul fears his labor in evangelizing them will eventually be wasted (4:11). Their course of action is to the missionary Paul as inexcusable as it is inexplicable, and his astonishment forces him to take up once again, though now with new intensity, his discussion of the deadly character of legalism.[55]

Accordingly, we believe that the most consistent answer to the problem of *stoicheia* in 4:9 is found when the term is understood as referring to elemental stages of religion whereby both Jew and Gentile sought to

---

52. According to Bandstra (*Law and Elements*, 61–71), the two most important basic forces in the *stoicheia* are the law and the flesh. Therefore the yielding of the Galatians to the observance of feast days is at the same time an act of submission to the flesh; the observance itself is but evidence of their enslavement to the *sarx*.

53. *Palin* does not mean "back" (*retro*) but "again" (*iterum*), though the notion of "going back" to the elements is clearly implied in the prepositional prefix of *epistrephein*.

54. The participle is *gnontes* (4:9), not *eidotes* (cf. 4:8). On this distinction see Burdick, "*oida* and *ginōskō*," 344–56, esp. 351–52.

55. One must, however, distinguish between Paul's evaluation of the situation and what the Galatians' point of view was. In Paul's mind the Galatians were about to give up Christianity and return to paganism (i.e., "slavery"). The Galatians, on the other hand, desired only to switch from the Pauline form of Christianity to the Jewish form that required circumcision and law-obedience. They never imagined that the acceptance of the Torah meant a return to paganism, that being *hypo nomon* was the same as being *hypo ta stoicheia tou kosmou*; cf. Betz, *Galatia*, 217; Boice, *Galatians*, 476; Ridderbos, *Galatians*, 161. Therefore Paul is anxious to show the Galatians that the opponents are actually enemies of the gospel who seek to destroy the church (1:6–9). He who chooses to follow their way not only falls back into the servitude of the elements, but is obligated to do the impossible: keep the whole law (5:3).

gain salvation. According to the context, service under the *stoicheia* must be wide enough to embrace both the service of the Jews under the law of Moses and that of the Gentiles under the false gods. If this interpretation is correct, Paul virtually identifies the religious celebrations of the Jews, who worship the true and living God, with those of the heathen, who worship *tois physei mē ousin theois* (4:8). This is in perfect agreement with Paul's earlier teaching that the purpose of the Mosaic Law was not to deliver, but to hold Jews captive in preparation for the deliverance that was to come through the promised "seed" (3:19–22).

However, it should be noted that Paul's use of *stoicheia* for the common enslavement of both Jew and Gentile does not involve an identification in every respect. The Jew still sought to worship the true God, while the Gentile *deisidaimonia* involved objects of worship which "by their very nature" (*physei*) could not be considered "gods" in any sense (4:8). Still, both situations are equal in the single point that they both involve a bondage, in contrast to the glorious liberty and freedom enjoyed by the "sons of God" (3:26–4:7).[56] In this sense, Jewish law is simply one particular manifestation of that which inevitably enslaves all humans in a helpless condition that only faith in the promised Messiah can remedy (4:3–5). Thus, while there is not identity, there is such a similarity between the heathen *cultus* and the Mosaic ritual that both may be described by the same epithet, *ta stoicheia tou kosmou*.

This brings us to the problem of the specific meaning of *asthenē* in 4:9. If our interpretation of the *stoicheia* that bring enslavement is correct, then the addition of the adjectival modifiers *asthenē kai ptōcha* will be Paul's way of emphasizing the total powerlessness of the law and its observance to gain the favor of God. This is an important facet of the apostle's overall argument in Galatians, fighting as he must against an over-evaluation of the law by which obedience to its commandments becomes a way of salvation. To the preachers of Judaism, Paul's gospel was in this respect woefully deficient and therefore merely *kata anthrōpon* (1:11), for it needed to be "corrected" by the observance of special days, months, seasons, and years (4:10), and especially by the observance of the markedly Jewish rite of circumcision (5:2–3, 6, 11; 6:12). Incredibly, the Galatians were on the verge of adopting the entire ritualistic system of Judaism as a means of completing what had begun only "imperfectly" under the tutelage of Paul!

---

56. On the significance of the motif of sonship in Galatians, see the excellent monograph by Byrne, "*Sons of God*," 141–90.

Since the Galatians do not regard their course as a dangerous one, Paul must try to convince them that their present drift toward legalism is in reality a return to slavery. Contrary to the claims of the Judaizers, the *stoicheia* are ineffective for giving life, for they are *asthenē* and lack the inherent power to accomplish salvation. The Mosaic Law, as a member or component part (*stoicheion*) of the *stoicheia tou kosmou*, requires what God demands, but is powerless to accomplish anything ultimately positive. The law provokes sin and transgression (Rom 5:20), condemns sin (Rom 4:15; Gal 3:10), and serves as a *paidagōgos*[57] (Gal 3:23–25), but it also is the power of sin (1 Cor 15:56) and the occasion for sin (Rom 7:8, 11) and inevitably leads to death. Thus in Paul's mind the "weak" law is in one aspect definitely a *force* to be reckoned with as it operates in the sphere of the flesh and ultimately issues in sin and death. The opponents, and now the Galatians, understood the elements as life-bringing forces, but Paul knows that they are really "weak and beggarly," completely ineffectual to do what the law preachers have promised.

Because the law involves religious bondage, it is not surprising to find Paul's warnings against it in this passage and indeed throughout the entire letter (cf. 1:9; 2:4–5, 15–21; 3:1–5; 5:1–4; 6:7–8, 12–13). Inherent in the Christian life is the potential danger of a believer once again seeking to live according to the law and flesh. But this course of life brings people into bondage, "be it the bondage of the immature heir, the Jew, or that of the slave, the Gentile,"[58] or, we might add, that of the misdirected Christian. Therefore, since any observance of Jewish ritual practices by Gentile converts amounts to nothing less than a return to bondage to the *stoicheia tou kosmou*, Paul must go to great lengths to convince the Galatians that these ritualistic celebrations are valid only for those who are still controlled by the old aeon. With regard to the salvation and sanctification of Christians, the elements are both *asthenē* and *ptōcha*, and indeed are a stumbling block to the Christian life.

---

57. The term *paidagōgos* stresses the positive, but purely preparatory aspect of the law's function. Because the Judaizers attempted to extend that function *beyond* the time of Christ's coming, Paul must stress its provisional status. If MacGorman is correct, the English rendering of *paidagōgos* should emphasize the *custodial* (i.e., "custodian," "guardian") rather than the *educative* (i.e., "schoolmaster," "tutor") function of the law in Gal 3:24–25. See his article, "Law as Paidagogos," 99–111, esp. 110. See also Longenecker, "Pedagogical Nature," 53–61.

58. Bandstra, *Law and Elements*, 65.

Paul's view that the law in its weakness works spiritual death finds its main parallel in his acknowledgment that in the death and resurrection of Christ the law and the *stoicheia* have been conquered. This fact is not insignificant in our quest to understand Paul's weakness language in Galatians, nor is it without parallel in the apostle's other writings: "God did what the law, weakened as it was by the flesh, could not do; sending his own son in the likeness of sinful flesh and for sin, he condemned sin in the flesh" (Rom 8:3). Paul rejects the works of the law because God has rejected in the person and work of Christ a life dedicated to nomistic service. The condition of humanity under law has now in Christ been superseded by a new set of conditions, namely, faith in Christ and his confession before others. God's people are therefore marked by faith, as indeed Abraham was (3:6–9), not by the works of the law.[59] Thus Paul insists that legalism is a betrayal of the whole gospel (5:2–4), for righteousness before God is a result only of faith and is a free gift that cannot be merited (5:5). *Nothing* therefore is able (*sthenos*) to earn salvation or sanctification—neither circumcision nor uncircumcision (5:6).

Having condemned such behavior, the apostle adds that life in Christ involves a different kind of bondage, which he defines explicitly in 5:13–14 as love of neighbor. With six Greek words he reduces all of the statutes of the Jewish law into a single one: *agapēseis ton plēsion sou hōs seauton*; "you shall love your neighbor as [you love] yourself" (5:14). His purpose of course is to show that in the single commandment to love of Lev 19:18 are summarized all the requirements of the Christian faith.[60] Here Paul can speak favorably of the law, for when Christians love and serve others, the law is fulfilled. This fact, however, in no way weakens Paul's argument against law and in defense of a gospel of pure grace. The law as a system of rules and regulations has no place in the life of a Christian, for it cannot effectuate its own fulfillment, but the essential ends of the law can and will be met through those who live in and are led by the Spirit (5:16–18). This life in the Spirit (*pneumati*) is characterized neither by legalism nor by license, but by a life of faith and love that Paul discusses in concrete terms[61] in the following verses (5:19–26).

---

59. Cf. in this connection Tyson, "'Works of Law,'" 430–31. See also Barth's discussion of Paul's use of *pistis* in Galatians, in "The Kerygma," 143–45.

60. Furnish, *Love Command*, 96–97, offers an excellent discussion of this subject.

61. Cf. Schrage, *Die konkreten Einzelgebote*, 231–33.

This being the case, there is a certain presumption in viewing the *stocheia* (and the law) not as something positively evil *per se*, but as elements that are *asthenē* and ineffectual, and therefore open to the dangerous possibility of enslaving people who were redeemed by Christ and through him have begun a new existence in the Spirit. Or to use Paul's terms, while the *stocheia* are not inherently harmful, they are "weak," for they are incompetent to bring salvation and life, and "beggarly," for they have no wealth whereby they can provide an inheritance. Since they are operative in the *kosmos*, within the sphere of human activity, and among a fallen humanity, they are unable to set people free as Christ has done by redeeming them through his death on a tree (3:13).

The accent in Gal 4:3 and 9 would therefore appear to lie on the modifying expressions *tou kosmou* and *asthenē kai ptōcha*. The latter expression can be considered as a substitute for the former, for the words "weak and beggarly" in 4:9 describe what in essence is meant by the genitive "of the world" in 4:3.[62] The noun *kosmos* here does not mean "the universe" or "the material world," but "the world of humankind," the present eschatological age, and hence the *stocheia* are those elements that enslave the members of the old aeon to which the Galatians are tempted to return. The adjectives *asthenē* and *ptōcha* are therefore only too appropriate to describe the impotence of the *stocheia* of the *kosmos* to provide salvation for humans and deliverance from their present bondage. The ascription *asthenē* does not deny the harmful potential of the enslaving powers, but emphasizes their identity with the sphere of human activity that belongs to the old aeon and that is passing away, and signifies the total powerlessness of commandments with reference to spiritual deliverance. Thus the *stocheia* are *asthenē*, "parce qu'ils ne peuvent pas opérer ce qu'ils pretendent, conduire les hommes au salut."[63] They are also *ptōcha*, a term that in classical Greek referred to basic economic deprivation but came to mean, metaphorically, deprivation of power and dignity.[64] Its meaning here is that the religious elements of the old age are not only powerless but also resourceless to supply what is needed to extricate humans from their bondage to sin and the flesh, in contrast to "the unsearchable riches of Christ" (Heb 7:18).

62. So Reicke, "Law and World," 264–65; cf. Delling, "*stoicheō, ktl.*," *TWNT* 7:685: "Man kann fragen ob *asthenē kai ptōcha* nicht den Genitiv *tou kosmou* interpretieren; jedenfalls ist mit beiden negativen Wendungen alle vorchristliche Religion zusammenfassend abgeurteilt."

63. Lagrange, *Galates*, 107.

64. Bammel, "*ptōchos, ktl.*," *TWNT* 6:885–915, esp. 909.

Therefore, while it is not necessary to restrict the meaning of *asthenē* too rigidly,[65] in view of the emphasis in this section upon the inadequacy of the law, it would seem that the apostle is thinking especially of the impotence of legal enactments to secure salvation or progress in holiness, regardless of whatever beneficial side-effects such "fundamental religious elements" might have.[66] These *stocheia*, common to both pagan and Jewish religion, not only cannot procure spiritual blessings, but ultimately bring people into bondage to their own impulse to be made perfect in the flesh (3:3) and are thus to be avoided by the Christian at all costs.[67]

Galatians 4:13

The second occurrence of weakness-termini in Galatians is found at the beginning of the highly enigmatic paragraph (4:12–20) discussing the Galatians' former attachment to Paul and why they should now follow his earnest counsel to reject the gospel of the false teachers. Considerations of space preclude a disproportionate treatment of the critical problem concerning the chronology of Galatians raised by *to proteron* in v. 13. Within the scope of this study we must accept the possibility that the words can mean "on the former of two occasions," though in our view 4:13 does not demand two visits of Paul to Galatia (according to Koine usage *to proteron* can just as easily be rendered "originally," or "previously").[68] Certainly the

---

65. E.g., Boice (*Galatians*, 473) offers the interesting suggestion that there is a subtle link between the ideas of redemption and adoption in 4:5 and the phrase "the weak and beggarly elements." Schlier (*Galater*, 203) correctly emphasizes the powerlessness of the elements "gegenüber der Macht und dem Leben Gottes und seiner 'Söhne,' und erweist sich ihre Verehrung als die angestrengte und furchtsame Leistung an überwundene und verfallende Götter." Many other parallels and points of contrast could be noted.

66. More recently, Martyn, *Galatians* concludes (405–6): "In a word, Paul employs the ancient equation of the world's elements with archaic pairs of opposites to interpret the *religious* impact of Christ's advent. Following the baptismal formula, he applies that tradition not to the sensible elements, but rather to the elements of religious distinction." Martyn's excursus "Christ and the Elements of the Cosmos" is worth reading in its entirety (393–406). See also Longnecker, *Galatians*, 166: "Thus when talking about the Jewish experience, it was the Mosaic Law in its condemnatory and supervisory functions that comprised the Jews' 'basic principles' of religion. Later in v. 9 after talking about the Gentile experience, it was paganism with its veneration of nature and cultic rituals that made up the Gentiles' 'basic principles' of religion."

67. Fitzmyer (*First Corinthians*, 447) translates as follows: "*For this reason many among you* are weak and *infirm, and a number are dying*" (italics in original).

68. See BDAG, 888.

question of whether 4:13 does or does not support the south-Galatian hypothesis cannot be resolved here; regardless of one's position on that issue, however, these verses clearly refer to Paul's preaching on the occasion of the founding of the Galatic churches.

There are few NT phrases that can boast of such a variety of interpretations as *astheneian tēs sarkos* in Galatians 4:13. Paul makes it clear that the Galatians know what his "weakness" actually is, but his readers today have not had their eyewitness advantage, and they are left to infer from the context the identity of Paul's *astheneia*. This means that in order to gain an accurate knowledge of the content of the term *astheneia* in 4:13, it is once again necessary to study the word in the context of Paul's wider argument in this portion of the letter.

At this juncture in Galatians 4 Paul has turned from formal argument to an appeal to the former bond of unity that existed between him and the Galatian churches. The intensely personal quality of this appeal is seen throughout, but especially in v. 19, where the apostle compares himself to a mother enduring birth-pangs and the Galatians to a human embryo in the process of being formed. The metaphors need not be pressed too far; indeed, the whole image seems to break down because the formation of a child in the womb can hardly be said to *follow* labor pains. This is, however, no reason to regard this verse as a later interpolation:[69] Paul simply wants to emphasize by the use of word-pictures his great pastoral concern and love for his converts.

This intensely personal and highly enigmatic entreaty poses an interesting question of interpretation: Why does the apostle suddenly bring up, in the middle of his discussion of the Christian's freedom from the law, the subject of the particular circumstances of the founding of the Galatian churches, including his *astheneia*? The Galatians were already quite aware of the situation (cf. *oidate*, 4:13). How can this intimate account be an argument against those who were wooing the Galatians into legalism?

The obscurity of this passage perhaps cannot be explained in a purely logical way; it is possible that Paul was so overwhelmed by emotion at this point in writing that he simply lost his train of thought. For this reason, many scholars are of the opinion that Paul has ceased argumentation and has turned to emotional begging and appealing.[70] But psychological in-

---

69. Cf. O'Neill (*Galatians*, 61–62) who ascribes the words *mechris hou morphōthē Christos en hymin* to a glossator.

70. According to Lagrange (*Galates*, 110–11), Paul's appeal is "moins un

terpretations of the passage, while properly pointing to the intensity and passion of Paul's appeal, fail to recognize the rhetorical character of these verses.

Betz[71] has demonstrated the remarkable similarity between this section and the standard Hellenistic literary topos of "friendship" (*peri philias*), which calls for a change between heavy and light sections and an emotional appeal to offset mere abstract argumentation. Both the Galatians and Paul would have been acquainted with this theme, and if the similarity here is more than coincidental, Paul will be arguing that his relationship with the Galatians (his "true friendship") now, as then, requires the reciprocity of his converts. The force of the argument lies in the fact that, when Paul needed help the most, the Galatians did not hesitate to provide without reservation the assistance required to restore him. And though they could have found cause to despise him, they had proven their friendship by accepting Paul as an *aggelon theou, hōs Christon Iēsoun* (v. 14). But they had not only received Paul with open hearts—they had also accepted the message of life that accompanied him to Galatia, thus creating between them a bond of Christian *philia*. It is this "friendship" that forms the basis of Paul's present appeal to the Galatians.

This means that the present passage in Galatians "is neither inconsistent nor lacking argumentative force,"[72] but serves to accentuate the paradox that these same ones who had once so enthusiastically received Paul now consider him as their enemy and reject his gospel. The appeal of this section, then, is an argument for the reestablishment of a good personal relationship that each party had once enjoyed but that the Galatians' present inclination to live by the law has soured.

Paul opens his appeal with the puzzling words *ginesthe hōs egō hoti kagō hōs hymeis*, "become as I, for I also as you" (4:12). The expression is capable of a wide variety of interpretations. In view of the preceding reference to law and the elements (4:1–11), the probable meaning is that Paul

---

raissonnement qu'un desir passionné d'union par une bonne volonté réciproque. Paul a fait les premiers pas: que les Galates en fassant autant!" The same idea is expressed by Oepke, *Galater*, 140–41; Burton, *Galatians*, 235; Mussner, *Galaterbrief*, 304–5. Robertson writes: "It is just in writers of the greatest mental activity and vehemence of spirit that we meet most instances of anacoluthon. Hence a man with the passion of Paul naturally breaks away from formal rules in the structure of the sentence when he is greatly stirred, as in Gal. and 2 Cor." (*Grammar*, 435).

71. *Galatians*, 220–23.
72. Ibid., 221.

is asking the Galatians to enter into the freedom from law that he now enjoys, while at the same time reminding them of his former identification with the Gentile Galatians in order to win them for Christ (cf. 1 Cor 9:20–22). If this interpretation is right, we can paraphrase the expression as follows: "Become as I am, for I also became as you were."[73] In other words, in seeking to win them to Christ, the end of which was to make them like himself—free from the *stoicheia*—Paul had made himself like the Galatians by disclaiming any special privilege as a Jew and by renouncing the Mosaic Law. On that basis, he now appeals to the Galatians to rid themselves of the nomists and become like him in regard to his Christian liberty.

Paul's original reception by the Galatians is described in vv. 13–15. The brief statement in v. 12, "you have done me no wrong" (*ouden me ēdikēsate*), which really belongs with these verses, is a litotes and should be understood as expressing an affirmative idea: they had treated him properly.[74] Exactly how properly is recounted in what follows.

In these verses there are six major statements, three concerning Paul, and three in regard to the Galatians. Concerning himself, the apostle first reminds his readers that he had preached the good tidings among them, but that he did so on account of bodily infirmity (or, notwithstanding it), and that his condition had subjected the Galatians to the temptation to reject him and his message. Regarding the Galatians, he affectionately recalls how they had resisted their[75] impulse to condemn or loathe him on account of his infirmity, and how they had received him with enthusiasm—so much so that they would have parted with anything, even their own eyes, as an expression of the depth of their attachment to him. It is in this context—where Paul states his desire that the Galatians might return to the true gospel by recollecting what they had once gladly accepted from

---

73. Greek reconstruction: *ginesthe hōs egō eimi, hoti kagō egenomēn hōs hymeis ēte*; cf. Lagrange, *Galates*, 111.

74. It is imprecise to say, as Schlier does (*Galater*, 209), that the statement also applies to the present situation. Although the aorist, as a tense, does not necessarily refer to past time (cf. Smith, "Errant Aorist Interpreters," 207–9), the aorist indicative *ēdikēsate* probably should be given a past signification, as should also the following series of verbs in the aorist indicative.

75. *hymōn* ("your temptation"), read by ℵ* A B D* F G it (most) vg Ambrosiaster, appears to have better external attestation than the reading *mou* ("my temptation"), supported by p46 C*vid Db,c K P Ψ *Byz* ita Chrysostom. The latter pronoun may have replaced the former "in order to alleviate the difficulty of the expression *ton peirasmon hymōn*" (Metzger, *Textual Commentary*, 596).

him—that the apostle uses for the first time the noun *astheneia* (or any of its cognates) to refer to himself.

There is some discussion as to the correct translation of the preposition *dia* in v. 13. A number of scholars think *di astheneian* refers to an *accompanying circumstance*,[76] while others construe the expression causally, making the illness the *occasion*[77] of Paul's preaching in Galatia. Though the former meaning is not impossible,[78] on the whole it seems most likely that the latter significance of *dia* is to be preferred here. The continuous or characteristic condition of the preacher would be expressed by *dia* plus the genitive,[79] not the accusative; but in the Greek text the only reading that was transmitted is *astheneian*. And while examples of *dia* plus the accusative in inexact usage can be cited (e.g., Rom 3:25; 8:20), the most natural meaning of the word in terms of the context is plainly "because of."

The preposition, then, signifies either that Paul was detained in Galatia through which he had merely intended to pass, or else that he was forced for his health's sake to visit Galatia which he otherwise would not have visited. In the latter case, even if the illness was the occasion of Paul's visit to Galatia, the problem most probably persisted for a period of time while he was there. But while it is best to understand *di astheneian* as the *specific* cause for Paul's preaching in Galatia, the *general* cause or motivation for preaching lay grounded in the appointment of God that Paul carried out in obedience as a *doulos* of Christ (Gal 1:10) and an *oikonomos* of God (1 Cor 4:1), compelled by a deep sense of devotion to the Lord (2 Cor 5:14–15) and for his sake (2 Cor 4:5, 14). As the latter verse clearly indicates—*hē gar agapē tou Christou synechei hēmas*—Paul preached the gospel in the first place *dia Christon*, not *di astheneian*.[80]

It is generally agreed today that *astheneia* refers to a physical condition of the apostle, and not to an unimpressive appearance, timidity, the emotional scars from persecution, sexual desires, human frailty in general, or some other figurative meaning. However, a few modern scholars still

---

76. E.g., Oepke, *Galater*, 105, "den begleitenden Umstand"; Ridderbos, *Galatians*, 166; Güttgemanns, *Der leidende Apostel*, 175.

77. E.g., Eadie, *Galatians*, 321–22; Betz, *Galatia*, 224; Boice, *Galatians*, 478; Schlier, *Galater*, 210; Mussner, *Galaterbrief*, 307.

78. Lagrange (*Galates*, 112) overstates the case when he says that the expression "ne peut avoir qu'un sens: 'à cause d'une maladie de la chair.'"

79. Cf. 2 Cor 2:4, *dia dakryōn* ("in tears"); Rom 4:11, *di akrobystias* ("in the condition of circumcision").

80. Cf. Zahn, *Galater*, 215.

prefer the metaphorical meaning of the phrase *astheneia tēs sarkos* over the literal. For example, H. Binder, in his article entitled "Die angebliche Krankheit des paulus,"[81] argues that "seine asthéneia, d.h. seine 'Schwachheit', bestand nur darin, dass er teilhatte am menschlichen Wesen."[82] A purely physical interpretation of *astheneia* is excluded because "in der Sprache des Paulus bedeutet asthéneia nie 'Krankheit', sondern immer 'Schwachheit', 'Kraftlosigkeit.'"[83] If this premise is true, the following conclusion is natural: "Hier wie dort vertritt Paulus den Gedanken der Armseligkeit, der Bedürftigkeit, der Schwäche, der Kraft—und Hilflosigkeit, des zum Scheitern Verurteiltseins—nicht der 'leiblichen' Beschaffenheit des Menschen sondern—seiner Existenz in der 'Fleischlichkeit,' im 'Fleisch,' in der Gottesferne."[84]

Although this interpretation is possible—especially in view of the fact that Paul must have had an especially sturdy bodily constitution to endure his travels and trials (cf. 2 Cor 11:23–33)—the plausibility of Binder's argument diminishes when one considers his major premise in greater detail. Binder expresses the "fact" that Paul never uses *astheneia* or its cognates to refer to a physical condition, and concludes from this that therefore Paul cannot have bodily infirmity in mind in Gal 4:13. But Binder's argument at this point is a pure *petitio principii*: his conclusion is not surprising, since it was also his premise! It is not sufficient merely to state that Paul never uses *astheneia* in a physical sense; in light of Pauline usage elsewhere this premise is tenuous indeed. Certainly if Paul did ever use the word to describe the illness of others, he could conceivably have employed it to describe his own, and the force of Binder's argument would be considerably weakened.

It is, in fact, manifest that Paul does on occasion employ the word-family to refer to a purely corporeal condition. In the Pastorals we learn that Trophimus remained in Miletus because of an incapacitating illness (2 Tim 4:20), and Timothy was urged to drink wine for medicinal purposes because of his frequent ailments (1 Tim 5:23). Certainly Epaphroditus's distressing condition involved a physical sickness of some sort (Phil 2:26, 27).[85] In each of these cases an *astheneia*-word is employed. This euphe-

---

81. 1–13.

82. Ibid., 13.

83. Ibid., 4.

84. Ibid., 7.

85. That the nature of Epaphroditus's condition was physical and not psychological is clear from the context: Only a grave physical condition can account for (a) the

1 Thessalonians and Galatians

mism usually implies in Greek (and the Pauline letters are evidently no exception) poor health.[86] In Gal 4:13, the phrase *astheneia tēs sarkos* as well as the context of the passage itself is clearly in keeping with this euphemistic usage, meaning "bodily infirmity." It is not surprising that Paul employs this expression for a physical condition, for bodily illness is an inherent quality of the *sarx*,[87] the old aeon, and the sphere of human activity that is temporal and weak.

Therefore, though it is not completely certain that the words *astheneia tēs sarkos* must be understood in a literal way as an actual distressing physical condition, it is nevertheless the most probable meaning in this context. This usage is entirely consistent with that in the Pastorals and Philippians where the word-group appears with the obvious meaning of sickness, and harmonizes perfectly with the common meaning of *astheneia* in the Synoptic Gospels. We must, however, register our agreement with one emphasis of Binder's interpretation, namely, that Paul was, generally speaking, a healthy man. It is evident from both the epistles and the Acts that, in spite of the constant attacks made upon him by Jews and Gentiles alike and the many dangers he continually faced, the apostle remained a surprisingly strong individual. This point is well taken, but it does not exclude the possibility of an occasional prepossessing physical condition, as Binder maintains. We thus agree with the majority of commentators[88] that the statement *di astheneian tēs sarkos* should be explained to mean that Paul was suffering from some sort of physical indisposition.

If we are certain that an unpleasant physical condition lay behind Paul's initial visit to Galatia, we cannot be certain of its precise nature. The difficulty of finding an answer lies primarily in the poverty of source

---

Philippians' severe distress of mind, and (b) the expression *paraplēsion thanatō* ("at death's door") in 2:27.

86. Binder's treatment of these passages, found only in a footnote, is inadequate: "Epaphroditus war nicht krank geworden, sondern in eine Situation geraten, der er nicht gewachsen war (Phil. 2:26). Trophimus blieb nicht krank in Milet zurück, sondern in einer schwierigen, fast aussichtslosen Arbeit (2 Tim. 4:20). Vielleicht war auch Timotheus nicht krank, als Paulus an ihn 1 Tim. 5, 23 schrieb" ("Krankheit des Paulus," 13n.).

87. Robinson, *The Body*, 20. According to Schweizer ("*sarx, ktl.*," *TWNT* 7:124) *sarx* in this context should be understood in its physical sense; so also Reicke, "Body and Soul," 201.

88. Cf. Schlier, *Grundzüge*, 101: "körperliche Hinfälligkeit"; Oepke, *Galater*, 105: "leibliche Krankheit"; Zahn, *Galater*, 215: "eine Krankheit des Leibes"; Betz, *Galatia*, 224: "illness of the flesh"; Eadie, *Galatians*, 323: "infirmity of the flesh"; Hendriksen, *Galatians*, 171: "physical infirmity"; Jewett, *Paul's Anthropological Terms*, 154: "bodily frailty."

materials. The apostle is always reticent to recount his own personal experiences, and when he does it is only briefly and without exception in polemical or argumentative contexts that do not lend themselves to precise forms of expression. That we know little of the person of Paul is not surprising, for his letters, though personal, are basically *pastoral* communications to congregations and are intended for public reading in the context of the churches' meetings. Therefore revelations about "Paul the Man" are largely incidental and usually of ancillary importance to the writer's overall purpose.[89] This means that we should not expect Paul to define his *astheneia* for us in any specific terms. Paul is aware that the Galatians know already what it is, and its mention might have detracted from his main appeal that is based not so much on his condition but on the Galatians' warm reception of him and his gospel.

In spite of these difficulties, research has fostered a wealth of hypotheses and inferences concerning the precise nature of Paul's *astheneia tēs sarkos*,[90] but neither Acts nor Galatians mentions it specifically, and even the most careful examination of the text will reveal no significant clues. The attempt to link Paul's illness to his "thorn in the flesh" (*skolops tē sarki*, 2 Cor 12:7) is common, but despite the similarities in language and subject matter, it is not necessary to find a reference to his *skolops* in this text. As Bring notes, to introduce the idea of a chronic ailment here is to introduce a Corinthian nuance that is foreign to the atmosphere of this letter.[91]

If one adopts the South Galatian hypothesis—that Paul is writing to the churches in the *province* of Galatia—it can be argued that Paul's *astheneia tēs sarkos* was the result of what he suffered from his enemies on the so-called first missionary journey (Acts 13–14). If so, *astheneia* refers not to a particular sickness or disease, but to the physical abuse and resultant weakened physical condition that occured to Paul in the form of maltreatment at Antioch (Acts 13:50, along with Barnabas) and of stoning at Lystra (Acts 14:19), the latter incident being so severe that Paul was left for dead

---

89. For a brief but excellent discussion of the autobiographical Paul, see Furnish, *Theology and Ethics*, 10.

90. E.g., migraine headaches, epilepsy, malaria, rheumatism, chronic ophthalmia, etc. For extensive listings of scholarly opinion on this issue, see esp. Schmidt, "*kolaphizō*," *TWNT* 3:818–21; Lightfoot, *Galatians*, 186–91; Eadie, *Galatians*, 329–45.

91. "Es scheint sich dort aber eher um ein chronisches Leiden und hier um einen akuten Krankheitsfall zu handeln;" see Bring, *Galater*, 185. But even *skolops* in 2 Cor 12:7 may not refer to a chronic physical problem (see our discussion in chap. 3).

1 Thessalonians and Galatians

(cf. 2 Tim 3:11).[92] The advantage of this view is that it accords with the Lukan account of Paul's travels in Acts, but it carries conclusive weight only with those already convinced of the South Galatian theory and the early dating of the letter.

The desire of the Galatians to pluck out (*exoryxantes*) their eyes—which they would have done had not the restriction in *ei dunaton* intervened—is evidence to some that Paul's *astheneia* was a form of ophthalmic disorder (4:15). If the gift could have relieved Paul's poor vision, so the argument goes, the Galatians would have parted with their own eyes quite willingly. However, although some type of eye disorder may have been involved in Paul's infirmity, it is not necessarily the meaning of this verse. The expression "to pluck out the eyes" is a common one both in the OT as well as in a great variety of secular authors,[93] and is most likely used here proverbially to emphasize the willingness of the Galatians to sacrifice their all for Paul: "Cela peut vouloir dire simplement qu'ils étaient prêts à sacrifier pour lui les biens les plus precieux."[94] Thus *tous ophthalmous* is here a synonym for that which is most precious to a person. As to the question, however, whether or not Paul was suffering from an eye ailment, we can draw no certain conclusions of any kind from Gal 4:15.[95]

On the basis of 4:14—"the temptation to you in my flesh you did not despise nor loathe (*oude exeptysate*[96])"—others have supposed that Paul was epileptic, taking the aorist of *ekptyō* literally with the meaning "to spit." While it is true that the ancient Greeks would expectorate at the sight of an epileptic seizure, the word *ekptyō* contains also a metaphorical sense of loathing or rejecting,[97] and because the verb is coupled with *exouthenein* ("to despise"), and follows it, the figurative meaning here is the most likely.

Many other attempts to account for Paul's *astheneia* could be listed, but most of the suggestions carry the point too far, and all are open to

---

92. So, e.g., Ridderbos, *Galatians*, 30, 166–67.

93. See Eadie, *Galatians*, 327, who cites such examples as Deut 32:10; Ps 17:8; Prov 7:2; Zech 2:8; Horace, *Sat* ii.5,33; and Terence, *Adelph*, v. 7–5.

94. Viard, *Saint Paul*, 95.

95. The reference to "large letters" (*pēlika grammata*) in 6:11 is said to support this view, but the expression is better understood to mean that Paul enlarged his writing to emphasize his personal greeting and impress his authority upon his readers than on the hypothesis that he so wrote because of age, infirmity, or lack of practice in writing Greek characters; cf. Lightfoot, *Galatians*, 220–21.

96. P46 lacks these words, no doubt an oversight of a scribe due to homoioteleuton.

97. BDAG 309; Thayer, *Lexicon*, 199.

legitimate inquiry and controversy. Whether or not Paul had one of the specific conditions mentioned above is finally a matter of pure conjecture. At any rate, in his use of *astheneia* the writer assumes that his readers are familiar with the word and the idea it connotes so that no further explanation is required.

As to the specific identity of the illness, then, it is possible to reconstruct only the most general description. We can infer from the context that the malady was suitable to give at least the impression that Paul's person and message were weak, even an object of derision to those who saw him in such a condition. We know further that this situation hindered Paul—at least he felt it could—but was overcome by the gracious reception of the Galatians who accepted the ill missionary as if they had been receiving the Lord himself. The illness must have also been severe enough to hinder Paul's mobility, yet not so severe as to prevent him from preaching the gospel. At the same time Paul must have found enough relief to permit him to continue his journey later.

But all we can say with certainty is that *astheneia* refers to some bodily infirmity that befell Paul and that was a potential source of offense to the Galatians. Since we do not have enough information for a diagnosis, all the suggestions as to the exact nature of his illness must remain conjectures.

CONCLUSION: WEAKNESS LANGUAGE IN GALATIANS

In Galatians Paul's main object is to show that believers are free from the law and that faith in Jesus Christ, not works of righteousness, brings salvation and eternal life. An essential part of his argument is the reference to "the elements of the world" that belong to the old aeon and bring men into bondage. Because the *stoicheia* are set over against both God and humankind, Paul's attitude toward the elements is always negative and fiercely polemical. His concern time and again is to demonstrate the total superiority of Christ over all powers, be they *archai, exousiai, dunameis, kyrioi, kyriotētes, archontes, thronoi, aggeloi* or, in our passage, *ta stoicheia tou kosmou*.[98] This is because to be subservient to the elements means to be in bondage to sin and, eventually, death. Servitude to the *stoicheia* finds its only remedy in the incarnation, death, and resurrection of Christ, who triumphed over them on the cross.[99] It is therefore beyond Paul that anyone

98. See Leivestad, *Christ the Conqueror*, 92–95.

99. The imagery of humanity's enslavement to and eventual triumph over the

delivered from these elements could desire to return to a position of slavery under them, especially if he or she had already appropriated the victory of Christ by "coming to a knowledge of God or, rather, being known by God" (4:9).

In Galatians Paul includes in the same category—the *stoicheia* —the Mosaic Law (the rudimentary teaching of the Jews) and the heathen systems from which the majority of the Galatians had been emancipated. These *stoicheia* are wholly inadequate to secure spiritual deliverance or progress in holiness, a fact that the religious past of all Christians—whether Jew or Gentile—has shown to be true. It is only through the sending of the son (4:4) that status as sonship is conferred. This is achieved by pure grace working through faith. Therefore the *stoicheia* can be described as *asthenē kai ptōcha*, "denn sie können nicht bewirken und verleihen, was Gott durch die Sendung seines Sohnes bewirkt und verliehen hat."[100] They are no longer applicable to children and heirs of God since they have been overcome by Christ the Conqueror and because the situation of slavery has been resolved.

It is therefore important for the apostle to emphasize the helplessness of all people *hypo ta stoicheia tou kosmou* in his attempt to contrast the situation of slavery with the present situation of salvation in Christ. In comparison with the power and wealth of the gospel, the old religious systems fade into insignificance. Even the Jewish law, which is both good and God-given (Rom 7:12, 22), when distorted into a means of earning salvation, can be used by Satan to bring men into bondage. Paul can therefore refer to a return to the elements and the adoption of the Mosaic Law in the same breath, for the rudimentary teachings of the Gentiles correspond exactly to the ritualistic element in the law that is *asthenēs* to produce life.

In view of this, it is clear that Paul's main contention, and his primary purpose in ascribing to the *stoicheia* the modifier *asthenē*, is to show that since a person is not justified by the keeping of the law, there are no Jewish requirements to be submitted to. Circumcision, feasts, clean and unclean meats, fasts, special days, etc., are now obsolete and have no meaning for the Christian. It is therefore unnecessary to adopt Jewish (or pagan) ordinances, for their observance is a return to the slavery involved in the

---

elements of the world is one of the major Pauline salvific motifs; see Epp, "Diverse Imageries," 105–8.

100. Sieffert, *Galater*, 238.

elements and inevitably will destroy the work of Paul and the faith of his Galatian converts.

Amid the multitudinous possibilities of interpreting Paul's *astheneia* in 4:13, it is not easy to find one's way. But if our interpretation of the word's context is correct, then Paul there describes with the term his own corporeal condition that forced him to visit Galatia and that was at first a temptation to the Galatians to despise him. While the translation "illness" is perhaps a tendencious paraphrase for *astheneia* in this phrase, it best and most plainly conveys what the author desires to express with the words *astheneia tēs sarkos*. Of this illness, however, we know only that it existed and had an impact on his travel plans.

Since Paul's entire apostolic ministry was one of travels, the hopes and disappointments involved with his itinerary must have had special significance. In spite of, or better, because of the many frustrations encountered along the way, Paul had a firm conviction that his travel plans were in the Lord's hands. Even the physical problem that stranded him in Galatia proved to be a blessing in disguise: Paul was able to evangelize an otherwise untouched area, thus accomplishing more than he had originally set out to. He learned through that experience that even an illness could be the occasion for preaching, just as later his imprisonment in Caesarea and Rome would work for the dissemination of the gospel.[101]

Through his Galatian experience Paul had also been reminded of his own *Menschlichkeit* and the power of God in spite of it. Just as the *stoicheia* belong to the old aeon, so in a sense does Paul. But this continuing participation in the *kosmos* through suffering, weakness, and illness forces him to look away from himself to the power of God for strength and sustenance. Paul's existence as an "apostle of weakness" in an earthen pot (2 Cor 4:7) has tremendous significance in that it serves to make clear to others that the source of his power is God and not himself. Evidently the Galatians recognized this, for they did not receive him on the basis of his personal appearance, physical health, or rhetorical prowess, but because he was indeed the messenger of God bearing the word of Christ (Gal 4:14).

---

101. Mussner (*Galaterbrief*, 307) aptly states: "Für einen Mann wie Paulus wurde alles zum *kairos*, wenn es galt, das Evangelium zu verkündigen."

3

The Corinthian Correspondence

INTRODUCTION TO THE CORINTHIAN LETTERS

THE CORINTHIAN CORRESPONDENCE IS the most voluminous in the Pauline corpus and *de facto* constitutes the most valuable source for our understanding of the Pauline weakness motif. In these two letters alone the words appear twenty-nine times, or 66 percent of the total, in Paul, while the largest single convergence of weakness language in the NT is in 2 Corinthians 10–13, where the words occur a total of fourteen times. Along with Romans (8 occurrences), these documents embody the most fertile soil of knowledge concerning the apostle's unique understanding of weakness and its implications for Christian living.

Nothing brought Paul more forcefully to the place of expressing with such clarity his perception of *astheneia* as the controversy with the Corinthian church concerning the apostle's apostolic authority. The writer employed the idea of weakness as a central motif in these letters because he had no choice: the concept had become an element of the serious disturbances at Corinth and demanded redress. Both the urgent practical problems in the church and the dispute with the opposition in Corinth indicated to Paul the liability of the concept to error through misunderstanding or falsification. Thus, for the first time the apostle's ideas on weakness are given a prominent position in his correspondence. We might say that in these two letters (and to a lesser degree in Romans) he develops weakness into a *theological* formulation. Elsewhere the usage of *astheneia* and its cognates is little more than peripheral to the mainstream of thought; in 1 and 2 Corinthians the apostle integrates the words in a most skillful manner into the major themes that he has chosen to expound.

Despite the many investigations into the situation behind Paul's letters to the Corinthians, there is still substantial disagreement on a variety of issues. Therefore, it will be helpful to establish at the beginning a series of working assumptions concerning the historical and literary circumstances behind the Corinthian correspondence. Of particular importance for our study are: (a) the identity of Paul's main opponents within the Corinthian congregation against whom he does battle, particularly in 2 Corinthians; (b) the literary-critical problem of 2 Corinthians raised by the sudden shift in tone and subject matter between chaps. 1–9 and chaps. 10–13; and (c) the date and main motive of each letter.

The Opposition at Corinth

All scholars agree that there was in the church at Corinth a group that disputed Paul's apostolic authority and professed to follow certain leaders whom Paul names "false apostles" (*pseudapostoloi*, 2 Cor 11:13), but virtually nothing is certain of their activities and teaching. That they were Jewish Christians is clear from 2 Cor 11:22–23, but whether they were Judaizers from Palestine who demanded the strict observance of the Mosaic Law (as in Galatia),[1] or Hellenistic Jews of the dispersion who held to Gnostic views,[2] has been debated. If they were Judaizers, it is strange that Paul did not directly attack their doctrine, though this does not exclude the possibility altogether. And while they exalted their own *gnōsis* (2 Cor 10:5), it is unlikely that the opponents were merely Gnostics; Gnosticism was not so highly developed in the first century,[3] nor does it seem likely that

---

1. So, e.g., Oostendorp, *Another Jesus*; and Harris, *2 Corinthians*, 312–14. Harris, however, limits the strategy of the Judaizers to the imposition of the provisions of the Apostolic Decree in Acts 15:20, 29, without insistence upon circumcision or calendrical observances (p. 313).

2. Schmithals, *Gnosis in Korinth*; and Wilckens, *Weisheit und Torheit*. See also Georgi, *Gegner des Paulus*, who views Paul's rivals as Hellenistic-Jewish itinerant preachers who claimed to be *theioi andres*.

3. See Yamauchi, "Alleged Evidences," 46–70, esp. 68–70.

The Corinthian Correspondence

Gnostic Christians would carry commendatory letters from the church in Jerusalem.

What *is* clear about those who were opposed to the apostle may be inferred from various statements in the second letter itself.[4] Because they had presented letters of commendation (3:1) and had "invaded" Paul's territory of preaching (10:13–16), it is evident that they were intruders from without. They arrived preaching a different gospel (*allon Iēsoun*, 11:4) and attacking the person of Paul directly (10:1, 10; 11:6), as well as his teaching (10:12–18; 11:7–12; 2:17) and honesty (1:15–18; 10:9–11; 12:16–19). Priding themselves in their Jewish distinctives (as *Hebraioi, Israēlitai, sperma Abraam*, 11:22), spiritual ecstasies (5:13; 12:1, 7), and special relationship to Christ (5:16, 10:7; 11:23), they claim the apostolic authority they deny to Paul, who only at a distance is bold (10:1, 10) and whose behavior and message are weak and offensive (5:11–13; 6:3–10; 10:2). In bold opposition to Paul's gospel they exalt their own philosophy of knowledge against the knowledge of God (10:5). Glorying in fleshly wisdom (*en sophia sarkikē*, 1:12), boasting in their assumed superiority to Moses (3:4–11) and in worldly things (*kata sarka*, 11:18), and encouraging indiscriminate behavior (6:14—7:1), they have nearly succeeded in bringing the community to open revolt against Paul.

The specific allegations against Paul made by these *pseudapostoloi* will be discussed in greater detail when we come to 2 Cor 10:10. Worthy of special attention here, however, is the determination of Paul's adversaries to undermine his authority and thus bring about his downfall, at least at Corinth and perhaps throughout his sphere of influence. What they found especially helpful to their purpose was the inconsistency between the apparent strength of Paul's writing and the weakness of his presence, which threw doubt upon his claim to be "of Christ" (2 Cor 10:7) and the veracity of his gospel (4:3; 6:2, 3). Paul did not deny that weakness was a valid characterization of his apostolic ministry—indeed, we shall see that weakness was at the very center of his self-identity and was that which authenticated his message. What he had to do, however, was to take the concept of weakness that his opponents used against him and redefine it according to its proper explication. To Paul, this faulty understanding of weakness among the Corinthians, pressed to an extreme, was leading to a faulty and dangerous misunderstanding of the more important fact—the Christ event (2

---

4. Excellent summaries in Guthrie, *Introduction*, 422–24; Feine et el., *Einleitung*, 246–48; Lohse, *Die Entstehung*, 42–44; Hughes, *2 Corinthians*, 356–58.

Cor 13:3–5); in that the Corinthians failed to understand *Paul's* weakness, they failed to understand who *Jesus* was. This is the underlying motive and significance of weakness language in the Corinthian correspondence and the reason why 2 Corinthians 10–13 is the *locus classicus* on weakness in the Pauline corpus.

The Literary Unity of 2 Corinthians

To what extent 2 Corinthians is the result of redaction is still a debated and debatable point. Even a merely cursory survey of the whole question in its larger implications would be impossible here. Although several pericopes are disputed—notably the Pauline origin of 2 Cor 6:14—7:1 and whether 2 Cor 2:14—7:4 is a separate, earlier letter of Paul to Corinth—the crucial problem is the question whether chaps. 1–9 and 10–13 could have been parts of the same letter. That 2 Corinthians 10–13 belongs to a separate writing of Paul suggests itself by an apparent illogical break between 9:15 and 10:1, the obvious shift in subject matter and tone between these two sections, and the harshness of the apostle's long invective in the latter section. The question arises: Are these four chapters an integral part of 2 Corinthians, another letter, or a fragment of a letter, perhaps to be identified with the "severe" letter (2 Cor 7:8) written in tears (2 Cor 2:4)? While intelligent defenses of the traditional view of unity are still to be found, the dominant view today is that 2 Corinthians 10–13 was written earlier than 2 Corinthians 1–9 and forms part of the "severe" letter written "out of great distress and anguish of heart with many tears" (2 Cor 2:4). Several features in chaps. 10–13 correspond to what is known of the "severe" letter, although its principal subject, the "offender" of 2 Cor 2:5–11, is not found there.

First, the obvious change in tone between these two sections (from joy and confidence to self-defense and indignation) can be explained on the hypothesis that the final portion of the "severe" letter begins here. Otherwise it would seem tactless of Paul to append such harsh and sarcastic words to his previous words of commendation. On the other hand, the possibility that Paul began his letter with praise[5] with a view to leaving till the end any criticism of his converts[6] cannot be ruled out altogether. Moreover, careful exegesis reveals that the tone in chaps. 1–9 is not always irenic nor

---

5. Cf. 1 Thess 1:2–10; 1 Cor 1:4–9; Phil 1:3–11.
6. Cf. Gal 6:12–17; Phil 3:2—4:3; 2 Tim 4:14–18.

is the tone in chaps. 10–13 always angry;[7] it may be that not until chaps. 10–13 does the battle between Paul and his opponents reach its full force.[8]

It is also argued that Paul's attitude toward self-commendation (*kauchasthai*) has undergone a change between the "severe" letter and 2 Corinthians. For in 2 Corinthians 10–13 Paul openly commends himself (11:5, 18, 22–29; 12:1, 12), but in chaps. 1–9 he states that he will not commend himself "again" (*palin*, 3:1 and 5:12). However, Paul's attitude of *kauchēsis* in chaps. 1–9 and 10–13 is not necessarily contradictory; the apostle throughout the letter is operating on the basis of a single principle: it is the Lord, not Paul himself, who gives Paul his commendation (cf. 10:12–18), so that he *may* boast—only "in the Lord" (10:17). Therefore he refuses to boast as the false teachers do, according to worldly standards (5:12, 16), even though he could out-do his opponents even on that basis, as he shows in 11:18–29.

Furthermore, it is sometimes argued that the references to a visit to Corinth are unintelligible if 2 Corinthians 10–13 is later than chaps. 1–9. However, each of the visit-references may be understood equally as satisfactorily on the hypothesis of unity: 1:23 and 2:3 may simply refer to the apostle's change of itinerary and to a letter in which that was announced (e.g., 1 Cor 16:5–9), whereas 13:2 and 10 may be references to his forthcoming visit that he is announcing in 2 Corinthians.

Therefore, although the hypothesis that the "severe" letter is contained within 2 Corinthians 10–13 cannot be disregarded out of hand, it does not appear necessary. The integrity of the transmitted letter has the unquestioned support of the entire textual tradition, a fact that cannot be set aside gratuitously. Furthermore, it seems incongruous to charge Paul with incoherency because scholars cannot now determine his train of thought as he moves from 9:15 to 10:1. "Les difficultés et les obscurités de notre lettre," writes Collange,[9] "proviennent de ce que Paul répond à une situation très précise et concrète, claire à ses yeux et à ceux de ses correspondents, cachée aux nôtres." In our present ignorance of all the facts concerning the circumstances of the letter's composition, should we be so quick to charge the apostle with inconsistency, or should we not rather admit that he knew better than we do how to frame the epistle for the audience he knew so well? 2 Corinthians is, after all, a personal document, and it reveals a spontaneity

---

7. See Stephenson, "A Defense," 94.
8. See Bates, " Integrity," 56–69.
9. Collange, *Énigmes*, 320.

that is unknown in Paul's other letters and that does not demand absolute consistency in every detail.[10]

Though the choice is not an easy one, in this study the integrity of 2 Corinthians is tentatively assumed. The greatest weakness of the "severe" letter hypothesis is the absence of any reference in 2 Corinthians 10–13 to the "offender" who was its occasion and most important subject. Accepting the unity of the letter relieves us of the obligation of finding traces of this "severe" letter in chaps. 10–13 or of explaining why a later editor would have removed them. Therefore, because sufficient unity of thought in the document as it stands can be demonstrated,[11] and because the abrupt break between chaps. 9 and 10 can be explained in a variety of ways without sacrificing the letter's essential unity,[12] the integrity of the transmitted letter need not be surrendered. Most importantly of all, even if it were necessary to assign chaps. 10–13 to a different letter, we would still have Paul as the author.

The Date and Purpose of 1 and 2 Corinthians

While it is not possible to date 1 Corinthians with any certainty, it was clearly written from the city of Ephesus (1 Cor 16:8) on Paul's third missionary journey, probably in the year AD 55. Two factors prompted Paul to write the letter. The immediate occasion was the letter Paul had received from the believers in Corinth seeking guidance on several questions. There were also reports of dissension and immorality that had come to him from Chloe's people that in turn called for a response. At the same time, Paul took the opportunity of introducing doctrinal teaching, particularly instruction concerning the resurrection of the dead (15:1–58).

2 Corinthians was almost certainly composed in the late autumn of A.D. 56 from a city in Macedonia, probably Philippi. The main purpose of the letter was to prepare the Corinthians for Paul's third visit to them. On his last visit to Corinth he admittedly had shown some weakness, but

---

10. Turner (*Style*, 80) writes: "Changes in mood are especially evident in 2 Corinthians and they tend to mar its literary excellence, as compared with 1 Corinthians, although chapters 9–12 are powerful in style. The polishing function of an amanuensis does not seem so evident in 2 Corinthians."

11. See, for instance, Tasker, *2 Corinthians*, 34–35; also Hughes, *2 Corinthians*, xix–xxi.

12. See the list of suggestions, some more, others less convincing, in Harris, *2 Corinthians*, 379–80.

this will not happen again (13:1-4). On this visit he will be ready to punish the disobedient, who should therefore examine themselves before he comes and so relieve him of the unhappy task of having to act with severity (13:5-6). Titus, in the meantime, will return to Corinth to deal with the matter of the collection and to prepare for Paul's arrival (8:16-24). The letter may therefore be understood as an explanation of Paul's itinerary. The following scheme has been suggested[13] and is adopted in the present study:

(a) The change of itinerary explained (1-7);

(b) The preparation for the upcoming visit (8-9); and

(c) The certainty and imminence of the visit (10-13).

EXEGESIS OF THE TEXTS: 1 CORINTHIANS

1 Corinthians 1:25, 27; 2:3

The main theme of the opening chapters of 1 Corinthians—divine judgment upon human wisdom—is stated clearly in 1:19 (Isa 29:14, LXX): "For it is written, 'I will destroy the wisdom of the wise, and I will bring to nothing the intelligence of the intelligent.'" The key phrase is *sophian apolluein*, which is paraphrased throughout by such phrases as *sophian mōrainein* or *mataioun* and *synesin athetein* or *kryptein*. What follows are three treatments of this theme in 1:20-25; 1:26-31; and 2:1-5. In the first section (1:20-25) appears Paul's theological *Prinzipienlehre* concerning wisdom and foolishness, which is succeeded by two sections that demonstrate the wisdom of God as exemplified (a) in the community of the elect (1:26-31), and (b) in his own life and preaching (2:1-5).[14] In each of these sections, weakness language occurs in support of the central idea found at 1:19. Because God's wisdom and power are misunderstood by a proud mankind to be "foolish" and "weak" (1:25), he elects those who have no confidence in the flesh, like the "weak" Corinthians (1:27) and the "weak" apostle (2:3), in order to humiliate those who possess worldly strength (*ta ischyra tou kosmou*, cf. 1:27).[15]

---

13. Hughes, *2 Corinthians*, xxi.

14. See Conzelmann, *1 Korinther*, 57.

15. "Der Erweis göttlicher Kraft ist an einer Stelle erfolgt, an der niemand es erwartet hat," writes Lohse (*Grundriss*, 81) with reference to the cross of Christ but with a significance that equally applies both to the elect in Corinth and to Paul their spiritual father.

Paul, Apostle of Weakness

1 Corinthians 1:25.

In 1 Cor 1:25 Paul states that "the foolishness of God is wiser than people, and the weakness of God [*to asthenes tou theou*] is stronger than people." In order to ascertain the meaning of the expression *to asthenes* it is necessary to begin our discussion at 1:18, the beginning of Paul's treatment of Christian *sophia* ("wisdom, broad and full intelligence"). In 1:18–25 the apostle contrasts the false wisdom of humans and the apparently foolish wisdom of God as displayed in the death of Christ on the cross. Christ, who is "the wisdom and power of God" (1:24, 30), is rejected by those who prefer their own brand of *sophia* to that of God's. In 1:18–25 Paul is anxious to communicate to the Corinthians a more mature, indeed the only correct, understanding of *sophia*, but finds them unprepared to accept it, being *sarkinoi* and *nēpioi* (1 Cor 3:1).

Paul proceeds here, as in 2:6–13, to show that rather than accepting divine *sophia* by faith, people have rejected it by a proud reliance on human wisdom (cf. 2:8). Christians, on the other hand, recognize the apparent foolishness of the cross to be true wisdom, perceiving in the death and resurrection of Christ God's working out his mysterious plan of salvation on behalf of a lost, fallen, and hostile humankind (1:18, 21). Paul, therefore, develops his response to the carnal difficulties among the Corinthians by introducing a series of contrasting themes: true and false wisdom; divine and human wisdom; the *apparent* foolishness of God's wisdom and the *real* foolishness of ours; and the necessity of rejecting the false and accepting the true *sophia*.

The exact connotation of the false wisdom in these verses has been disputed. The Corinthian *sophia* may be identified either as Greek philosophy, a Hellenistic gnosis, or some sort of Jewish concept in opposition to the gospel of Paul. But "whether it was Greek rationalism and rhetoric, a pre-Christian gnosis or a Jewish reaction to the Gospel that confronted Paul in Corinth and lay at the heart of the difficulties there, Paul saw that the root of the problem was the radical opposition between human wisdom and divine wisdom."[16] That this contrast is fundamental to Paul's argument is evident in that the word *sophia* appears in 1 Corinthians almost exclusively in 1:18—4:21, the section where the apostle draws out most clearly

---

16. O'Donnell, *Education in Wisdom*, 149–50.

The Corinthian Correspondence

the antithesis between the *sophia tou kosmou* and the *sophia tou theou* (1 Cor 1:20, 21).[17]

To present emphatically the greatness of God's wisdom as contrasted to human wisdom the apostle resorts in 1:25 to hyperbole. God, of course, does not have foolishness or weakness, but by saying that he does Paul shows the paradoxical nature of our attempt to rely upon our own wisdom and strength. The Greek construction plainly reveals the intentional parallelism:

(1) *to mōron   tou theou sophōteron   tōn anthrōpōn estin*[18]

(2) *to asthenes tou theou ischyroteron tōn anthrōpōn.*[19]

To this must be added the statement in v. 24 that v. 25 is written to explain (cf. *hoti*): *Christon theou dynamin kai theou sophian* ("Christ, God's power and God's wisdom"). As Conzelmann[20] correctly notes, *to mōron* corresponds to *sophia*, and *to asthenes* corresponds to *dynamis*, so that v. 25 is really a statement about Christ. "Christ crucified" (*Christon estaurōmenon*, 1:23) is the supreme instance of the weakness and foolishness of God and stands against the world's wisdom because he contradicts the idea that victory is gained through the display of force.

For this reason both the form and the content of Paul's message were repugnant to those who were lost (*apollymenois*, 1:18).[21] Paul refused to preach with convincing arguments and insisted on limiting his message to a man who had died on a cross. Therefore the world, and now some of the Corinthians, rationalized that the apostle's gospel was absolute foolishness and impotence. Against this notion Paul asserts that Christian wisdom is an acceptance of the foolishness and weakness of God, that is, the reception of Christ crucified as preached in the Pauline kerygma. The *logos tou*

---

17. See Ellis, "'Weisheit,'" 115.

18. DG read *sophōteron estin tōn anthrōpōn*.

19. The expression *tōn anthrōpōn* ("of the people") has no particular people in mind, but refers to the totality of people, i.e., all humankind (cf. Germ., "die Menschen," Fr. "les hommes").

20. *1 Korinther*, 69.

21. A Christ on the cross was a stumbling block to the Jews and absolute folly to the Gentiles (1:23), and constituted a most despicable message to human ears; cf. Cicero, *In Verrem* 5, 165: "crux, crudelissimum taeterrimumque supplicium" (cited by Grosheide, *The First Epistle*, 49n.). On the significance of crucifixion in the ancient world and its relationship to 1 Corinthians, see Hengel, "MORS TURPISSIMA," 125ff.

staurou is a *skandalon*, *mōria*, and *asthenē* only to those who are perishing but is God's wisdom and power to those who are being saved by it.

Thus by saying that God has foolishness and weakness, and by contrasting that with human wisdom and power, Paul wishes to assert that God has complete control over humans and fully accomplishes his purposes, so that the plans and actions of mere human beings are nothing in comparison. What the world considers to be *mōron* and *asthenes*, i.e., the crucifixion of Christ, is really a revelation of the wisest council (*sophia*) and providential power (*dynamis*) of God, salvation for believers, and the only valid ground of glory and boasting (1:31).

The abstract words *to mōron* and *to asthenes* are, then, to be understood in concrete terms as referring to the cross of Christ.[22] As he will do throughout the Corinthian letters, Paul takes up terms or concepts the Corinthians had used in a negative sense and redefines them through his understanding of the Christ-event in a positive way. It is to protect the gospel and its core, the cross, that these concepts are given such a prominent place in the apostle's argument. Hence, what Paul means by *to asthenes* here is that God's power to save, though misunderstood by humans and labelled "weak," is greater and more efficacious than the mightiest efforts of humans.

1 Corinthians 1:27

Having asserted that salvation is in Christ and not in the wisdom of people, and that therefore we have no ground for boasting, Paul now (1:26–31) carries forward his argument with a summons to consider the circumstances under which God has called his people. The Corinthian believers themselves are the proof that the "folly" of God is wiser than human wisdom, for (1:26, *gar*) he chooses those who by worldly standards (*kata sarka*) are neither intellectually (*ou polloi sophoi*), politically (*ou polloi dynatoi*), nor socially (*ou polloi eugeneis*) important and gives to them eternal life. By this *argumentum ad hominem* the apostle does not intend to say that all Christians belong to the lower, less-educated, or poorer classes of society, nor does he wish to assert that the *sophoi*, *dynatoi*, or *eugeneis* are excluded from the kingdom. His statement does imply, however, that the majority of the Corinthians were slaves or freedmen (cf. 7:21ff.; 12:13), even though it is certain that a few of the community came from the privileged class.[23]

---

22. Cf. Wendland, *Korinther*, 23.

23. E.g., Crispus (1 Cor 1:14) *ho archisynagōgos* of the local synagogue at Corinth

In the following two verses (27–28) Paul describes those whom God has chosen as *ta mōra* ("the foolish"), *ta asthenē* ("the weak"), *ta agenē* ("the base"), *ta exouthenēmena* ("the despised"), and *ta mē onta* ("the nothings"). By using the neuter plural forms of the adjectives Paul wishes to emphasize not the individuals but their qualities and characteristics. The last three terms are especially appropriate to the situation in Corinth where there were so many slaves. As in v. 25, so here the descriptive terms in vv. 27–28 are used to explicate what was said in the preceding verse (v. 26). The writer's ultimate purpose, however, is to show that all the glory must be rendered to the Lord (v. 31), for it is because of Christ (*ex autou*, v. 30) that salvation has been accomplished.

God chose for himself (*exelexato*)[24] *ta asthenē tou kosmou* (1:27). In the category of "weakness" Paul has thus far used the neuter singular *to asthenes* to indicate the opposite of *dynamin* (1:24, 25). He now adds the neuter plural *ta asthenē*, "weak things," in order to make the statement general enough to include not only persons who may be considered weak but anything at all that could be designated as such. God chose *ta asthenē* in order to shame *ta ischyra*, what the world considers to be strong, whoever or whatever it may be. Things that are considered mighty in the world (*kosmos*) have been disgraced by God's choice of the weak things of the world, in order to show that there is another, higher, divine power that truly makes strong.

Lenski and others[25] have noted that the first four groups mentioned proceed to a climax that is found in the fifth and final statement representing the lowest step: *ta mē onta*, "things that do not even exist" (1:28). The absence of *exelexato ho theos* suggests that this final description of the elect is comprehensive and embraces the four preceding ones. In all four groups there is an element of nonexistence of something specific—wisdom, strength, wealth, etc.—but when Paul adds *ta mē onta* he refers to nonexistence itself.[26] God chooses "things not existing" in order that he might bring

---

(cf. Acts 18:8), and Erastus (Rom 16:23) the city treasurer (*ho oikonomos tēs poleōs*). See also 1 Cor 11:27–34, where the social distinctions in the church are evident at the Lord's Supper.

24. *Eklegomai* is always in the middle voice in the NT and means "to pick or choose out for one's self" (Thayer, *Lexicon*, 196). Its threefold repetition in vv. 27–28 emphasizes the deliberateness of God's action (Vincent, *Word Studies*, 3.194)

25. Lenski, *Corinthians*, 73–74; Conzelmann, *1 Korinther*, 72; Barrett, *1 Corinthians*, 58; Wendland, *Korinther*, 23.

26. See Lenski, *Corinthians*, 77. Paul's use of the expression *ta mē onta* is curious.

to naught the things that are (*ta onta*, 1:28) with the ultimate purpose that "no flesh should glory in the presence of God" (1:29). This means that no one can merit the election of God, neither the wise, great, noble, etc., whom he does not elect, *nor* the foolish, weak, despised, etc., whom he does. There can therefore be no merit in weakness, for the fact that God chooses, and that he chooses as he does, is due solely to his grace and divine providence. The Christian existence of all believers, including "weak" ones, depends not on their virtue but on God's sovereign election, so that they too must learn to boast solely *en kyriō*. God's act of grace in election silences all human glorying including that of the elect, for they glory *en Christō Iēsou* (v. 30). Therefore, Paul does not praise weakness, nor does he develop a cult of the social lower class, for election rightly understood demands the renunciation of self-glorification by all.

1 Corinthians 2:3

"And I was with you *en astheneia* and in fear and much trembling," is Paul's description of his preaching. This statement and the section in which it is found (2:1–5) illustrate the main point of 1:18–31, namely, that the power of the gospel depends neither upon the intelligence of the hearer nor upon the rhetoric or eloquence of the preacher. The gospel alone is the *dynamis theou* and the *sophia theou*, a fact that is reflected not only in the lives of the Corinthians but also in the activities of Paul.

Because the gospel was considered "foolish" by the world, Paul did not preach "in persuasive words of wisdom"; because the gospel was "the weakness of God," he came preaching "in weakness"; because the gospel was the "power of God," his preaching consisted of a "demonstration of the Spirit and power." Hence Paul's method of preaching corresponded in a remarkable fashion to the message that he proclaimed. That he was aware of this antithesis between weakness and power is seen most clearly in the ongoing

---

According to Barrett (*1 Corinthians*, 58) the words bear no relation to Greek philosophical usage, but Wendland (*Korinther*, 23–24) thinks that "vielleicht nimmt Paulus hier den griechischen philosophischen Fachausdruck 'das Nichtseiende' auf" in order to make the strongest possible contrast with the Greek world of thought. However, he cites no evidence or parallels for his position. The words *ta mē onta* are more probably a general reference to those things and persons that in the opinion of the world are simply unimportant and therefore lack authority; so Thayer, *Lexicon*, 175; Grosheide, *The First Epistle*, 52; Fisher, *Corinthians*, 33. Conzelmann (*1 Korinther*, 72n.) notes that the expression is used "sozial, nicht kosmologisch."

expression of the *logos tou staurou* in his own life.[27] Paul had erased from his thinking everything but "Jesus Christ and him crucified" (2:2), the most repelling aspect of the evangel, so that the faith of his converts "might not rest in human wisdom but in the power of God" (2:5), that is, in the crucified Messiah.

Broadly speaking, *astheneia* here first is a general term to describe the apostle's feeling of personal inadequacy in view of his message that requires us to admit our own helplessness and rely upon the sacrifice of Christ. It is possible to identify it more specifically with the *skolops* of 2 Cor 12:7, for if the "thorn" affected his physical appearance his adversaries would have had reason to complain, "His letters are weighty and strong, but his bodily presence is *asthenēs* and his speech is of no account" (2 Cor 10:10). More probably, however, here as well as in 2 Cor 10:10 *astheneia* is a reference to an unimpressive personal presence that has its emotional counterparts in *phobos* and *tromos*,[28] the nervousness or anxiety which, in this case, may have resulted from the loneliness and discouragement of his disappointing visit to Athens (Acts 17).

Paul's personal weakness and the kerygma of the cross that accompanied him to Corinth may also be understood christologically as the paradoxical expression of the *dynamis* of God that offends the worldly strong. Here it is not the message (cf. 1:25) that embarrasses the *dynatoi*, but the weak and frail messenger whom God has chosen to bear it. For what Paul preaches and what Paul does are inseparable: the cross of Christ is not limited to a past event but is demonstrated continuously in his daily experience. In that the bearer of the *logos tou staurou* reflects his own self-understanding of the cross and allows himself to be crucified with Christ, the *logos* becomes a *logos tēs katallagēs* (cf. 2 Cor 5:18–6:2) to those who believe. Therefore, while *astheneia* does refer to a poor personal presence (or physical condition), in view of the emphasis in v. 2 upon the message of his preaching ("Christ crucified") and in v. 3 upon the manner of his preaching, the state in question must include a theological sense as well. Paul rejected oratory, not because he was physically or mentally not up to it, but because his preaching in Corinth had been absolutely subjected to

---

27. See Bultmann, *Theologie*, 301–3. For Paul, nothing was more inextricably tied to his life and apostleship than the gospel, "the word of the cross," as Schütz has shown, *Apostolic Authority*, 35.

28. *Phobos kai tromos* is a Pauline expression (cf. 2 Cor 7:15; Phil 2:12; Eph 6:5) that designates an uncertainty based upon humility, arising from an appreciation of the importance and difficulties of the apostolic ministry. See Lietzmann, *Korinther*, 11.

the message of the gospel and performed in the Spirit's power only. Thus his conformity to the gospel of Christ is *both* inward and outward.

The negative characteristics of weakness, fear, and trembling are enlarged upon in the corresponding positive statement in v. 4. Paul succeeded in his ministry in spite of his weaknesses because he discarded mere human helps and relied solely upon the divine *pneuma* and *dynamis*. It is interesting that the three catchwords of v. 3 correspond directly to the threefold characterization of Paul's ministry in v. 4:

en astheneia: *ouk en peithois sophias logois*

en phobō: *en apodeixei pneumatos*

en tromō: *kai dynameōs*

The last two positive statements of v. 4 correspond antithetically to the final two negative statements of v. 3, while *ouk en peithois sophias logois* is the corresponding negative description of *en astheneia*. This idea fits the emphasis the apostle makes upon his refusal to impress his audience with the wise choice of words rather than the substance of his message, for preaching *en sophia logou* would empty the cross of its power (1:17). God rejects the philosopher who delights in discussion and dispute (*syzētētēs*, 1:20) as well as those who are proud of their superficial sophistries (1:22), but takes pleasure in those who continue proclaiming (*kēryssomen*, 1:23) Christ as the crucified Savior. Paul therefore resolves (*krinein*) not to preach anything except Christ and him crucified (2:2). This necessarily involves also a corresponding decision to cast aside eloquence (*logos*) and wisdom (*sophia*) as instruments of his proclamation (2:1).

Hence, Paul's choice of method at Corinth was not determined solely by the pseudo-intellectuality of the Corinthians, though he was aware of their infatuation with eloquence and rhetoric, but by the content of the message itself to which the bearing of the preacher perfectly conformed. Paul's method of preaching demonstrated that indeed *the gospel alone* was the power of God unto salvation.

1 Corinthians 4:10

In 4:1–21 Paul discusses the character of the servants of Christ (*hypēretas Christou*, 4:1) who are entrusted with the handling of God's truth (*oikonomous mystēriōn theou*, 4:1). The Corinthians are admonished to have the proper attitude toward apostles and teachers and to leave the estimation of their value and service to God, "who will bring to light the hidden things of darkness and will disclose the purposes of [their] hearts" (4:5). Paul had applied this principle of judgment to himself and Apollos for the benefit of the church in Corinth (4:6–7).

Whereas the Corinthians claim to be spiritually rich and take pride in their charismatic leaders, Paul and Apollos are considered weak and a shameful *theatron tō kosmō kai angelois kai anthrōpois* (9). In a rare outburst of sarcasm Paul condemns their feeling of self-sufficiency (8–13), beginning with a series of pointed questions about their spiritual attainments (8), which is followed with a remarkable statement about the sad condition in which he and other preachers of the gospel find themselves (9). He concludes with a series of comparisons between the imagined superiority of the Corinthians and the position of the apostles (10–13). His purpose in all of this is to reestablish his position of preeminence among them as their spiritual *patēr* (14–15), not to shame them.

The plural of the adjective *asthenēs* occurs in v. 10 where a short series of three contrasts between the condition of the apostles and that of the Corinthians appears. These three antitheses follow each other closely and may be regarded as detailed illustrations of Paul's derisive rebuke of the inflated self-satisfaction of the Corinthians found in vv. 8–9.[29] The chiastic form is seen clearly in the exchange in the third sentence of *hēmeis* and *hymeis*, which heightens the contrast and smoothes the transition to v. 11 ("we"):

hēmeis mōroi dia Christon, hymeis de phronimoi en Christō.

hēmeis astheneis, hymeis de ischyroi.

hymeis endoxoi, hēmeis de atimoi.

The catchwords *mōros*, *ischyros*, and *asthenēs* recall the thought of 1:18ff., where it was stated that the gospel and those who preach it are considered foolish and weak by the world. Here, as in 2:3, Paul admits that he is foolish, weak, and held in dishonor, but he has become such a person in order to be wise, strong, and honorable in a Christian sense. The fact that he uses *ischyros* for the antithesis of *asthenēs* instead of *dynatos* (cf. 2 Cor 13:9, *hotan hēmeis asthenōmen, hymeis dedynatoi ēte*) is merely a rhetorical variation without intrinsic significance, the distinction between "power" (*dynamis*) and "strength" (*ischys*) being at best only implicit in Paul, who can write of himself, *panta ischyō en tō endynamounti me* (Phil 4:13).

---

29. So Fisher, *Corinthians*, 65; Lietzmann, *Korinther*, 20; Grosheide, *The First Epistle*, 107.

Whereas the Corinthians imagined themselves to be *ischyroi*, they considered Paul's message, and the means by which he presented it, to be ineffective and weak. Paul thus became to his antagonists an object of disdain, for he rejected rhetoric and persuasion in order to rely exclusively upon the power of the indwelling Christ. In Christ he *is* weak (2 Cor 13:4), but this very fact enables him to manifest divine strength (2 Cor 12:9). Just as the gospel, the *dynamis theou eis sōtērian* (Rom 1:16), conceals itself in weakness, so also the weakness and mortality of Paul, rather than hindering his apostolic ministry, afford the best platform from which to display the glory of Christ. Only *en dynamei theou* (2 Cor 6:7) can he accomplish his mission and overcome the limitations of human existence that otherwise would impede his activities.[30]

Fisher[31] is correct in seeing in vv. 11–13 a series of illustrations[32] that directly parallels v. 10 and demonstrates that the apostles are indeed foolish, weak, and disreputable. That they are fools in the eyes of people is proved by their undergoing hardships for Christ's sake (11–12a). That they are without honor in the world's eyes is proved by its maltreatment of them (13b). And that the apostles are weak when viewed from a human standpoint is proved by their refusal to retaliate when wronged (12b–13a). If reviled (*loidoroumenoi*), persecuted (*diōkomenoi*), or slandered (*dysphēmoumenoi*) because of Christian service, they respond as Jesus would (cf. Matt 5:5, 10ff.) by blessing, patiently enduring, and seeking conciliation. These qualities would quite naturally be despised by the Greeks as signs of weakness and cowardice. For this reason the apostles are scorned and held in the lowest possible disrepute "as the world's scapegoats, the scum of the earth, to this day" (13).

---

30. However, Pickett (*Cross in Corinth*) maintains that Paul's reference to his own weakness in 4:10 carries social connotations that have been overlooked by most commentators. He writes (43n15), "Black fails to recognize the social connotations of the weakness terminology in Paul and sees it instead as denoting the powerlessness, transitoriness and bodily frailty of humanity, especially in relation to God (cf. pp. 228–34)." In our view, there is nothing in the immediate context that would require the term *asthenēs* to refer exclusively or even primarily to Paul's social status or value.

31. *Corinthians*, 66.

32. For other catalogues of hardships ("Peristasen-Kataloge"), cf. 1 Cor 15:30–32; 2 Cor 4:8–11; 6:4–5; 11:23–29.

1 Corinthians 8:7-12

At 8:1 Paul turns to a fresh theme raised in the Corinthians' letter: *peri de tōn eidōlythytōn* ("Now, about things offered to idols . . .").[33] The question of the eating of meat offered to heathen idols would arise in two situations: (a) at religious festivals held in the temple of the pagan deity, and (b) in social settings where such food was being served or at the marketplace where sacrificial meat was often sold. Could Christians eat meat that had been part of an animal sacrifice to a pagan god? Was one bound to decline an invitation to a feast in which such food was served? And could one, even unwittingly, purchase meat in the public market, a part of which may have come from one of the pagan sacrifices so common in Corinth?

There were two opinions within the Christian community concerning the matter, and both were wrong. Some Corinthians, reveling in the knowledge that "an idol has no real existence" and "there is no God but one" (8:4), reasoned that they were absolutely free to purchase and eat the sacrificed meat. Others, less knowledgeable brothers and sisters, believed that meat offered to idols still carried the taint of the pagan god and, therefore, eating it even in private meant participating in the pagan sacrifices. These two groups are commonly referred to as the "Strong" and the "Weak" respectively, even though the former ascription is not mentioned explicitly in 1 Corinthians (as it is in Romans 14) and neither group can be identified with one of the several factions in Corinth referred to in 1:12.[34]

Paul's treatment of the problem divides itself into five parts. In 8:1-13 he asserts first the basic principle that the liberty of the strong is to be disciplined by love. They must therefore exercise responsibility toward the weak who do not share their knowledge that idols have no real existence. Next, he cites his own situation as an example of the suspension of personal rights for the good of others. Paul waives his right to marry and to receive material benefits from his converts for the sake of the Corinthians (9:1-18); he accommodates himself to the customs of others to win them to Christ (9:19-23); and he subjects himself to spiritual discipline lest people suspect his motives (9:24-27). Third, he illustrates the dangers of idolatry from the history of Israel (10:1-13) that leads, fourthly, to a warning against

---

33. See Barrett, "Things Sacrificed," 138-53; Fee, "*Eidōluthuta*," 172-97.

34. This is the conclusion of Rauer, whose excellent study of the weak, (*Die "Schwachen"*) is the result of careful research and constitutes a major contribution to the discussion. A short, but penetrating study of the question is that of Theissen, "Starken und Schwachen," 155-72.

participation in pagan festivals (10:14–22). Finally, he suggests a series of practical ways to make decisions in social circumstances (10:23—11:1).

Chapter 8, where the weakness-termini appear, can be further subdivided into three paragraphs with the following themes: (a) the superiority of love to knowledge (1–3), (b) the significance of the pagan system of gods (4–6), and (c) the proper exercise of Christian freedom (7–13). Paul concludes the discussion by expressing in the first person the Christian ideal that all should follow: "Therefore if what I eat causes my brother or sister to fall [into sin], I will *by no means* [*ou mē*] eat meat again, lest I cause my brother or sister to stumble" (v. 13).

The terms for weakness, which appear five times in this discussion, are embedded in every occurrence in a slightly different expression:

(1) v. 7 *hē syneidēsis autōn asthenēs ousa molynetai.*

(2) v. 9 *hē exousia hymōn autē proskomma gennētai tois asthenesin.*

(3) v. 10 *ouchi hē syneidēsis autou asthenous ontos oikodomēthēsetai eis to ta eidōlothyta esthiein;*

(4) v. 11 *apollytai gar ho asthenōn en tē sē gnōsei.*

(5) v. 12 *typtontes autōn tēn syneidēsin asthenousan*[35] *eis Christon hamartanete.*

The fact that weakness language is found in vv. 7–13, and not earlier, is in itself significant. Only after he has established his basic premise and corrected the thesis of the strong does Paul proceed to positive instruction and application. In fact, if it were not for the relative length of this paragraph, one might be inclined to think of the discussion of the weak as an afterthought, since what Paul says applies more to the strong than to those with weak consciences. Here it is not the principles of the weak that are called into question but the distorted *gnōsis* of the strong. Nor does Paul give any advice on how the weak consciences could be strengthened, or even if they should be. He says nothing in this passage about the inner disposition of the person whose conscience is debilitated. His only concern is to protect the weaker Christians from returning, even part way, to pagan worship because of the example of a more enlightened brother or sister.[36] We must therefore

---

35. The omission of *asthenousan* by p46 and Clement is best explained by homoioteleuton, even though some have suggested theological motives for its absence (e.g., Metzger, *Textual Commentary*, 557).

36. Cf. Horsley, "Consciousness and Freedom," 586–87. See also Ruef, *1 Corinthians*, 73–74.

The Corinthian Correspondence

resist the temptation to glean more from this passage than Paul has put into it. He neither denounces, defends, nor defines the weak Corinthians, nor does he deal with them as a separatistic party but as certain ones (*tines*) who consider freedom dangerous and whose consciences (*syneidēsis*)[37] is overscrupulous.

When one attempts to trace the train of thought in Paul's usage of weakness vocabulary in vv. 7–12, the following pattern emerges. The first occurrence (v. 7) is the adjective *asthenēs* that modifies *hē syneidēsis*, "the conscience" of those who cannot cease to believe in the reality of the spiritual beings behind idols.[38] To eat food sacrificed to these idols is contrary to their unenlightened awareness, and if they do eat their conscience is defiled. After a short interlude in which Paul asserts the neutrality of food (v. 8), the substantive *tois asthenesin* ("to the weak") appears in v. 9: "Be careful lest this liberty of yours somehow become a stumbling block [*proskomma*] to the weak." Here it is not the conscience that is weak but the men and women who bear it. Metaphorically, a *proskomma* cannot cause a conscience to "stumble," but it may lie in the path of an individual and induce him or her to fall. Contrary to the opinion of the stronger members, the verdict of even a weak conscience is valid and hence Paul does not dispute it. It is therefore not a matter of correcting the faulty knowledge of the weak, but of bridling the unrestrained exercise of freedom that could lead to their destruction. Specifically, "the weak" in v. 9 is a reference to those

---

37. In 1 Cor 8:7–13 and 10:23–11:1 *syneidēsis* appears eight times (out of 20 in Paul): 8:7, 10, 12; 10:25, 27, 28, 29 (twice). Interestingly, the term is not found in Paul prior to 1 Corinthians and is missing in the parallel passage in Romans 14. This would suggest that Paul picked up the term from the enlightened Corinthians who had confronted him with their concept of "conscience." Later in writing Romans Paul could discard the term.

38. Three times in 1 Corinthians 8 weakness is related to *syneidēsis*, the conscience. The term refers to one's perception of something, an "awareness" or "consciousness," without any necessary moralistic overtones. Stendahl correctly criticizes the tendency to modernize the concept in terms of a psychological, introspective attitude, which makes Paul "a hero of the introspective conscience" ("Introspective Conscience," 199–215). The Pauline conception is not to be confused with the modern idea of an autonomous, subjective freedom of choice; rather in Paul *syneidēsis* means "judgment": the ability to know one's self, to critically judge one's own actions in the light of the concrete revelation of God (cf. Conzelmann, *Grundriss der Theologie*, 204–206). In Romans 14, in place of *syneidēsis* Paul says *pistis*, "faith." Only in later times did *syneidēsis* come to be thought of as a selective, inner power enabling one to know what is right *before* one does it; cf. Whiteley, *Theology of St. Paul*, 210. On *syneidēsis* in general, see Maurer, "synoida, syneidēsis," *TWNT* 7:897–918. Reicke ("Syneidesis," 157–61) discusses the *locus classicus* of the Pauline use of *syneidēsis* (cf. idem, *Disobedient Spirits*, 174–82). On the different functions of the conscience, see Zuck, "Conscience," 329–40.

who possess weak consciences and refers to v. 7, but the term also recalls 1:27 where it is said that God chooses "the weak" to confound the strong. In a general sense, therefore, Paul is defending the place of the weak man and woman in the church, for they too are chosen by God and deserve the love, respect, and care of stronger Christians.

At v. 10 Paul introduces a hypothetical situation (*ean gar*) in which a person with a weak conscience might be encouraged to eat food offered to idols. He takes one Corinthian (*tis*) with a weak conscience as a representative of them all. In v. 10 *syneidēsis* reappears, but here again it is not the conscience that is weak but the person (*asthenous ontos*). The unusual wording of the statement is more prominent in Greek than in most English versions. A cumbersome but suggestive translation would be, "For if someone sees you who have knowledge reclining [at table] in an idol-shrine, will not his or her conscience, this weak person's [conscience], be emboldened to eat things sacrificed to idols?" The irony is meant for the strong: You should be "building up" the weak but instead you are encouraging (*oikodomein*) them to idol worship; you do exercise freedom, but in such a way as to destroy the freedom of your brother or sister!

If Paul's use of *oikodomein* in a negative sense is an intentional contrast to its meaning elsewhere in his letters, it may be inferred that the stronger members were attempting to justify their inconsiderate behavior by claiming that they wished only to "build up" or edify the weak. Paul's answer to this is that there is a proper and an improper way to edify, and that the proper course of action is to defer to the weaker members.

Paul does not answer the question he raised in v. 10, preferring simply to state the tragic results when the strong act out of *gnōsis* rather than *agapē*: "For the weak person [*ho asthenōn*] perishes by [*en*] your knowledge, the brother or sister for whose sake Christ died" (v. 11). According to the context, "perishes" (*apollytai*) must refer to a lapse into paganism and not to eternal destruction (cf. John 3:16). It is not the strong person's exercise of liberty *per se* that accomplishes this but, as the preposition *en* shows, also the weak person's attempt to live according to the knowledge of the strong, trying to suppress his or her own scruples. Though the situation is purely hypothetical, the argument at this point is at its highest: If the sophisticated Corinthians continue to abuse their freedom, weaker Christians may return, even part way, to the worship of pagan deities and thus bring upon themselves their own destruction. Here the weak person is described as "the brother or sister for whom Christ died," a stark contrast between the indifference of the strong and the love of Christ for the weaker Christian.

Finally in v. 12 the drama reaches its culmination with Paul showing the dire consequence this action has on the selfish actors themselves: *hamartanontes eis tous adelphous kai typtontes autōn tēn syneidēsin asthenousan eis Christon hamartanete*. The two present tense participles are instrumental, meaning "by sinning" and "by wounding" and emphasize a continuous course of action. The point is that a wrong done to a brother or sister in Christ is a wrong committed against Christ: *eis Christon hamartanete*. Paul hopes that if anything will alarm the strong it will be this fact.

The plurals in this verse (Paul has changed from the second person singular to the broader second plural) need not imply that Paul has in mind sizable groups of offenders or offended, for he often changes the number in midstream, here evidently in the interest of generalization.[39] Here the conscience is viewed as being weak (*tēn syneidēsin asthenousan*) and capable of being wounded. Specifically, the sin here is against the conscience of the weak believer who is driven in a direction in that he or she would not have gone otherwise.

Paul's argument in these verses may be summarized as follows. He rejects the argument of the "enlightened" that as long as one has the knowledge that idols are nothing any relationship with pagan ceremonies or partaking of idol-meats is harmless. Nor does he accept the arrogant suggestion that the consciences of the weak could be bettered by a good dose of healthy *gnōsis*. For Paul, *gnōsis* is a proper and beneficial gift, but if misused this knowledge is nothing more than carnal wisdom, a wisdom of the world.[40] Paul's view is that a Christian may freely buy sacrificial meat and eat food of any kind whatsoever provided no other Christian is hurt by that action, so that eating or not eating is to be decided on the basis of how that decision will affect "the brother or sister for whom Christ died" (8:11).

Because moral action is never a matter of an isolated act of choosing from a variety of options but is always an act of choosing and doing what is good for one's Christian neighbor and what will edify the Christian community, Paul never tires of exhorting his readers to seek their neighbor's good (cf. 1 Cor 10:24; Rom 15:2; Phil 2:4). The supreme motive for all Christian behavior is love: "For you were called to freedom, brothers; only do not use your freedom as an opportunity for the flesh, but through love

---

39. See Lenski, *Corinthians*, 347.
40. See Ellis, "'Weisheit' und 'Erkenntnis,'" 126.

[*dia tēs agapēs*] be servants of one another" (Gal 5:13). Because godly *agapē* is paramount (1 Cor 13:13), every Christian should be willing to limit his or her own freedom of action out of concern for the welfare of others. Love, however, should not merely be regarded as a restriction of one's freedom; it is more accurate to say that, for Paul, love is an *act of freedom* by which a believer demonstrates that he or she has been liberated from self and sin.[41]

Therefore, the stronger Christians in Corinth must exercise their freedom to eat sacrificed meat without attempting to cause the weak to stumble.[42] Their consciousness has been permeated with the awareness that idols are real and that when they eat such meat, they think of it only as an offering to an idol rather than as food provided by God. Their awareness, or "conscience" (*syneidēsis*), is weak and unable to discriminate in such matters. Once again it is important to note the role of "conscience" in Paul's argument. Though the term may have had a stoic origin, Pierce[43] is probably correct in describing Paul's usage of *syneidēsis* in terms of the popular, non-philosophical Greek thought. Even so, the difference between the Pauline usage and that of Greek philosophy is more a matter of emphasis than of content. Paul is not concerned whether the conscience of a weak person is going to hurt or bother him or her, but he does worry that a believer will be tempted to return to paganism through the faulty example of a more sophisticated Christian. The distinction that Paul makes is not between those who have a strong conscience and those who have a weak one, but between those who are knowledgeable and those who are not. It is therefore not a question of a good or a bad conscience, but of a conscience in a weak person that is capable of being inadequately informed (8:7), weakened (8:12), and even defiled (8:7).[44] The strong, on the other hand, have *gnōsis* and *exousia* that permit them to do this thing or that. *Syneidēsis* does not

---

41. See Furnish, *Love Command*, 111–12; Friedrich, "Freiheit und Liebe," 81–98.

42. In agreement with Hays (*First Corinthians*, 142–43): "Thus, 1 Corinthians 8 must be read as a compelling invitation to the 'strong' Corinthians to come over and join Paul at table with the weak."

43. Pierce, *Conscience*, 16f.

44. Referring to those scholars who contend that the "weak" here are those who belong to a higher social stratum, Garland (*1 Corinthians*, 382) writes: "Paul explicitly connects weakness to their conscience, not their socioeconomic status, and his case assumes that idol food was readily accessible to the weak. D. Black (1984: 84–168, 228–46) shows that Paul uses the term 'weakness' . . . anthropologically to refer to humanity's general powerlessness in relation to God, christologically to refer to weakness as the place where God exhibits his power, and ethically to refer to weakness as a characteristic of immature believers who must not be condemned."

refer to them, only to the weak who do not enjoy the same knowledge and liberty of action. However, the strong *are* to live according to conscience: according to the conscience of the weak, not their own.[45]

1 Corinthians 9:22

The paragraph that comprises 9:19–23 has as its main theme Paul's self-accommodation to the customs of those he sought to win for Christ. The basis for this accommodation is stated at the outset in v. 19: "For though I am free from all people, I have made myself a slave to all, in order that I might win the more." Paul's primary goal in life was to glorify his Lord by winning men and women to the gospel, and this desire dominated everything he did or said. In discussing his self-sacrificing ambition to gain new believers in vv. 20–23, Paul enumerates three groups to which he, on various occasions, had accommodated his lifestyle: the Jews, the Gentiles, and "the weak" (*hoi astheneis*). Even though he did not always live according to Jewish customs, in order to win Jews Paul became like them and when necessary conformed to the practice of the Mosaic Law. Where Judaism was in direct and open conflict with Christianity, Paul was unmovable (cf. Gal 2:4, 5); but in situations where his conduct would unnecessarily alienate Jews he did not hesitate to defer to others, as the circumcision of Timothy in Acts 16:3 illustrates.

"To those under the law" (*tois hypo nomon*) is probably another description of the Jews, though the reference is broad enough to include proselytes and other Gentiles who accepted, in part at least, the requirements of the Mosaic Law. While Paul was not under the dominion of this law (*mē ōn autos hypo nomon*) and therefore not obligated to observe its rigorous ceremonies, as the occasion demanded he would live up to its requirements if that meant the salvation of a Jew or others who considered themselves bound to its traditions.

The second major group to which Paul had accommodated himself was *hoi anomoi*, literally "the lawless." Paul is speaking of those who do not now nor ever did observe the ordinances of the Jewish law. He must mean the Gentiles who, although they were not without some kind of law (Rom 2:14), did not have a written code of commandments such as the Jews possessed.[46] In this case, in order to win Gentiles Paul lived *without* observing

---

45. See further Maurer, "Glaubensbindung und Gewissensfreiheit," 107–17, esp. 114.
46. Fisher, *Corinthians*, 149; Ruef, *1 Corinthians*, 84; Barrett, *1 Corinthians*, 212.

the various restrictions of the law of Moses. He hastens to add, however, that although he did not always practice the Mosaic Law, he did observe a higher law—the law of Christ (Gal 6:2)—so that he is not *anomos theou all ennomos Christou*.[47]

The apostle concludes his list in v. 22 with the statement: *egenomēn tois asthenesin*[48] *asthenēs, hina tous astheneis kerdēsō* ["to the weak I became weak, that I may win the weak"]. In light of Paul's earlier discussion of believers who possess a weak conscience (8:7–13), it is usually suggested that "the weak" in this verse "are Christians not yet fully emancipated from legalism."[49] But if this is true, in what sense does Paul speak of "winning" (*kerdainein*) them? Barrett[50] suggests that Paul is using the verb loosely to mean "keep" them in the church instead of forcing them out by wounding their consciences. Accordingly, Paul "became weak" when he abstained from sacrificed food and observed whatever other scruples the weak had.[51] This view, however, destroys the obvious parallel the apostle is drawing with the previous clauses by concluding each statement with *hina . . . kerdēsō*, "that I might win [them]." It is unlikely that Paul would have used the expression with reference to the evangelization of non-Christians three times and then, without explanation, use it with reference to the edification or preservation of Christians. More probable in our opinion is the view that the weak are non-Christians, whether Jewish or Gentile, who are powerless (*astheneis*) to work out any righteousness for themselves.[52] It is useless to argue that because the verb "gain" (*kerdainein*) is wider in meaning than "save," the weak whom Paul desires to reach can indeed be believers.[53] All four occurrences of *kerdainein* (9:19, 20, 21, 22a) are defined in v. 22b by the verb *sōzein*, which expresses Paul's ultimate purpose in regard to all of the classes already mentioned: "I have become all things to all people that I by all means might save some [*hina pantōs tinas sōsō*]." The verb *sōzein*

---

47. See Dodd, "*Ennomos Christou*," 134–48.

48. Against p46 ℵ A B 1739, several MSS (CDFG) add *hōs* on the analogy of vv. 20–21.

49. Barrett, *1 Corinthians*, 215. Others who see the weak as Christians are Wendland, *Korinther*, 75; Conzelmann, *1 Korinther*, 199; Lenski, *Corinthians*, 379–80. Lietzmann (*Korinther*, 43) curiously refers to the weak as "Halbchristen"!

50. *1 Corinthians*, 215.

51. Ibid.; cf. also Fisher, *Corinthians*, 149; Bruce, "'All Things to All Men,'" 89–90.

52. Cf. Rom 5:6: "When we were still powerless [*ontōn hēmōn asthenōn eti*] Christ died for the ungodly."

53. So, e.g., Lenski, *Corinthians*, 380.

here explicitly states what *kerdainein* can only imply,[54] namely, that Paul's ultimate purpose in accommodating himself to others is the preaching of the gospel and the consequent conversion of non-believers.

Understood in this way, "the weak" becomes a broad and general description of those Paul seeks to win for Christ and encompasses the preceding categories of Jew and Gentile. This interpretation of *hoi astheneis* does not deny the fact that Paul did indeed, for the sake of the weaker Corinthians, respect their scruples and refuse to eat sacrificed meat lest he burden their consciences (8:13). But the immediate context demands that the meaning of *asthenēs* at 9:22 be subordinated to the main subject of 9:19–23, which is the winning of all people for Christ. Though he is free and independent, Paul voluntarily brought himself under bondage and was willing to accommodate his actions to others if only he might see some of them won to the gospel, for whose sake he does all things (*panta de poiō dia to euangelion*, 9:23). In view of this emphasis upon *to euangelion/euangelizesthai* in 9:12, 13 (twice), 16 (twice), 18 (twice), 23 and 27, it seems better to modify somewhat the meaning of *asthenēs* than to give a completely different sense to *kerdainein*. Only if Paul had in mind non-believing Jews, who may have held to similar scruples as the weak in Corinth, can the sense of *asthenēs* here be the same as that in chapter 8.

1 Corinthians 11:30

In the present passage (11:17–34) Paul moves from a discussion of the veiling of women (11:2–16) to the disorders that are connected with the observance of the Lord's Supper (*kyriakon deipnon*). The present pericope must constitute another interruption of Paul's reply to the questions the Corinthians asked, for a new topic is introduced only in 12:1 (again with *peri*). In dealing with this problem, he discusses three matters: (a) abuses at the *agape*—the love feast that accompanied the Supper (17–22); (b) the institution of the Supper by the Lord on the night he was betrayed (23–26); and (c) participation at the table "in an unworthy manner" (*anaxiōs*) that ensues in the discipline of the Lord (27–34).

---

54. Thayer, *Lexicon*, 345; also Schlier, "*kerdos, kerdainō*," *TWNT* 3:672: "So 1 K 9,19ff., wo es [*kerdainein*] den Sinn von 'zum Christen machen' erhält und mit *sōzein* wechselt, 9, 22." Cf. 1 Pet 3:1: "... so that some, though they do not obey the word, by the behavior of their wives might be won (*kerdēthēsontai*) without a word."

The reference in v. 30 to the "weak, sickly, and sleeping" (*astheneis, arrōstoi, koimōntai*) within the congregation falls in the third paragraph and must, therefore, be treated in the light of what has preceded. Verses 27–34 are generally understood as introducing a final section rounding off the whole passage (17–34). Here the topic is the judgment (*krima*) of God upon those who partake of the Lord's Supper in a sinful and irreverent way. The judicial setting is obvious from the array of terms bearing upon judgment: *dokimazein* (28), *krima* (29), *diakrinein* (29), *krinein* (31), and *katakrinein* (32).[55] This emphasis upon judgment follows quite naturally from Paul's earlier criticism of the Corinthians, who "come together [at the table] not for the better but for the worse" (11:17). Indeed, abuses at the Eucharist were just one of the several grave improprieties that had crept into their meetings (cf. the problem of the charismata in 12:1ff.), demanding a lengthy redress.

It is immediately apparent that the problem dealt with in 11:17–34 had two aspects to it. First, the Corinthians were insensitive to the needs of the poorer members of the congregation, and second, they failed to recognize the special character of the meal as the *Lord's* supper.[56] The fact that "each goes ahead with his or her own meal" (v. 21) is a hint that there were different social strata in the Corinthian church. Evidently some could not bring food to the Eucharist because they could not afford to do so, whereas others, the rich, presumably brought more than they needed in order to make provision for the needy. The implication is that the richer members were eating and drinking the extra supplies themselves. Paul asserts that social barriers cannot be maintained between the rich and the poor, especially not at the Lord's Supper. His rebuke of these abuses eventually led to a separation of the Eucharist celebration from the common meal.

Paul's criticism and correction of the manner in which the Corinthians celebrated the Eucharist extended also to their inadequate *gnōsis* of its purpose. Instead of discerning the Lord's body, that is, recognizing the presence of Christ at the Eucharist, many treated it like an ordinary meal. They brought what they could afford and, disregarding the feelings of others, ate and drank what they liked, often to excess. These actions were more consistent with the conventions of pagan feasts than with the Lord's table. Paul's solution to the problem was basic and simple: if Christians wanted

---

55. See Roetzel, *Judgement in the Community*, 136–37.

56. The sevenfold reference to the Lord in this passage can hardly be coincidental; see vv. 20, 23 (twice), 26, 27 (twice), 32.

merely to enjoy a good meal together, they were to do so at home (*en oikō*). But at the *agape* meal, the Corinthians must show respect for their fellow believers' physical as well as spiritual needs by waiting for each other and eating together. Otherwise the eating and drinking of the elements was unworthy of the Lord whom they ostensibly were honoring. Unworthy participation meant being guilty of the Lord's body and blood and resulted in the punishment of the communicant. The Eucharist itself was no guarantee of escaping this *krima* of God; if the church will not chasten itself and persists in sin, the Lord will act to judge it. This judgment should be understood as chastisement, and has as its end not the condemnation of the church, but its sanctification and salvation. It is a grace in that it is *hypo tou kyriou* and keeps the church from being condemned with the world (11:32).

No one can with certainty explain the causal connection between illness and death and unworthy partaking of the elements. Nevertheless, the basic principle involved is clear: those who fail to discern the body offend against the Lord himself, and as a result incur divine judgment upon themselves. The view that failing to discern the body is the same thing as failing to distinguish the body of Christ from an ordinary piece of bread has little to commend it. Paul never speaks of eating the body or drinking the blood, only of eating the bread and drinking the cup. Much more probable is the view of Higgins that eating and drinking without discerning the body refers to "conduct at the Lord's Supper which is due to failure to recognize the Church for what it is, the body of Christ, in which the living Lord is present."[57] The resultant judgment of such unworthy participation is oriented not to the substance of the meal, but to the act of administration and of participation at the Eucharistic celebration.

In v. 30 Paul states that this judgment works itself out in several concrete expressions: *dia touto en hymin polloi astheneis kai arrōstoi kai koimōntai hikanoi* ["This is why many among you are weak and sick and a number are sleeping"]. The verb *koimōntai* is present tense, while *eisin* must be supplied with the adjectives *astheneis kai arrōstoi*, indicating that the judgment has already begun among the Corinthians. In the present context these ascriptions cannot refer to spiritual ailments, for *koimōntai* is obviously used here euphemistically, as in 15:18, for "die."[58] These instances of sickness and death among those who eat and drink unworthily are, first, Paul's explanation of the events taking place at Corinth; but they also are

---

57. Higgens, *Lord's Supper*, 72–73.
58. Thayer, *Lexicon*, 351.

an indirect warning directed against any who might be tempted to misuse the Lord's Supper.

It would seem from this context that the adjectives *astheneis* and *arrōstoi* both refer to physical ailments,[59] and since they are both predicates of *polloi*, there cannot be much of a difference of meaning between them. Etymologically, both adjectives denote that which lacks strength. *Arrōstos* ("sick") is a negative compound of *rōstos*, "strong," and is used only once by Paul (and never by Luke). Here its meaning could be equivalent to the basic idea in *asthenēs*, "without strength," but in light of the implicit progression of thought from *astheneis—arrōstoi—koimōntai* its Hellenistic meaning "sick" seems preferable.[60] This would imply that *astheneis* is not synonymous with *arrōstoi*, but is a term denoting a physical punishment of a less serious nature. "Weak" would suffice as a translation for the word, but perhaps the better term would be "sickly," a disposition towards illness that *arrōstoi* more explicitly connotes.[61]

As we have already noted, the illnesses and untimely deaths attributed by the apostle to abuse of the Eucharist are not acts of condemnation by the Lord, but are merciful chastisements to bring the Corinthians to repentance and to impel them to observe the true nature of the Supper. Thus, the Eucharist is either an occasion of voluntary self judgment (11:28–29) or else of liability to God's judgment upon those who abuse it.[62] Whereas the improper observance of the Lord's Supper may lead to the judgment of the physical body, proper use does not necessarily protect one from illness and death. There is no warrant in Scripture that the Eucharist will produce a beneficial effect upon the sick, nor does Paul say that the penalty for unworthy participation is *invariably* physical sickness or death.[63]

---

59. In the article "Glaubensmangel in Korinth," Sebastian Schneider argues (3–19), that Paul is not referring to physical ailment but rather to people who are weak, sick, and sleeping in regard to the Christian faith. He suggests the following translation for our verse: "Deshalb (sind) unter euch (geistlich gesehen) viele Schwache und Kranke und schlafen sogar Zahlreise" (19). I remain unconvinced.

60. Cf. Buck, *Selected Synonyms*, 302.

61. Cf. Fitzmyer, *First Corinthians*, 447, who translates this verse: "*For this reason many among you* are weak and *infirm, and a number are dying*" (italics in original).

62. Moule, "Judgment Theme," 472.

63. See Bornkamm, "Herrenmahl und Kirche," 312–49, for a more thorough discussion of this question.

1 Corinthians 12:22

At 12:14 Paul begins a long and sometimes involved treatment of the physical body as a picture of the church. This section (12:14-26) is part of a larger discussion of the nature of the Christian congregation as the body of Christ composed of gifted members (1 Cor 12-14), in which Paul treats (a) the purpose of spiritual gifts (12:1-31), (b) the supremacy of love over all gifts (13:1-13), and (c) the superiority of the gift of prophecy over the gift of tongues (14:1-25).

In 12:14-26 the discussion concerns the human body in all its diversity as an analogy of Christ's church. There are many points of comparison between the physical body and the church: both are composed of many parts, yet each organism is complete only when the various parts function properly; each member of the body is dependent upon every other member; the mutual interdependence of the various parts of the body can be destroyed by discord. Therefore the mutual care of each member is vital to the body's health and ability to function properly.

The basic proposition is stated in v. 14: "For the body does not consist of one member, but of many." Among these members Paul is careful to include in v. 22 "those members of the body that seem to be weaker" (*ta dokounta melē tou sōmatos asthenestera*). Because the comparison between the human body and the congregation is implied throughout chap. 12, we may assume that the reference is to the "weaker" members of the Corinthian church. It is already clear that in Corinth there are stronger members who exalt themselves over the weak, and presumably Paul has the same or similar idea in mind in 12:22. As he has shown before (cf. 1:27; 8:7-13), even the least attractive and most inconspicuous members of the church are important and should be treated with respect. The weaker members not only have a proper place in the church, but are in fact "much rather necessary," for all the members of the body are interdependent and interrelated. Therefore, because they are actually indispensable, Paul says they only "seem to be" (*dokounta . . . hyparchein*) weaker and unnecessary.[64]

---

64. In a very helpful discussion, Chow (*Patronage and Power*, 178) notes the radical implications of Paul's exhortations: "Paul argues that the presence of the weaker parts is necessary in order to have a sound body. God not only places the necessary weaker members in the body, but also gives more honor to them (1 Cor 12:24)." Paul's notion of the complete interdependence of the body thus forms the basis for his insistence on the inclusion of the weak members.

1 Corinthians 15:43

The final reference to weakness in 1 Corinthians falls in the paragraph (15:42–49) where the apostle, resorting once again to analogy, contrasts the believer's present mode of existence and his or her future resurrection life. He states in v. 43 that the condition of our transitory life on earth is characterized by *astheneia*, but our resurrection existence will be a life of *dynamis* in perfect harmony with God's own essential being. It is necessary to consider even this singular occurrence of *astheneia* in its proper context in order to correctly explicate its meaning.

In 1 Corinthians 15 Paul passes on to the subject of eschatology, including a discussion of the somatic aspect of the resurrection.[65] After a brief introduction (1–3a) there follows the traditional account of the death and resurrection of Christ (3b–7), including an enumeration of those to whom the risen Savior had appeared. The remainder of the chapter is taken up with the apostle's own interpretation and defense of the doctrine of the resurrection in reference to his opponents' claim that "there is no resurrection of the dead" (15:12).[66]

When he comes to vv. 35–39 Paul addresses the questions that many of the Corinthians had been asking: by what power and in what manner is the resurrection of a sinful, mortal body to be accomplished (v. 35)? His answer is extremely skillful and his reasoning exceedingly careful. After establishing on the analogy of terrestrial and astral creatures that God is able to take similar matter and organize it differently to accomplish his purposes (36–41), he refers in vv. 42–44 by analogy again to the existence of the resurrected man or woman. By a series of four contrasts between the body that is sown (*speiretai*) and the body that is raised (*egeiretai*), he illustrates the different order and functions the earthly body has from the spiritual body:[67]

1. perishable — imperishable
2. dishonour — glory
3. weakness — power
4. a physical body — a spiritual body

---

65. Dahl, *The Resurrection of the Body*, discusses in detail the many problems relating to the subject of the resurrection.

66. On Paul's response to his opponents, see Sandelin, *Auseinandersetzung*, 13–15.

67. Cf. Ruef, *1 Corinthians*, 172.

These terms contrast the preeschatological and eschatological bodies of people, the former being broadly designated as *psychikon*, whereas the latter is characterized as *pneumatikon* (v. 44). Paul uses the adjective *pneumatikon* to express the quality of the body in the resurrection state without implying any sense of immaterialness or etherealness. This is the state in which the *pneuma* rules.[68] The *pneuma* gives to the resurrection body the threefold characteristic of *aphtharsia*, *doxa*, and *dynamis*. This pneumatic body stands over against the psychic body (*sōma psychikon*), which is characterized by *phthora*, *aitimia*, and *astheneia*, a distinction that Paul can also express by *ex ouranō* and *ek gēs*, respectively (15:47).

It is not surprising that among all the terms at his disposal Paul should use *astheneia* to characterize the psychic body, for "weakness" describes well the condition of human life on earth. For the present, believers still continue to die and the body continues to be liable to disease. Only the inward person is being renewed day by day (2 Cor 4:16). While the Holy Spirit is already active in the bodies of Christians in a proleptic sense,[69] he must wait until the parousia to change their carnal bodies into spiritual ones. In the meantime, even believers who are relatively strong remain subject to illness, disappointment, failure, and eventually death. Cultivate the present body as they would (and the Greeks did develop it highly), it is but a weak instrument subject to change, decay, and ultimately physical decomposition.

Just as the present body is characterized by *astheneia*, so the future resurrection body will be characterized by *dynamis*. This is the divine power that is now concealed in the weakness and mortality of the flesh but that will be triumphantly and gloriously manifested when it finally asserts itself in the resurrection.[70] Meanwhile, in their present bodily existence, Christians groan for freedom from their physical afflictions and limitations; but they also realize that the limitation of their human existence is the necessary presupposition for the operation of the *dynamis* of God, which is made perfect in weakness (2 Cor 12:9). Hence Paul could express

---

68. H. Clavier ("Brèves remarques," 361) writes, "On peur assurer que le caractéristique essentielle du *sōma pneumatikon* selon Paul, n'est pas d'être ou non un corps en esprit, mais un organe de l'esprit, commandé par l'Esprit, par le Saint-Esprit."

69. Cf. Cullmann, "Proleptic Deliverance," 166; cf. also Lietzmann, *Korinther*, 84.

70. See Bauer, *Leiblichkeit*, 97–106. Vos, "Paul's Teaching on the Resurrection," 193–226, discusses the possibility that this emphasis upon the transformation of one's body represents a second stage of development in Pauline eschatology, following the first stage in 1 Thessalonians.

his confidence in the accomplishment of his apostolic mission (Phil 4:13), for his weak and corruptible earthly existence has become a vessel for the outworking of the divine power and the life of Jesus (2 Cor 4:7–12). This antithesis between weakness/power and death/life previews the usage and meaning of *astheneia* in 2 Corinthians, where the physical afflictions that hindered Paul in his apostolic work become the center of the manifestation of the divine power (cf. esp. 2 Cor 11:30; 12:5, 9–10; 13:3–4).

EXEGESIS OF THE TEXTS: 2 CORINTHIANS

Preliminary Remarks

In order to gain a proper perspective from which to assess accurately the weakness motif in this letter, the following preliminary comments should prove helpful. In this section of 2 Corinthians (chaps. 10–13) the whole complex of words for weakness is used with remarkable frequency. The noun *astheneia* occurs six times (11:30; 12:5, 9 [twice], 10; 13:4). The verb *asthenein* is found a total of seven times (11:21, 29 [twice]; 12:10; 13:3, 4, 9). The adjective *asthenēs*, so frequent in 1 Corinthians, occurs here also (10:10). Unlike 1 Corinthians and Romans, where the references to weakness are fairly well-spaced, those in 2 Corinthians (with the single exception of *asthenēs* in 10:10) occur in "lumps" in chaps. 11, 12, and 13. In most instances mention is made of the concept without any clue as to its precise connotation, so that an investigation of each word in its own context is the only reliable guide to the correct understanding of the motif as Paul employed it in this letter. However, the reader will discover that the distinctive usages, although essentially separate from each other, like various threads woven through the fabric of Paul's concept of weakness all together ultimately form a unified tapestry that conveys a single, unmistakable impression. This one fact alone is sufficient to establish the uniqueness of the weakness vocabulary in 2 Corinthians.

These chapters contain material so rich that a full appreciation of their contents would be possible only after a thorough investigation of many details. Nevertheless, even a superficial glance at the material enables one to discern recurrent themes and phrases from which an overall perspective of the passage may be acquired. Perhaps the major element we may note is the idea of "boasting" or "glorying" (*kauchasthai*).[71] Although Paul will

---

71. 2 Cor 10:1—13:13 contains a unique concentration of terms for confidence,

not claim the Lord's authority for producing his apostolic credentials, he is convinced that boasting is the only way of reestablishing his authority with the Corinthians. However, while Paul condescends for a time to boast on the same low level as do his opponents (11:21–29), his true boast is in his weaknesses (11:30; 12:5, 9, 10) and in the corresponding power of Christ (12:9). If *kauchasthai* is the main concept of these chapters, *asthenein* runs a close second because weakness is the only valid ground for the apostle's boasting.[72] Thus when Paul discusses himself, which he is always reticent to do, what he says centers on the term *astheneia*. For this reason, "weakness" is fully expounded and developed as one of the key themes of 2 Corinthians.

The recurrence of the "apostleship" motif suggests that this theme was also important to Paul. Indeed, one of the main reasons Paul wrote this letter was to defend himself by setting forth at length and in great detail his own private understanding of his existence as an apostle. This apology reaches a particularly sharp point in chaps. 10–13.[73] Even a superficial reading of these chapters clearly reveals how central weakness is to Paul's understanding of apostleship, for when all the arguments are condensed and combined, the difference between Paul and his adversaries is essentially this: one represents an apostolate in weakness, the other in (false) glory. Therefore Paul feels compelled both to denounce the attempt of some to use his weaknesses against him and to urge the Corinthians to accept his weaknesses as true and valid expressions of the apostolic office. Although this emphasis runs as a thread throughout the letter, it is most clearly seen in the formal apology contained in the final chapters, where the weakness terminology is used fourteen times.

Here the charges of the false apostles are not scouted by Paul; he knows that there exists no real proof against him, yet he cannot ignore the attempts of his opponents to discredit him. However, Paul's concern in these chapters is more than a protest or apology, for this detailed explanation

---

including not only the common *kauch-*word group, but also *tolman, elpis, tharreō, elpizō,* and *ouk aischynomai*. See Olson, *Confidence Expressions*, 1–5, esp. 4, Table 1.

72. According to Zmijewski, "mit *asthenein* . . . begegnet eines der die gesamte 'Narrenrede' bestimmenden Leitwörter" (*Stil*, 273). The other major term in his opinion is *kauchasthai*. In this way Zmijewski *equates* their importance.

73. Betz, in his monograph *Paulus und die sokratische Tradition* suggests that Paul has adopted in these chapters a rhetorical pose that enabled him to indulge in self-praise without damaging his personal integrity. Betz's exegesis on the whole considerably reduces the autobiographical value of 2 Corinthians 10–13; this, however, is unnecessary when these chapters are considered to be an integral part of the entire letter (cf. Henrichs' review of Betz' monograph in *JBL* 94, 310–14).

of the meaning of *astheneia* is motivated not only by the confrontational setting but also by Paul's deep-felt concern that the concept, rightly understood, be a source of encouragement and strength for other Christians. By refusing to evade the issue he is afforded the unique opportunity to state in a positive manner what is perhaps his most basic understanding of weakness, which may be paraphrased thus: "My weakness is *Christ's* weakness, the only legitimate representation of the crucified Messiah and his gospel, the assurance that God is now manifesting his son in and through my life, and the promise that one day I will fully participate in the resurrection's glory, power, and incorruptibility." It is abundantly clear that, although the discussion was initially forced upon Paul by circumstances, the negative character of his defense in these verses is not so immense as to overshadow the positive significance of *astheneia*.

We have already noted that, cogent as the arguments are for separating chaps. 10–13 of 2 Corinthians from 1–9, they are not in our opinion convincing.[74] Most of the arguments against the letter's integrity can be explained by supposing that there was a group in the Corinthian church that had not as yet been reconciled to Paul and that was still attempting to lead the majority of the Corinthians away from the apostle. Before embarking upon his journey to Corinth, Paul therefore finds it necessary to make one final appeal to the church to reject the enticements of this recalcitrant minority. Because they have called into question *Paul's* authority, he purposely disassociates himself from his coauthor Timothy (1:1) and begins a personal appeal to this disloyal group—*Autos de egō Paulos parakalō hymas*, "I, Paul, *myself* beseech you . . ." (10:1).

The progression of thought in Paul's appeal is extremely difficult to discern, yet it exists. Most scholars agree that the material in chaps. 10–13 can be divided into three major parts that follow closely but do not perfectly correspond to the traditional chapter-divisions. The first section comprises 10:1–18 and is an entreaty to hold fast to the gospel of Christ as preached by Paul. The second section comprises 11:1—12:13 and is considered to be "the heart of the last four chapters"[75] and "unique in all Paul's writings."[76] In it Paul descends for a moment to the level of the false

---

74. Contra Wan, who argues that the "differences between chapters 10–13 and the rest of 2 Corinthians are so pronounced and so pervasive that they cry out for explanation. The best explanation seems to be that these four chapters belong to an altogether different letter" (*Power in Weakness*, 127).

75. Fisher, *Corinthians*, 406

76. Lenski (1963), *Corinthians*, 1232.

apostles by foolishly boasting about himself in an attempt to prove that his credentials of apostleship are superior to theirs. Finally, in 12:14—13:10, there is an entreaty for the church to prepare itself for Paul's forthcoming third visit, which he mentions three times (12:14; 13:1, 10). The conclusion of the letter (13:11–14) includes a final appeal, personal greetings, and the usual benediction. The clearest statement of Paul's purpose in writing these chapters is found in 13:10: "This is why I write these things while I am away from you, in order that when I come I may not have to be severe in my use of the authority that the Lord has given me for building you up, not for tearing you down."

Before proceeding now to actual exegesis, we may note one final point. In the Introduction we stated that our guiding principle is that Paul's special use of *astheneia*-vocabulary is intimately related to the specific historical situation. Nowhere is this more clearly seen than in 2 Corinthians 10–13, where Paul is an apologist attempting to defend himself against attacks and misunderstandings emanating from Corinth.[77] However, it should be recognized that the Pauline concept of weakness is nowhere elaborated on theologically in these chapters, but rather is merely alluded to by means of several short and pithy statements. The only exception to this fact is the discussion in 12:7–10, where Paul describes in more detail what it means to be weak. Even here, however, the language is not the language of deep contemplation but the speech of a man recounting his own personal experiences in a remarkably intimate manner.

2 Corinthians 10:10

In 2 Cor 10:9–10 Paul turns his attention directly to the comments of his opponents in Corinth. This minority was attempting to undermine his authority by comparing his weakness with their own impressive appearance. What was confusing to the majority of Corinthians was the fact that both Paul and his opponents were claiming to be "servants of Christ" (11:23) and "apostles" (11:5), but based on two different criteria. The opponents base their claim on outward, visible manifestations of strength and wisdom,

---

77. Notes Heckel (*Kraft in Schwachheit*, 12): "Auch bleibt angesichts dieser Frontstellung zu bedenken, daß in 2. Kor 10–13 kein systematischer Abriß der paulinischer Theologie bzw. einzelner Themenkreise vorliegt, sondern die Antwort auf konkrete Vorwürfe gegeben und trotz aller emotionalen Aufgewühltheit in einem klar aufgebauten Gedankengang apologetisch und paränetisch auf die Gemeinde hin zugespitzt wird."

including visions (12:1ff.) and mighty works (12:12). Paul, on the other hand, bases his claim on his participation in the sufferings, or "weakness," of Christ (11:23ff.; 12:10). To his adversaries, this weakness is a sign that Paul cannot wield apostolic authority. Moreover, they claim that Paul seeks only to terrify his readers by his letters but dares not act with the same vigor when he is face to face. Paul cannot have apostolic authority since he lacks the gift of eloquence (11:6), which for them is the outward sign of the Spirit's presence.[78]

In v. 10, Paul responds to this criticism concerning his letters and personal presence, showing that he is neither fearful nor ignorant of such slander. He quotes the very words of his calumniators: "His letters are weighty and strong, but his bodily presence is weak [*asthenēs*] and his speech of no account." This criticism, circulating behind his back, had the potential of being greatly damaging to his authority. The particular charge was that between his letters and his conduct there existed the greatest discrepancy, that his writings were forceful and authoritative, whereas his manner and speech were marked by cowardice and indecision. In short, the charge was that Paul was inconsistent, superficial, even "two-faced."

Paul has no desire to give substance to this charge, but since his apostolic authority is at stake, he cannot allow his weakness to continue to be misunderstood. The gentleness and paternal love that characterize his relationship with the Corinthians will not be discarded; however, should the situation require it, he will not spare them the next time he comes to their city. Those in Corinth who may wish to remain unrepentant will have proof enough of Paul's apostolic authority on his third visit, when he will act in precise accord with his letters (cf. 13:1–3). If he comes and discovers that they still will not accept his authority, they will learn the hard way that he can indeed be stern in person (v. 11).

These considerations show that Paul's adversaries in Corinth were looking for some pretext to undermine Paul's credibility so that they could eventually enhance their own authority. They were essentially correct in their assessment of his letters as *bareiai* and *ischyrai*; but they were wrong in supposing that Paul on paper and Paul in person were two incompatibles. While he desires to avoid on his forthcoming visit to Corinth a display of boldness, Paul indicates his readiness to come with rod in hand if the Corinthians do not shape up (cf. 1 Cor 4:21). Those who laud his epistolary

---

78. See Wilckens, *Weisheit und Torheit*, 46ff., 218.

boldness yet scorn his personal weakness will stand self-accused when Paul is present with them (cf. 13:2, 10).

The opponents' charge that Paul's bodily presence (*hē parousia tou sōmatos*) was *asthenēs* has given rise to the tradition, ancient yet widely accepted today, that Paul was small in stature, frail, and unattractive in his personal appearance. The words used here do not support this tradition. Although it is entirely possible that in physique Paul was unimpressive, the context indicates that his opponents were not criticizing his personal or physical condition, but his *general deportment*. Their accusation may be paraphrased as follows: "He is bold when he writes (at a safe distance!), but when it comes to taking action (personally) he is feeble and vacilant. The vigor, authority, and severity of his written words are altogether lacking when he dares to show his face." As Hughes notes, a disparagement of Paul's character would have been much more serious than merely ridiculing a physical debility.[79] Likewise, the accusation that Paul's manner of public speaking lacked eloquence does not mean that he was an ineffective communicator of the gospel. By the standards of Greek eloquence and rhetoric to which the Corinthians were accustomed, Paul's *logos* was indeed "contemptible" (*exouthenēmenos*), but he had purposely eschewed oratorical devices lest he distract his hearers' attention from the simplicity of "Christ crucified" (1 Cor 2:1-5). Paul had already admitted as much to the Corinthians in a previous letter when he stated that his original entrance into Corinth was attended by a feeling of personal insufficiency and simple speech: "I came to you in weakness and fear, and with much trembling. My message and my preaching were not with persuasive words of wisdom" (1 Cor 2:3-4a). But his speech had also been attended by "a demonstration of the Spirit's power" (1 Cor 2:4) in order that their faith should stand "not in human wisdom, but in the power of God" (1 Cor 2:5). Therefore the statement *hē parousia tou sōmatos asthenēs* is not (as it has often been taken to be[80]) a reference to Paul's physical appearance, but refers to his general character or deportment,[81] so that it is impossible to deduce from it any physical description or portrait of him.

---

79. Hughes, *2 Corinthians*, 362.

80. See, e.g., Fisher, *Corinthians*, 402; Heading, *2 Corinthians*, 187.

81. Hughes, *2 Corinthians*, 362-63; Tasker, *2 Corinthians*, 138-39; Lietzmann, *Korinther*, 142; Harris, *2 Corinthians*, 381; etc.

Paul, Apostle of Weakness

2 Corinthians 11:21, 29, 30

In 2 Corinthians 11 Paul is very conscious of his own weakness: "To my shame I admit that we were too weak for that!" (v. 21); "Who is weak, and I am not weak?" (v. 29); "If I must boast, I will boast of the things that show my weakness!" (v. 30). These passages are striking in one regard: Paul's reference in each of them is remarkably personal. He does not speak of his "weakness" in abstract or theoretical terms but relates it in every instance to very specific situations in which he has been intimately involved. Whether the reference is to the greed and tyranny of the false apostles who have slandered him without cause (v. 21), the care of the churches and their demands upon his charity (v. 29), or the humiliations and sufferings involved with his missionary journeys (v. 30), in every situation—be it opportunity or crisis—Paul is compelled to admit that he feels "weak." This admission, however, had the potential of being seriously misunderstood when viewed through the jaundiced eyes of his enemies.

Paul's opponents are impressed only by externals, but the adequacy of their credentials—in Paul's mind at least—is suspect: commendatory letters (3:1), authoritarian behavior (11:20), spectacular visions and remarkable ecstatic experiences (12:1–7), rhetorical ostentation (11:6), and "authentic" Jewishness (11:22) are invalid criteria for testing apostolic credentials; for, as Paul argues most clearly in 11:21—12:10, the only incontestable vindication of apostleship is weakness and humility in Christian service. According to this criterion, Paul can lay claim to superiority, not simply equality, over his rivals.

Paul, therefore, accepts the charge of his opponents that he is weak, for weakness is a sign of apostleship. Christ himself was "crucified in weakness, but lives by the power of God" (13:4). Far from contradicting the gospel, the sufferings, limitations, and weaknesses of the apostle are wholly consistent with it because the sufferings, limitations, and weaknesses of Jesus comprise the very core of the gospel's message. Therefore, if being weak means acting like a father instead of like a ruler, speaking with simple instead of proud words, preaching the gospel free of charge instead of demanding apostolic wages, humbling oneself instead of boasting in oneself, leading the churches by example instead of forcing one's will upon them, Paul is more than happy to admit, "I *am* weak." This acknowledgment makes its first explicit appearance in 2 Corinthians at 11:21, where Paul prepares himself to begin to indulge in what he calls "a little foolishness" (11:1).

2 Corinthians 11:21

In order to justify the harshness of their dealings in Corinth, Paul's rivals had been saying that his personal presence was characterized by a despicable weakness (cf. 10:10) that proved Paul could not be "of Christ" and therefore could not be a true apostle. Having been deceived by the false claims of these false apostles, the Corinthians could not see the irony in accepting men of "true" apostolic authority even though that meant they had to tolerate the worst of indignities at their hands (11:20). Paul, therefore, with biting irony asserts, "I confess to my[82] shame that [when compared with these 'super-apostles'] we have been weak [*ēsthenēkamen*[83]]." This admission is meant to be a rebuke to the Corinthians whose tolerance of such tyranny apparently had no limits, yet whose criticism of the one who had treated them with great consideration was excessively harsh. If tyranny, arrogance, and violence are the credentials of true apostleship, then to his own shame Paul must admit he had failed as a leader in Corinth, for he has indeed been too "weak" to employ the ruthless tactics of the opposition. It is clear from these verses (vv. 20–21) that Paul's rivals boasted a great deal in their ability to enslave Paul's converts and, having brought them under their power, to use and abuse them in any way they deemed necessary. These verses also indicate the grief and sorrow the apostle must have felt to see those whom he had evangelized reduced to such a pitiable state of utter bondage (*katadouloun*). It has now become necessary for him, their true father in the faith, to authenticate himself in their eyes by proving that his credentials are in no way inferior to those of the "superlative" apostles. Though speaking only "in foolishness" (v. 21b), he is going to enter a boasting contest with his adversaries (11:22–29) so that, acknowledging again Paul as a legitimate apostle, they may overthrow the false teachers and return to a pure faith.[84] Paul is equal to them in the matter of nationality (v. 22) and superior to them in achievement (vv. 23–29). He had endured more hardships and confronted more dangers, had been more frequently in

---

82. Because (a) Paul is reproaching himself, and (b) the phrase *kata atimian legō* governs the *following* clause, the pronoun "my" is to be supplied instead of "your" (cf. RSV, NIV).

83. The correct reading is most likely the perfect, which, possibly to omit any reference to the present time, was changed in other witnesses (DFG) to the aorist *ēsthenēsamen*.

84. For an examination of the structure and style of this and other "catalogues of suffering" (Leidensparänesen), see Kamlah, "Wie beurteilt Paulus?" 217–32, and Hainz, *Ekklesia*, 167–68.

prisons, more horribly beaten, more despised and more severely treated by Jew and Gentile alike. But above all there was the daily pressure (*epistasis*) of caring for all the churches (11:28) with their problems, defections, and divisions, necessitating frequent visits, at times lengthy letters, and always intensive prayer. These adversities, hardships, and arduous responsibilities are an expanded commentary on what Paul wrote in 4:10, that he always carried in his body the dying of Jesus, who demanded of his followers, "Take up your cross" (Mark 8:34). This is the type of conduct that is the mark of true servants and apostles, who are ready to suffer bodily and mentally, to be hated and despised, to expend physical and spiritual energy in the service of others, for Jesus' sake. If this is weakness, then Paul can boast that he has not been strong in the manner in which the "super-apostles" have been strong.

2 Corinthians 11:29

With reference to the daily pressure (*epistasis*) and anxiety (*merimna*) involved with the wardenship of the churches he has founded, Paul now adds in v. 29 two examples of his identification and sympathy with his converts: "Who is weak and I am not weak? Who is made to fall and I am not indignant?" The care of the Christian church in its multiplicity of locales made great and continual demands upon the apostle's time and energies. Two aspects of that care—perhaps the two that required the most compassion—involved sympathy with the weak and indignation at the perpetration of evil among Christ's "little ones" (Mark 9:42).

These two attitudes are the expression of Paul's love, first, for those who are over-scrupulous, and second, for those who stumble so as to fall into sin. These two groups may indeed be one and the same. Paul has already admonished the strong Christians in Corinth to exercise their liberty in such a way that would not offend the weak members of the congregation, saying that if they did so they really sinned against Christ himself (1 Cor 8:9–13). The abuse of Christian freedom by the strong who place stumbling-blocks in the way of the weak and impose upon them moral burdens too heavy for their unenlightened consciences to bear is ample reason for the apostle's feeling of indignation. Though he himself is strong, he is willing to identify with the weak so that their weakness becomes his own. Should one of them stumble in his or her Christian walk, Paul treats it as though it were his own stumbling, enduring the same pain and feeling the same vexation. Here Paul's thought is remarkably like that of the author of Hebrews, who writes of the high priest of old, "He can deal gently with the ignorant and erring, since he himself is beset with weakness" (5:2), and of Christ, the Great High Priest, "For we do not have a high priest who is unable to sympathize with our weaknesses" (4:15).

It is this sympathetic statement in 11:29—*tis asthenei kai ouk asthenō;*—that closes the preceding catalogue of persecutions and sufferings (11:22–28) and prepares the reader for Paul's assertion that it is only in the things that reveal his weakness does he dare to glory (11:30)—what we are calling the principle of "boasting in weakness" (or, obversely, glorying in *God's* power). This principle is first hinted at in 11:21, then carefully developed within 11:22–29, and finally becomes the pervading feature in 11:30—12:10, reaching its climax in the words of the Lord himself, "My grace is sufficient for you, for strength is made perfect in weakness" (12:9). The record of Paul's afflictions as an apostle of Christ is then repeated in 12:10 (in an abbreviated form), which ends with a reiteration of the basic principle, "For when I am weak, then I am strong." Two specific instances that Paul describes in the intervening verses are the proof that this principle is true: his escape from Damascus (11:32–33), and his "thorn in the flesh" (12:7–8).

2 Corinthians 11:30

All during the preceding gasconade, where Paul has been matching boast with counterboast, what may be called the Pauline principle of "boasting in weakness" seems to have been formulating itself. The weakness about which he has been criticized (11:21) is really for him the only subject for boasting, for it is in weakness—his humiliations and sufferings—that Paul demonstrates his likeness to Christ, who was "crucified in weakness" (13:4).[85] The precise definition of Paul's *kagō kauchēsomai* at v. 18 emerges here and is set forth in its most basic form: "If I must boast, I will boast of the things that show my weakness." This paradoxical truth is a proper summary of all that Paul has said in vv. 23–29, for, though he is as much a Hebrew, an

85. Writes Martin (*2 Corinthians*, 382): "Both these ideas—physical weakness and a 'non-charismatic persona'—interlock, however. They fit into Black's analysis of *astheneia* as (1) weakness as a sign of humanity in its earthiness and dependence on God and (2) weakness as a Christological aspect of Paul's apostolic life, since his weakness is 'in Christ,' the one who was 'crucified in weakness' (2 Cor 13:4). See *Paul, Apostle of Weakness*, 228–40."

Israelite, a servant of Christ as the "superlative" apostles, and can claim all the qualifications that are demanded of the greatest apostles, when Paul gives up foolish boasting and returns to sound thinking, he realizes there is in the final analysis only one kind of boasting pleasing to the Lord: boasting in one's weakness. This distinguished in the end his boasting from that of his opponents, who would have never thought of priding themselves on evidences of their weakness, infirmity, and dependence upon God. For Paul, however, these were the very things that were developing him in his likeness to Christ. Since Christian character is paramount to all other requirements, weakness becomes an essential qualification for apostleship. The crowning illustration of the weakness of which Paul boasts in chap. 11 is his dramatic escape from Damascus through a window in a basket (vv. 32–33). While these verses present a variety of historical problems and the reason for their inclusion here is debated, it seems clear that the reference, partially at least, is to set the stage for what follows in 12:1–4 where Paul speaks of his visions and revelations. Harris's description of "an embarrassing descent to escape the hands of men and then an exhilarating ascent into the presence of God"[86] is probably an accurate one of the transition from 11:30–33 to 12:1–10.

Paul's ignominious escape emphasized his weakness at the outset of his public ministry, for it happened while he was yet a fresh recruit in gospel warfare. Paul's "thorn" (12:7), on the other hand, emphasized what is probably to be understood as a continuous, or recurring, disabling physical weakness with which the apostle had been afflicted to keep him from glorying in anything but his weakness. The narration of the Damascus experience connects chap. 11 with chap. 12 both by closing out the list of hardships and by introducing the apostle's glorying in private visionary experiences. These "visions and revelations of the Lord" (12:1) are then the prelude to the narrative about the thorn in the flesh and, like the previous list of experiences that have been catalogued in 11:23–28, are a response to the boasts of his rivals. Compelled again by circumstances, and with great distaste for the whole business, Paul begins to disclose what may be considered his most intimate and heavenly experience as a Christian. It is important to recognize, however, that nowhere does Paul abandon the principle he stated in 11:30, for he is still glorying in his weaknesses, the most obvious and lamentable of which is his "thorn in the flesh" (12:7).

---

86. Harris, *2 Corinthians*, 393.

The Corinthian Correspondence

Only in order to reveal his "thorn" does he now reveal the marvelous things he has never before publicly disclosed.[87]

2 Corinthians 12:5, 9, 10

In 2 Corinthians 12 Paul continues his arguments whereby he hopes to effect the repentance of those in who were still opposed to his apostolic authority.[88] Whereas in 11:23–29 Paul appeals to his sufferings as proof of his apostleship, now in 12:1–13, since his opponents extol ecstasy and visions, he appeals to his own ecstatic experiences in order to prove to his detractors that he too possesses the Spirit. The theme of boasting is continued throughout this chapter. Paul must (*dei*) boast even though he is fully aware it will gain nothing (*ou sympheron*). He would prefer simply to admit his own weakness and rely solely on God's grace, yet he feels compelled to "go on to visions and revelations of the Lord" (12:1). Had his opponents not forced him into it, Paul would never have mentioned—much less boasted—in these experiences. This chapter requires special attention for here, unquestionably, *astheneia* receives special emphasis. Nowhere do we see the subtleties of Paul's weakness terminology more clearly than in these verses in which the full force of Paul's apology for his weakness comes to the fore. His overall objective is to show that God's power is more clearly seen in weakness than in Paul's own strength, for *astheneia* is not a hindrance to God's working, but the requirement for it. The specific theme is *dynamis en astheneia*, which continues and yet more precisely defines the general theme of chaps. 10–13, *kauchasthai en astheneiais*.

Paul limits his "boasting" about visions and revelations to a single ecstatic experience that occurred "fourteen years ago" (12:2). Though the date is specific, none of the visions recorded in Acts can be identified with the revelation mentioned here, since it occurred during the so-called "ten silent years" (AD 35–45) that Paul spent in Syria and Cilicia (Gal 1:21). Therefore the reference cannot be to the apostle's conversion experience on the road to Damascus, which was accompanied by a vision of the resurrected Christ, for this Damascus vision took place more than twenty years before the writing of 2 Corinthians. The vision spoken of here appears to have been designed for Paul alone, having as its purpose strengthening and

---

87. Cf. Hughes, *2 Corinthians*, 429.
88. See Akin, "Triumphalism," 119–44.

reassurance before he would embark upon his mission to the Gentiles that began shortly after the apostle's arrival in the city of Antioch (Acts 11:26).

Paul cannot describe what he saw during his vision, nor can he relate with human words what he heard, for it is forbidden for a human to utter them (12:4). This reticence distinguished Paul from those who boasted long and loud about their revelations, for not only was the experience too intimate for Paul to relate, but also it was an undeserved gift for which he could claim no merit. For this reason Paul speaks of his vision as though another person had experienced it and declines to boast on his own behalf (12:2–5a). Though he values spiritual experiences, Paul purposely subordinates them to the promise of Jesus that strength is perfected in weakness. Spiritual experiences are not the only, and certainly not the major, proof that the Spirit is at work in Paul; the true strength of the apostle is, in fact, most clearly seen *apart* from them (12:5–10).[89]

2 Corinthians 12:5

Although God had allowed Paul to witness astonishing revelations of divine truth, he did not intend for them to make the apostle a proud man. Paul understood this, and even though he has had revelations of outstanding quality (*tē hyperbolē tōn apokalypseōn*), he realizes that he cannot elevate himself without deposing God from his proper place of exaltation. He has already been told by the Lord himself that his authority as an apostle should not rest on private, esoteric experiences (12:9). Indeed, his opponents have fraudulently deluded the Corinthians by making such claims for themselves, but they were fools for doing so (12:6). Paul therefore intends to make it clear that he will refrain from boasting about the exceptional experiences of the past, wishing only to be judged by what the contact of others with him led them to observe, namely, his weaknesses, "so that no one may think more of me than he or she sees in me or hears from me" (12:6b).

Thus Paul asserts that, though he could have boasted truthfully about "such a man" (*toioutou*) as was described in 12:1–4, "on my own behalf I

---

89. Whether Paul actively sought to cultivate ecstatic or pneumatic experiences (so Saake, "Paulus als Ekstatiker," 153–60) or to subordinate them to love and church order (cf. Barrett, *2 Corinthians*, 34) continues to be a debated question. Käsemann argues convincingly that God gave Paul the "thorn" to bring him from the heights of his mysticism to the reality of his office in order to *distance* Paul from his ecstatic experiences and to make weakness an acceptable standard of apostolicity (*Legitimität des Apostels*, 65).

will not boast except in my weaknesses [*en tais astheneiais mou*[90]]" (12:5b). It is clear from the context that *toioutou* is masculine (cf. *emautou* in the same verse), not neuter, and, therefore, must be a reference to Paul, who himself had received the vision but who wanted to make it clear that he felt it was based on no merit or virtue of his own. "Er will sich zwar dessen rühmen, dass jener Mensch in Christus, der er selber ist, und von dem er sich zugleich wie von einem anderen unterscheidet, solcher Begnadung gewürdigt wurde, aber eben seiner selbst als dieses irdischen Menschen hat er sich damit gerade nicht gerühmt, sondern des Herrn."[91] When he had walked in Paradise, he did so because he had been (involuntarily) snatched up out of himself and could, therefore, claim no special category for himself. Consequently, Paul did not use his visionary experiences of heaven as evidence for his apostleship, for it was not based on such experiences that could not add to his personal—or apostolic—status or importance.[92]

Understanding *ou kauchēsomai* in this way, it does not become necessary to distinguish between Paul "der Apokalypiker" (*toioutos*) and Paul "der Mensch und Apostel" (*egō autos*) as Lietzmann[93] suggests we do. Paul's concern here is to be judged (v. 6) not only correctly, but also by the correct criteria, and for him the *only* valid sign of apostolicity was his weakness through which God's power was being manifested.[94] Far from being valid marks of apostleship, ecstatic phenomena and "super-spiritual" experiences in which people boast actually have the greatest potential of impeding the display of divine power. The Corinthian intruders were themselves the best proof of this, for the divine power was scarcely perceptible in their "apostolic" activities. It is only when Paul is "weak"—persecuted, insulted, humiliated, poor, sick, despised, unloved by his own converts—that God's might comes into view and Paul can claim "I am strong" (cf. 12:10). To commend oneself in anything else is not only foolish, but also false.

---

90. p46 B D* and a few other witnesses lack the possessive pronoun. Whether *mou* was added by copyists, or was accidentally omitted in transcription, is difficult to decide. On the basis of the testimony of ℵ D2 F G *Byz* lat, the word probably should be retained in the text; indeed, B shows a tendency to shorten the expression (it omits *mou* also in 11:30 and 12:9, both times after *astheneia*). The thought is definitely that Paul would rather glory in *his own* weaknesses, not in another's.

91. Wendland, *Korinther*, 247.

92. See Lincoln, "'Paul the Visionary,'" 204–20, for a fuller discussion of Paul's vision of paradise.

93. *Korinther*, 154–55.

94. See Barrett, *2 Corinthians*, 312.

Paul, Apostle of Weakness

2 Corinthians 12:9a

Perhaps the most outstanding example of Paul's usage of *astheneia*, and certainly the most frequently cited reference in popular literature, is 2 Cor 12:9a: "But he [the Lord] said to me, 'My grace is sufficient for you, for power is perfected in weakness.'"[95] This verse is the "summit of the epistle"[96] and the crowning point of Paul's view of weakness.[97] From this vantage point the abject weakness of God's servant is seen in its proper perspective and the fundamental significance of *astheneia* for the Christian is most clearly revealed. The very *raison d'être* of Paul's existence as an apostle and as a Christian appears to have been grounded in these words of the resurrected Lord, "My grace is sufficient for you." This is why all boasting is excluded: for Paul all strength is a gift of God, the result of the free bestowment of the grace of God. This grace suffices (*arkei*); it suffices for all Paul's labors, all his trials, all his conquests, and especially it suffices for his thorn. This grace is mightier than any "angel of Satan," greater than any weakness, and more meaningful than any vision or revelation. By it Paul does not merely endure the hindrance of his *astheneia*, but overcomes it so as to carry out his ministry fully to its divinely appointed *telos*. This grace will never abandon Paul, but will support him in every circumstance of life so that the divine power, working through human weakness, accomplishes its purpose. Therefore, Paul can claim for himself *panta ischyō* (Phil 4:13); this is not a sufficiency in himself but *en tō endynamounti me*, so that he can speak of his own *autarkeia* only when it is coupled with Christian *eusebeia* (1 Tim 6:6).

This *astheneia* of Paul is not related for its own sake, but as a sequel to the lesson of "the thorn in the flesh" (12:7).[98] This disability, whatever its nature, afforded him the opportunity to display the power of Christ. Paul would far rather boast of his weaknesses than of his strengths, for it is in

---

95. It should be noted that the emphasis in this familiar verse is on the *introductory* words, "My grace is sufficient for you." The words, "for power is perfected in weakness," serve only to explain that statement.

96. Hughes, *2 Corinthians*, 451.

97. According to Heckel (*Kraft in Schwachheit*, 2), "Nirgends in den paulinischer Briefen begegnet die Verbindung von Kraft und Schwachheit so pointiert wie im 'Herrenwort' im 2. Kor 12, 9a: 'Es genügt dir meine Gnade, denn die Kraft kommt in Schwachheit zur Vollendung.'"

98. See Powers, "'Thorn in the Flesh,'" 85–99. She writes (98): "Paul tells of this 'thorn in the flesh' because he is so anxious that his Corinthian readers understand and enter into the world of the gospel. Paul wants the Corinthians to understand the reality to which his whole life and ministry point and to let that reality govern their lives."

his weakness that God's power has clearly been evidenced. The experiences related in 12:1–4 may well be boasted of; but because they are really only given him and are not of his own attainment, they tell one nothing of Paul's own character does like the *skolops tē sarki* does.

It is difficult, if not impossible, to know what Paul's "thorn in the flesh" was.[99] The usual interpretation, and one that many exegetes feel deals adequately with the available evidence, is that *skolops* refers to a physical handicap of some kind; but there is nothing in the text that demands this conclusion. Others have advanced the claim that the word refers to the opposition Paul encountered during his various missionary journeys. Again his thorn may have been carnal temptations, or spiritual trials of an unknown nature which he faced. Neither of these last two options are today widely defended. That Paul's thorn is persecution seems to find support in the context of this portion of 2 Corinthians, where so much has been said concerning his opponents and especially about one who may have been the ringleader.[100] That Paul was continually beset by personal enemies is not unlikely, as is shown for example by Paul's reference to Alexander the coppersmith, who "did me great harm; the Lord will repay him for what he has done" (2 Tim 4:14). The fact that the thorn is described as a "messenger of Satan" (*angelos Satana*) may be another indication that Paul is speaking of a person rather than a thing or illness. However, as plausible as this conjecture is, it is not altogether convincing. Paul's language suggests that the thorn he received was peculiar to him, which would not be the case if the reference were to persecution. Furthermore, the reference to Alexander in 2 Tim 4:14 implies that Paul reacted to personal enemies by committing them into the Lord's hands, not by praying for their removal. Moreover, the mention of a "messenger of Satan" need indicate no more than the satanic origin of the thorn which, like Job's suffering (Job 2:1–5), was attributable to demonic agency. The view that Paul's thorn is a reference to some physical affliction of the body therefore remains a viable possibility, and becomes a probability should one prefer to translate *skolops tē sarki* "a thorn *in* the flesh," rather than "a thorn *for* the flesh" (dativus incommodi).[101] This is

---

99. Thorough discussions of the problem may be found in Lietzmann, *Korinther*, 156–57; Wendland, *Korinther*, 249–50; Hughes, *2 Corinthians*, 442–48; and esp. Minn, *Thorn That Remained*, 8–31.

100. See Mullins, "Paul's Thorn," 299–303.

101. Hodge (*2 Corinthians*, 285) translates, "*pertaining to* the flesh," and compares the expression with Gal 4:14, *ton peirasmon en tē sarki*, though the parallel is dubious. Hughes (*2 Corinthians*, 447) purposely leaves the question open, as does Harris (2

true even if we do not connect it with the reference in Gal 4:13 to "an infirmity of the flesh" (*astheneian tēs sarkos*). There the reference seems to be to an exceptional illness that quite unexpectedly overtook Paul, whereas the language here is more indicative of a chronic and recurring ailment. Since Satan often appears in Scripture (and in the letters of Paul) as God's agent for the infliction of divine discipline in the body (cf. Job 2:1-5; 1 Cor 5:5; 11:30; 1 Tim 1:20), it is not hard to see how Paul could regard his thorn as a "messenger of Satan" that constantly tormented him (*kolaphizē*). But if the reference here is to a bodily malady, its precise nature must remain a conjecture. Since even this suggestion falls far short of certainty, we would be wise to withhold from it, and from any other theory, excessive confidence.[102]

There is no doubt that Paul had wanted to be rid of the dread affliction, for he had asked the Lord on three different occasions (*tris*) for its removal. His prayer had as its primary concern not merely personal benefit but the work of the ministry to which God had called him. He desired to be free from his thorn in the flesh in order to be able to carry out his life's work—as he supposed—more effectively and without any unnecessary hindrances. The language of this section suggests that this may have been the most intensive prayer struggle of Paul's life, although, as Stendahl[103] has shown, all of Paul's recorded prayers, including the epistolary greetings and doxologies, were shaped by issues of deep concern to the apostle.

Corinthians, 397) and Tasker (*2 Corinthians*, 174), following A. T. Robertson, who writes, "*sarki* may be either dative of advantage or locative" (*Grammar*, 538). In either case, it can be argued that *sarx* refers to the physical body here and not to one's sensual nature. Sand's suggestion that, because of its close connection with *mou* and *me*, *tē sarki* is only "eine verdeutliche Erklärung des Personalpronomens" is not convincing (*Der Begriff "Fleisch,"* 131).

102. However, some matters are clearer than others. We can be relatively certain that the reference to *skolops* is not literal, but "bildhaft," and that the word most likely is to be rendered "thorn," not "stake" (Delling, "*skolops*," *TWNT* 7:414). To say that, because the context involves persecution by adversaries, Paul's "thorn" and the "messenger of Satan" *must* allude to adversaries, not to an illness as Barré ("Qumran," 216-27) has recently argued, is a *non sequitur* and ignores the complex of *astheneia*-termini (cf. 12:5, 9) in Paul where the meaning is obviously "illness" (Phil 2:26, 27; 1 Tim 5:23; 2 Tim 4:20; probably also Gal 4:13). Thierry's suggestion that the words *angelos Satana* be considered the *subject* of *edothē*, resulting in the translation, "mir wurde als Dorn im Fleisch ein Satansengel gegeben," is not very convincing. See his article, "Dorn im Fleische," 301-10, esp. 303-04. No doubt what Delling (414) describes as the "ertraglosen Debatte" over the symbolic meaning of *skolops* will continue and give rise to many more conjectures.

103. Stendahl, "Paul at Prayer," 240-49.

The Corinthian Correspondence

The key to Paul's prayer life was the same as Jesus': *ou ti egō thelō alla ti sy* (Mark 14:36b). Christ, who himself in his earthly life had been so ruthlessly assaulted by Satan, prayed in the garden three times for the cup to pass, but in the end an angel from heaven came and strengthened him for the cross of suffering (Luke 22:43). One can only imagine with what compassion the Lord received Paul's thrice-repeated supplication to be free from his thorn in the flesh. But what was true in Jesus' situation was also true in Paul's (cf. Heb 5:7): "Im Gebet erkämpft er sich die Bereitschaft zum Leiden und sterben."[104] It was only through prayer (*in actu orationis*) that Paul came to recognize that his handicap (be it a medical or non-medical condition) was God's own way of keeping him from self-glory, and that *in* his suffering he was to fulfill his missionary calling. Now the apostle understood the meaning of the continual drain on his strength: in *that* very condition God's power would be made manifest and reign supreme. From then on, Paul accepted his thorn in the flesh, considering it to be both a messenger of Satan *and*—since it was a deterrent to spiritual pride and a platform from which to display divine strength—a gift of God.

2 Corinthians 12:9b

The sentence, "Most gladly therefore will I rather glory in my weaknesses [*en tais astheneiais mou*], that the power of Christ may rest upon me," should begin a new verse, since the words are no longer the Lord's, but Paul's. As a consequence (*oun*) of the Lord's promise concerning divine grace, Paul can rest in the assurance that his infirmities—which include his greatest disability of all, the *skolops*—are working together for his good (Rom 8:28) and for the benefit of others (2 Cor 13:9). Therefore, rather than pray for the removal of his infirmities, Paul glories in those things that reveal his weakness and utter dependence upon God. The phrase *en tais astheneiais* does not merely mean "in the midst of weaknesses," but "because of" them; there is nothing here of mere resignation or acquiescence. Instead, Paul "most sweetly" (*hēdista*) desires to boast in his infirmities, realizing the divine purpose in them.

Paul intends to boast in weakness rather than strength so that (*hina*) the power of Christ may rest upon him. The verb *episkēnoun* ("to take up residence in a tent") is reminiscent of the shekinah glory of God that filled

---

104. Jeremias, "Das Gebetsleben Jesu," 137. On the relationship of prayer and suffering in the life of Jesus, see also Rissi, "Die Menschlichkeit Jesu ," 28–45.

the OT tabernacle of Jehovah (Exod 40:34). It was not in weakness itself that Paul took pleasure but in the opportunity weakness afforded him to experience the "over-shadowing" power of the indwelling Christ. The idea is paradoxical, but true. Only when Paul is weak in human power can he be strong in divine power. What was only implicit in his earlier statements about boasting in weakness (11:30; 12:5) now becomes perfectly clear in this single desire to be lost in the grace, protection, and power of Christ.

The broadest sense of *astheneia* is in the Lord's statement in 12:9a, "for strength is perfected *en astheneia*," where the anarthrous noun is in the singular, representing "generell die ganze *irdisch-menschliche Existenz* in ihrer Schwachheit."[105] Paul now employs the plural *en tais astheneiais mou*. "In my weaknesses" includes the disability of the thorn by which he had so grievously suffered, and all the other disabilities, apparent or otherwise, of which he could boast. These weaknesses are spelled out in greater detail in the following verse.

2 Corinthians 12:10.

Paul not only boasts (*kauchēsomai*) about his weaknesses, he takes pleasure (*eudokō*) in the things he must endure *hyper Christou*, "for Christ's sake." Both verbs express the thought of Paul's willingness to be weak in order that the power of Christ might be in operation in him, but *eudokein* states the more positive, optimistic attitude of the apostle toward his weaknesses. When judged solely by human standards, Paul's life was less than satisfactory; but when judged in the light of the all-sufficient grace and power of Christ, it was a life of contentment, satisfaction, and happiness. Since Christ gave up his own life for the sake of others (2 Cor 5:14), Paul is happy to endure hardships for the sake of Christ (cf. Matt 5:11, 12). Far from being signs of one's estrangement from Christ, these hardships are the signs that a person is a true apostle of Jesus Christ, who "died for all, so that those who live should no longer live for themselves, but for him who died for them and was raised again" (2 Cor 5:15).

"Weaknesses" is the first of five words used in 12:10 to describe Paul's life. Because of the emphasis given to *astheneia* in the context (12:5, 9), "weaknesses" is most likely a general term, incorporating within it the following four groups that may be considered evidences or manifestations of the infirmities of the apostle. Because they were the occasions

---

105. Zmijewski, *Stil*, 383.

of manifesting his weaknesses—and consequently the power of Christ in operation through them—Paul was pleased to endure sufferings, whether they were insults (*en hybresin*), hardships (*en anankais*), persecutions (*en diōgmois*), or distresses (*en*[106] *stenochōriais*). "Insults" refers primarily to the verbal reproaches of others; "hardships" refers to the apostle's daily needs that were not always met because of untoward circumstances (cf. 11:26–28); "persecutions" refers to the physical abuse he was often subjected to for his faith; and "distresses" (literally, "tight places") refers to situations in which Paul could do nothing but pray and expect deliverance.

These situations are Paul's pleasure and delight, not in and of themselves, but because they maintain and extend the cause of Christ (*hyper Christou*). At the same time, Paul is not ignorant of the delivering power of God, even in situations where "the sentence of death" has already been issued (cf. 1:9). Where weakness exists, there exists simultaneously the power of "God who raises the dead" (1:9) and the hope of future deliverance from even the most hopeless of predicaments (1:10). If, therefore, Paul's own weaknesses provide a channel for the demonstration of God's might, then the path of suffering must be the proper one for the servant of God. It is in *this* representation of apostolic life that the power of Christ becomes visible and not in the portrayal of the false apostles. "Pour mener la vie d' un apôtre chrétien, Paul sait qu'il doit accepter l'humaine condition de 'faibless': sa vocation exceptionnelle ne peut être une raison de s'y soustraire, au contraire: son acceptation conditionne et protèe l' authenticité chrétienne de sa vie d' apôtre."[107]

Paul summarizes the thoughts of 9–10a by reiterating in 10b the divine standard of strength by which he has been operating: *hotan gar asthenō, tote dynamis eimi*, "for when I am weak, then I am strong." This statement is the final demonstration that Paul's attitude toward weakness has been correct. The reason (*gar*) he takes pleasure in infirmities, of which insults, hardships, persecutions, and distresses are continuous expressions, is because in all actuality Paul's moments of weakness are the moments of his greatest power. What was intended by Satan to destroy Paul became, not a handicap, but in the providence of a loving God a wonderful aid to making his ministry energetic and productive. Thus the more often he acknowledges his own weakness, the more evident Christ's strength becomes.

---

106. If one follows p46 ℵ* B in omitting *en*, then "persecutions" and "distresses" would be appositional, not two separate categories (cf. 6:4).

107. Cambier, "Le critère paulinien," 488.

Paul, Apostle of Weakness

2 Corinthians 13:3, 4, 9

The main subject of 13:1–10 is Paul's desire to restore discipline at Corinth on his forthcoming third visit. He has no intention of permitting it to turn out like his second "painful visit" (2:1; 13:2) when the influence of the false teachers was stronger than his own. He has now given the Corinthians ample opportunity to repent and take positive steps toward reconciliation. His failure to take judicial action on his second visit is no guarantee that he will restrain himself from acting severely on his third, since all charges against him are now proven false. Paul, therefore, resolves to exercise spiritual authority when he arrives at Corinth if that is what it takes to completely reestablish himself as an apostle of Christ.

2 Corinthians 13:3

Paul's opponents, as we have seen, have been challenging his authority by denying that he possesses the spiritual power of a true Christian apostle. The unmistakable evidence of this was (supposedly) his inability to be stern in person by asserting his opinions with impressive words (10:10). They want, he says, "proof that Christ is speaking in me." Paul now asserts that upon his third visit he will be happy to provide them with all the proof they desire by employing every appropriate severe measure. He will do this, however, not to prove that he has great power, but that *Christ*, working through Paul's weakness, is powerful.

The relative clause introduced by *hos* explains why Paul can claim that Christ is speaking to the Corinthians. The Christ who speaks in Paul is one "who is not weak towards you, but is powerful among you." In failing to recognize the authority of Paul, who claimed to be of Christ, the Corinthians had thought that Christ himself was weak and unable to manifest his power in their life as Christians. With the words, "He is not weak . . . but powerful," Paul wishes to correct this notion by pointing out that Christ is already demonstrating his power both "toward" (*eis*) them and "among" or "in the midst of" (*en*) them. Implicit in his statement is the idea that unless the Corinthians recognize the *saving* power of Christ and satisfy themselves with that, Paul will be ready to supply them with proof of the *disciplinary* power of Christ.

Exactly which manifestations of Christ's power Paul is reminding the Corinthians of is uncertain, but perhaps the first phrase *eis hymas* refers to the exhibitions of divine power in Paul's preaching (1 Cor 2:4) and miracles (2 Cor 12:12), while the phrase *en hymin* (i.e., "in the church") refers to the demonstration of the power of Christ in the spiritual gifts of which the Corinthians were inclined to boast (cf. 1 Cor 12:4–11). But if one feels the context permits a less specific reference, it is possible that Paul has in mind a more general manifestation, such as the work of Christ in their conversion or sanctification. Be the reference specific or general, however, the argument remains the same. Christ has demonstrated and is demonstrating his power toward and among the Corinthians, and will again manifest his power through Paul's disciplinary activity should that become necessary.[108]

2 Corinthians 13:4

The Corinthians had been seeking an experimental proof (*dokimēn*) of what kind of a being the Christ who speaks in Paul was. Paul's answer that the Christ who indwells them is not weak, but strong, necessitated further explanation. Christ will prove himself strong, even though (*kai gar*) "he was crucified out of weakness"—death being the ultimate weakness a person can experience. The expression *ex astheneias* does not simply mean that Christ was crucified because of weakness, as if he experienced a lapse from strength that then occasioned his death. He had no intrinsic weakness of his own, although he lived as man in the flesh. Christ's weakness was the weakness of obedience to God, an obedience that led him to assume human nature in all its poverty and to become obedient even to the point of dying on a cross. From a mere human point of view the crucifixion exposed the helplessness of Christ, but his death was completely voluntary and in complete accordance with the will of God.

However, just as weakness was characteristic of Christ, so also was power. Christ lives *ek dynameōs theou*, though he once was limited by *astheneia*. The power that Paul describes here is the power of the resurrection. Since his resurrection, Christ is alive and powerfully at work drawing upon the power of God. And the Lord is now, in a sense, repeated in the life of his servants. Because Paul is "in Christ" (*en autō*) he shares in both the weakness and power that are characteristic of his crucified, risen Lord. The occurrence of these two terms—weakness and power—together in the same passage, and the use of each of them in a similar way in other passages (notably 1 Cor 1:25, 27; 4:10), shows that we have here a set theological

---

108. See Nielsen, "*Dynamis*," 146.

motif: weakness, the showplace of God's power. On the cross, Christ proved that God's weakness is stronger than human strength. It was in Christ's weakness that the power of the resurrection was first revealed and made available. Paradoxically the dying of the body (its crucifixion) leads to a manifestation of life in that same body.

Paul thus relates Christian weakness to Jesus' own death and resurrection by asserting, "He was crucified in weakness, yet he lives by the power of God. Likewise, we are weak in him, yet by the power of God we will live with him." As Christ was crucified and raised from the dead, so Paul, as a participant in the existence of Christ, is himself a partaker of the weakness of Christ and the resurrection power of God. Even though they appear to be antithetical to each other, weakness and power are experienced *together*, being for Paul two aspects of the same reality. By emphasizing that he is *both* weak and strong in Christ, he seeks to avoid two possible misunderstandings among his readers: first, that he is too weak to act with authority toward them, and second, that he will act like the false apostles with an independent and selfish display of authority. Paul is neither totally weak nor totally strong, but both simultaneously. Should it become necessary to act with authority (and severity), it will not be Paul's strength that is evident, but the power of God working through a weak vessel. This is indicated clearly by the present tense of *asthenoumen*, by which the continuous aspect of weakness in Paul's life is emphasized. The continuing reality of weakness is necessary so that Paul might not confuse the power of God with his own power and consequently lose God's power by attempting to rely on his own strength. His apostolic legitimacy is based not on his own strength, knowledge, or religious experience, but solely on the extent to which he faithfully represents by word and deed "Christ crucified."

Paul, therefore, urges his readers to understand that in the weakness of Christ his own weakness is to be understood. The central expression is *asthenoumen en autō*. Paul does not assert that he is weak in himself, and strong in Christ, a statement that the Corinthians could have readily accepted and understood. Rather, he states he is weak *in him*. Paul's weakness is a reflection of his fellowship with *the Lord* and of his participation in *his* death and resurrection. This was more difficult for the Corinthians to understand. Paul's opponents, being Jewish Christians, have placed emphasis on Jesus the miracle-worker but not as one who was crucified in weakness. They have seen in Paul weakness and humility (10:1, 2) and have concluded that he walks *kata sarka* (10:2) and cannot be of Christ. They do preach

Jesus, but "another Jesus" (11:4), not the Jesus of the cross but a wonder-worker who is characterized by strength and authority. In their gospel God does not reconcile through the cross (5:18, 19) nor does he forgive through the cross (5:21).

Since the opponents of Paul have modeled themselves after their erroneous view of Jesus—a Jesus without suffering—it is not surprising that they consider the suffering of Paul as a natural result of his own foolishness. Paul, however, declares that "Christ was crucified in weakness." And while Christ does live, he is alive solely by the power of God, a power that comes only in the midst of weakness, as the Lord himself has said (12:9). The Christians must therefore suffer with Christ and accept their weakness, for only by daily bearing the sufferings of Jesus can the life of Jesus manifest itself in the body (4:10, 11). Paul therefore commends himself, not by his power but by his suffering for Christ's sake, because in weakness he is united with him. The final proof that Christ is in him and that he is in Christ is living as Christ lived: in weakness. And by sharing his weakness, Paul also shares his power. But because the resurrected Christ is no substitute for the crucified Christ, it is necessary that the Christian retain a permanent witness to the weakness of God.[109]

This weakness-power motif in 2 Cor 13:4 is given a specific apostolic[110] reference when Paul writes, "but we will live with him toward you by the power of God." The verb *zēsomen* ("we will live") is probably a simple future and refers to Paul's impending activity in Corinth when the power of which he speaks will become manifest in a concrete place and in concrete situations (cf. *eis hymas*, omitted by BD, which interpret *zēsomen* in its soteriological sense). Paul anticipates having to deal with the situation in Corinth on his forthcoming visit, at which time Christ will reveal his resurrection power through his apostle. The death and resurrection of Christ is in Paul's thought no mere speculative doctrine for which there is no corresponding reality in life. The resurrection power of God will shortly make an unmistakable impact upon the Corinthians.

---

109. Cf. Bouttier, *La Condition Chrétienne*, 58.

110. "Paul is speaking as an apostle, not just as a Christian" (Schütz, *Apostolic Authority*, 215). The plural, however, implies that the statement is normative for all Christians, not only for Paul as an apostle. All Christian life is dependent upon the power of God (cf. Rom 5:10; 6:3, 10; 2 Cor 4:10).

2 Corinthians 13:9.

Because God's power is at work in Paul and his assistants, they are willing to appear weak. Paul therefore writes, "For we are glad when we are weak (*asthenōmen*) and you are strong. What we pray for is your perfecting" (13:9). He is glad that he should be considered weak if such weakness is due to the strength of his converts, that is, the evidence of robust and mature Christian character (*katartisis*). Proof of their maturity will be shown in their willingness to oust the offenders and to renounce those sins of the flesh and spirit listed at 12: 20, 21. Before Paul can resume a normal relationship with them, however, they need edification (*oikodomē*, 12:19). If they bring their own congregation in order as it should be, Paul will gladly forego exercising strict discipline, even if it makes him look weak. What Paul writes here throws special light upon the apostolic office as he understands it. He shows no particular desire to display his authority by adopting stern measures, for he would much rather see the church discipline itself. He seeks only the upbuilding of the church (*oikodomē*), not its destruction (*kathairesis*, 13:10). If, at times, this requires a powerful display of divine authority, then he will act accordingly; but there is no place at all for a proud or overbearing spirit such as the false teachers display. If he writes with strong words when absent it is only in order to obviate any need for acting with authority when present. He therefore declines as it were the challenge of his opponents to take up the boasting match upon his arrival at Corinth to see who can be more tyrannical and domineering. *Paulus infirmus* is too weak to act that way; but so is *Paulus potens* who has no ambition for personal position or prestige. The apostle therefore prays for the perfecting of his converts (9b), since this is the only certain protection from the disciplinary authority of Paul. If the Corinthians rectify what is wrong, they will no longer deserve his severity.

CONCLUSION: WEAKNESS IN THE CORINTHIAN LETTERS

While Paul uses the root to describe somatic illness (1 Cor 11:30) and the mortality of the psychical body (1 Cor 15:43), by far the predominant usage of *astheneia* and its cognates in the Corinthian letters is nonliteral, i.e., ethical and soteriological. The first main meaning is "weak" in the sense of insignificant or powerless. Humans are unable to save themselves because of their inner poverty (1 Cor 9:22). However, God delights to choose the weak in order to magnify his own strength and shame the worldly strong, i.e., the self-reliant (1 Cor 1:27). Since all Christians belong to the body of Christ, the insignificance of certain members of the church in the eyes of the world (and in the eyes of self-exalting church members) is only apparent (1 Cor 12:22). However, believers may be described as weak in another, less beatific sense. In Corinth there are Christians who lack the *gnōsis* of more learned believers and whose consciences are still influenced by long-standing habits as nonbelievers. These Christians Paul labels *hoi astheneis* (*hoi asthenountes*), and he devotes a lengthy discussion to their situation (1 Cor 8:1–13).

Many members of the Corinthian church, perhaps the majority, were accustomed to participating in activities that would indirectly involve a sort of countenancing of idolatry. To others in the congregation, however, this type of behavior was considered to be permissive and scandalous. The "enlightened" Christians certainly had no desire to worship the many pagan divinities so prevalent in Corinth. Yet their actions were easily misunderstood by those with weak consciences, and therefore the possibility of scandalizing the extremely conservative members of the community was real, and no doubt had already occurred. The stronger Christians needed to be reminded that love has priority over knowledge and that the spiritual welfare of the weak Christian is their responsibility too.

The unlikelihood that the weak Christians could have comprised a definite faction within the Corinthian community has been demonstrated by Rauer,[111] though it remains a distinct possibility that they were closely associated with other groups. Possibly "the weak" are those church members who felt themselves bound to the traditions of the Jewish law. However, it is neither necessary nor proper to limit the ascription to Jewish Christians *alone*, for the usage is wide enough to embrace both Jewish and Gentile converts. Indeed, some scholars see here a problem more sociological in nature than ethical. According to Theissen, for example, the weak and the strong are members of different social strata. For socio-economic reasons, the lower classes (the weak) would not normally have enjoyed meat in their diet, whereas the upper classes (the strong) would.[112] This interpretation

---

111. *Die "Schwachen,"* 66f.

112. Theissen, "Starken und Schwachen," 155–72. The economic interpretation is predominant also in the dissertation of Schreiber, *Gemeinde in Korinth*. Cf. also Grant, "Economic Background," 96–114.

certainly contains an element of truth, but the casuistical aspect of the problem between the weak and strong Corinthians, indicated most clearly by the thrice-repeated reference to *syneidēsis*, must not be ignored. Rauer's conclusion that the weak are *mainly* Gentile Christians who maintain a belief in (and an unhealthy fear of) the demonic powers behind idols is perhaps still the most satisfactory: "Ihre 'Schwäche' aber ist nicht so sehr das Bewusstsein einer überirdischen Macht, die hinter den *eidōla* lauert—das teilt Paulus mit ihnen—, aber die damit verbundene religiöse Scheu und Furcht vor der Macht der abgeschworenen Götzen."[113]

Of far greater significance is the further development of *astheneia* in 2 Corinthians to refer to the sphere of divine activity. In this letter Paul's weakness language is motivated and developed in response to tendencies by some to interpret the concept in a purely anthropologic sense. Against this apologetic background the specific *christological* character of the weakness vocabulary is brought into its sharpest focus. In chaps. 10–13, where the words occur numerous times, the weakness motif is developed in great detail and its theological implications are all too evident. At this point in its evolution, Paul's view of weakness is essentially an embodiment of the tension between strength and weakness, a tension that can be alleviated only by refusing to accept one pole or the other. When this point became misunderstood, as it was by the Corinthians, there was no alternative left to Paul but to become explicit in his language.

In 2 Corinthians weakness is not only a sign of Paul's humanity but of his apostleship.[114] Therefore the apostle boasts in the things that reveal his weakness (2 Cor 11:30; 12:5, 9, 10) and gladly bears in his body the death of Jesus as the way to manifest his life (cf. 2 Cor 4:10).[115] Christ, in his humanity, became weak (2 Cor 13:3) in order to share in the same weakness that people experience as a matter of course (cf. Heb 5:2). At the crucifixion, the weakness of Christ's humanity was most evident, but even this display of divine *astheneia* was stronger than the strength of humans (1 Cor 1:25). Weakness has now become the place where the divine will is expressed. Christians share the same weakness that Christ experienced when they manifest the crucified Christ in their lives (2 Cor 13:4). This spiritual

---

113. Rauer, *Die "Schwachen,"* 31.

114. See Fuchs, "La Faiblesse," 243–46.

115. "The past dying with Christ and the present dying with Christ in suffering are not two unrelated things, but the same thing taking place on two different levels" (Tannehill, *Dying and Rising*, 117). This dying-rising motif is also very evident in Philippians; see Palmer, "To Die is Gain," 203–18.

weakness is the only legitimate grounds for boasting and a mark of honor, for it displays what the world considers *to asthenes tou theou* (1 Cor 1:25) but what is in actuality *hē dynamis tou theou* (2 Cor 13:4).[116]

Therefore, rather than plead for release from his "thorn in the flesh," Paul has learned to glory in it as a means to the realization of divine strength (2 Cor 12:7-10). In the midst of his inadequacy and apparent disabilities is at work the grace of God that enables him to be a more-than-conqueror (Rom 8:37). The thorn and its attendant weakness afford Paul the unique opportunity to witness the power of Christ residing in his life and expressing itself through it. The Lord himself had revealed to Paul that where weakness is given, grace sufficient to triumph through it is also given, and with that grace the promise that through human weakness divine power finds its full scope and ultimate mode of expression (2 Cor 12:9). Satan had desired the thorn to constitute a source of great discouragement to Paul and a hindrance to his work, but the Lord had graciously made provision to sustain Paul in the midst of it. By means of this disability God's will was made manifest to his servant: "My grace is sufficient; my strength is independent of human ability; my might is displayed in human weakness; and my will is performed despite infirmities of the body or soul." Paul therefore emphasizes that his authority comes from God alone and that his power is effective only when it is linked to the power of God in Christ (2 Cor 13:4). However, Paul's weakness does not mean that he can allow flagrant disobedience to continue in the Corinthian church (2 Cor 10:4ff.; 13:2ff.). Every sin must and will be challenged, even by the apostle in his weakness. But it is only to prove *the presence and power of Christ* that he "will not spare those who sinned earlier or any of the others" (2 Cor 13:2b).

---

116. Writes Furnish (*II Corinthians*, 550): "This is why weakness is the hallmark of his [Paul's] apostleship, because he has been commissioned to the service of the gospel through the grace of Christ—a grace where power is made present in the cross."

4

Romans, Philippians, 1 and 2 Timothy

INTRODUCTION TO ROMANS

SCHOLARS GENERALLY AGREE THAT the apostle Paul wrote his letter to the Romans from Corinth[1] during the winter of AD 56–57 as he prepared to sail to Jerusalem with his peace-offering for the relief of Christians in Palestine. Although the Roman church had been in existence for some time, Paul had never visited the congregation. He was, however, acquainted with several of its members (16:3–6).[2] Evidently he expected the Roman church to serve as a base of missionary operation in the West comparable to Antioch in the East. From there he intended to set out to lead his cam-

---

1. However, Taylor ("Origin of Romans," 281–95) held that Romans was composed in the city of Philippi after Paul's departure from Corinth for Jerusalem.

2. According to some critics, the greater part of Romans 16 is supposed to be addressed to the Ephesians. Attractive as this view is, it is not universally received, for despite the fact that one cannot rule out the possibility of the independent existence of 16:1–23 on *a priori* grounds (cf. McDonald, "Romans XVI?" 369–72), a stronger case can be made in favor of its Romans destination. See Harrison, *Introduction*, 307–11; Kümmel, *Einleitung*, 275–80; Guthrie, *Introduction*, 400–404; Michel, *Römer*, 471–72; Donfried, "Romans 16," 50–60; and esp. the thorough and detailed monograph by Gamble, *Textual History*. Lohse summarizes well these authors' conclusions: "So lässt sich kein zwingender Beweis dafür führen, Röm. 16 könnte nicht Bestandteil des Röm. gewesen sein" (*Entstehung*, 49).

paign in Spain. For this new undertaking he would need the support of the household churches at Rome for prayer, personnel, and finance. If this was to be realized, he would need to communicate to the church in detail the gospel he had been preaching for over twenty years. Moreover, should his apprehension about trouble at Jerusalem turn out to be a reality, this statement of the gospel as he preached it would be a fitting memorial of his ministry and an adequate basis for the Roman church to continue his work intelligently.

It is certainly true, as John Drane points out, that from the standpoint of occasion and purpose Romans is more a theological treatise than a response to events and issues in the Roman church.[3] Paul's desire to introduce himself to the Christians in Rome and to relate to them what he preaches affords him the opportunity to express at length and in detail the basic truths of his evangel. While motifs of earlier letters are discussed, they appear in Romans in a form so vague and generalized that the epistle "has almost nothing of the occasional character common to Paul's letters."[4] Paul's overriding concern is to demonstrate that the gospel is in full accord with God's nature and plan,[5] which he initially revealed to Abraham (4:1–25) and which is now being fulfilled in the inclusion of the nations on the basis of faith in Christ and in the final salvation of Israel.

At the same time, however, specific concerns relating to the actual situation in Rome cannot be ruled out altogether as motivations for writing. Although there are good reasons for doubting that Paul was as informed about the situation in Rome as he was about the needs in Galatia or Corinth, one can hardly underestimate his knowledge of church life in Rome in general. As the greetings in chap. 16 indicate, Paul had many friends and acquaintances in Rome, including close associates in the gospel-ministry (such as Aquila and Priscilla), from whom he could have gained first-hand knowledge of circumstances in Rome. The desire of these friends that Paul should journey to Rome may have resulted in

---

3. Drane, "Why Romans?" 208–27.

4. Harrison, *Introduction*, 306. This fact probably prompted the omission of geographical indications (Rom 1:7, 15) and personal names (chap. 16) in an early effort to "catholicize" the Roman letter, as has been argued by Dahl, "The Particularity," 261–71, and, more recently, by Gamble, *Textual History*, 128. Therefore, the generalized character of Romans is not a strong argument against a Roman destination. Elsewhere I have argued that the same phenomenon occurred in Ephesians, in "Ephesian Address," 59–73.

5. See Morris, "Theme," 249–63, who notes the dominance of the God-theme in Romans.

urgent communications to that effect. The constant coming and going of people in the Roman Empire—which inevitably would have included some Christians—suggests that Roman believers ultimately found their way to Paul. With his intention of visiting Rome, it would occur at once to Paul to inquire of the health and status of the Roman church. That in Romans he even bothers to deal with such matters as charismatic gifts (12:3–13), the issue of "weak" and "strong" Christians (14:1—15:13), and the political responsibilities of believers (13:1-7) is perhaps sufficient indication of his concern to deal with concrete and practical duties devolving upon believers (12:1—15:13). Actual, known situations in Rome quite possibly may have been lying behind these exhortations, even though the particular state of the Roman church is nowhere described in detail. The reason for this may lie not so much in Paul's ignorance of conditions in Rome as in his deference to the Roman Christians, the majority of whom he had never met. Thus, it is not unreasonable to suppose that both of these considerations—the fact that he was unknown by face to the Christians in Rome, coupled with the necessity of dealing with practical issues—dictated the character and content of his paraenesis in Romans 12–15.[6] This point of view will have special significance when we come to the occurrences of the weakness termini in Rom 14:1, 2 and 15:1, where Paul refers to "weak" Christians who comprised a part of the church's membership.

Accordingly, while the purpose of the epistle is impossible to define with complete precision, it is tenable that its occasion, at least partially, was to meet the immediate needs of the readers. This appears to be true not only of many of the practical exhortations found in chaps. 12–15 but also of the main body of the letter, where a constant interplay between "Jew" and "Gentile" emerges. The main problem there appears to have been what Guthrie describes as "the fundamental Christian principle of 'righteousness' as contrasted with the Jewish approach,"[7] including not only the question of Israel's rejection of the Christ (chaps. 9–11) but also the demonstration that all people, both Jewish and Gentile, are in need of "the gospel, because it is the power of God for the salvation of everyone who believes: first for the Jew, then for the Gentile" (1:16).

We have seen that in 2 Corinthians the gross misunderstanding of Paul's weakness by a group of his converts forced him to take up an emotional defense of his apostleship. In Romans we can discern a more balanced

---

6. See Kümmel, *Einleitung*, 273.
7. Guthrie, *Introduction*, 399.

approach in which Paul is free to take up the terms for weakness in connotations other than those that refer to himself. This is primarily because the words are no longer used for polemical purposes in a conflict setting. The apostle, now enjoying a respite from his normal strenuous work and travel, writes with an ease and tranquility that is traceable throughout the epistle. This usage of *astheneia* in a completely different manner represents a significant development of the weakness theme. In this respect Romans forms a bridge between the usage of the words in the mostly polemic contexts of the Corinthian letters and that in Paul's later letters, where for all intents and purposes the words were dropped from his vocabulary.

The closely-reasoned character of Paul's argument in Romans has given rise to the following widely-accepted structure. After an opening paragraph (1:1-17), the main body of the letter may be divided into four major parts. 1:18—8:39 contains the first two of these, but where one should break the passage into its sub-sections is debatable; the best possibility seems to be at 5:1. The third major division, comprising 9:1—11:36, treats the problem of the election of Israel; the fourth main section of the epistle (12:1—15:13) discusses specific duties relative to the Christian's relationship with God and others. The letter's conclusion (15:14—16:27) deals with Paul's program and plans and includes the familiar personal greetings and doxology, as well as an unusual (and problematic) warning against schismatics (16:17-20).

EXEGESIS OF THE TEXTS

Romans 4:19

In the first major section of Romans, Paul seeks to show that righteousness before God is righteousness by faith alone (1:18—4:25). He writes that all people are under divine judgment and in need of the gospel in which God's righteousness is being revealed through Jesus Christ (1:17). In this there are no exceptions for Jews (2:1—3:20), because a person's right standing before God is based not on heritage but on faith so that all boasting is excluded (3:27-31). Not even Abraham had a right to glory in his own works, because "he believed God and it was accounted unto him for righteousness" (4:3).[8]

---

8. On the general subject that our author treats, see Williams, "'Righteousness,'" 241-90.

Paul, Apostle of Weakness

A somewhat isolated reference to weakness comes toward the end of Paul's extended discussion of Abraham's justification apart from works (4:1–25).[9] After reminding the Romans of God's original promise to Abraham (Gen 15:5), which was fulfilled despite the advanced age of the patriarch through his hope and faith (4:18), Paul rehearses the circumstances that had made the fulfilment of the promise impossible apart from the special intervention of God (4:19–21):

> "Without weakening in faith [*mē asthenēsas tē pistei*] he considered his own body to be already dead—since he was about a hundred years old—and that Sarah's womb was also dead. Yet he did not waver in unbelief regarding the promise of God, but was strengthened in faith and gave glory to God, being fully persuaded that he was able to do what he had promised."

By this illustration of the faith of Abraham Paul is continuing his explanation of salvation by grace by emphasizing the antithesis between justification by works and justification by faith. Not by the energy of his own natural powers but by the exercise of faith did Abraham attain to justification with God. "Those who are of law" (4:16), therefore, cannot be the heirs of the promise unless they too exercise faith. This means that those who are of the Mosaic Law are not excluded if they are also "of the faith of Abraham," who is the father of all believers.

Exactly *how* Abraham became the *patēr pantōn hēmōn* (4:16) and the *patēr pollōn ethnōn* (4:17) is explained in vv. 19–21, which begins with the statement, *kai mē asthenēsas tē pistei katenoēsen to heautou sōma [ēdē] nenekrōmenon* ("without weakening in his faith he faced the fact that his body was as good as dead," NIV). To describe the nature of Abraham's hope and faith, Paul refers to the procreative impotency of the bodies of both Abraham and his wife Sarah.[10] Since Abraham was one hundred years of age and Sarah was past the age for conception (cf. Gen 18:11), childbearing should have been, humanly speaking, utterly impossible. Abraham recognized that fact (he "faced the fact"); yet, apart from a brief moment of hesitation (Gen 17:17), he did not waver in unbelief but fixed his attention

---

9. Paul is completely silent about the offering of Isaac, for what interests him is not what Abraham did for God but what God gave to Abraham *kata charin* (4:16). For a fuller discussion, see Ward, "Abraham," 283–90.

10. Here Paul uses *sōma* for the source and carrier of sexual power (Robinson, *The Body*, 28); cf. the OT usage of *basar* for the male reproductive organ in Gen 17:13; Lev 15:2; Ezek 16:26; 23:20. Cf. also the NT connection of the flesh with circumcision (Gal 6:12; Rom 2:28).

on the promise of God. Faith according to Paul does not ignore nor deny the realities of the situation: it overcomes in spite of it. As far as Abraham was concerned, he was "fully persuaded" (*plērophorētheis*) that God's ability could match his promise. Abraham could therefore consider all the unfavorable circumstances—even "fix his eye" (*katanoein*) upon the obstacles—and still not become weakened in his faith in God.[11]

The clause *kai mē asthenēsas tē pistei* is further described, both negatively and positively, in v. 20. This verse makes it clear that the faith that Paul is describing is not merely belief in the impossible for its own sake, but a trust based upon the promise of God (*eis tēn epaggelian tou theou*). "It is the promise on which it [faith] rests which is its power. It exists because a man has been over-powered, held and sustained by God's promise."[12] By fully recognizing his own impotency and that of his wife, Abraham was not being foolish since he knew God could not fail to keep his word. Therefore, in v. 20 Paul goes on to state that Abraham "did not waver in unbelief" but "grew strong in faith." The first statement, *ou diekrithē tē apistia*, specifically identifies being "weak in faith" with *unbelief* (*apistia*). Käsemann rightly observes that *apistia* denotes more than a mere negation of *pistis*: it denotes "die Absage an den Glauben, der Verzicht auf die angebotene Verheissung Gottes."[13] If Abraham had wavered at the promise of God, that would have entailed an active rejection of faith.

Instead, Paul writes that he "was strengthened in faith [*tē pistei*]." Although *tē pistei* may be taken in an instrumental sense, in view of the emphasis upon the objective basis of Abraham's hope it is much more probable that the expression is a dative of respect: "in faith." Isaac was begotten by Abraham and conceived by Sarah, not because Abraham was empowered *by* his faith, but because he rested in God's power and faithfulness. As a believer Abraham no longer looked to himself, for he recognized that the promise could not be realized unless God intervened with supernatural power by "calling into being that which does not exist" (4:17). This interpretation

---

11. This interpretation is based upon the reading *katenoēsen* (א A B C) as opposed to the negative *ou katenoēsen*, supported by D G K P and most other MSS. However, both readings are thoroughly compatible with the context. Should one prefer to include the negative, Paul's meaning would be that, because of Abraham's unweakened faith, he did not become *absorbed* with disagreeable circumstances regarding his or his wife's procreative ability to the extent that his faith was subverted.

12. Cranfield, *Romans*, 1.248.

13. Käsemann, *Römer*, 173. On the meaning of *pistis/pisteuein* in Romans 4 see further Lührmann, *Glaube*, 46ff.

best accords with the parallelism in the statement *mē asthenēsas tē pistei* (v. 19), where the meaning is obviously *in respect to faith*. After all, Paul is arguing that it is God, not Abraham, who is *dynatos . . . kai poiēsai* (v. 21). Only because God makes the dead to live can Abraham become the progenitor of the people of God. Thereby God's promise to Abraham makes him what he really is not—a father—by giving life to his body and to Sarah's maternal capacity.[14] "Indem Abraham klar und scharf seine Erstorbenheit sieht," writes Schlatter, "ohne sich den wirklichen Tatbestand zu verhüllen und doch irgendwie bei sich selbst die Kraft zu suchen, der Vaterschaft teilhaft zu werden, verzichtet er auf sich selbst, und damit kommt es nun zu einer unbeschränkten, ganzen Bejahung der göttlichen Zusage, die ihm die Vaterschaft nicht durch ihn selbst, sondern durch Gottes im Todten Leben schaffende Tat verleiht."[15]

The major value of Paul's citation of the example of Abraham is the standard his faith becomes for all believers.[16] "Against all hope" (4:18) he faced an impossible situation with unwavering faith in the power of the Almighty to keep his promise. The necessity of trusting in God's faithfulness to his word applies as definitely to Paul's present readers as to Abraham. Just as "he did not waver through unbelief," so the Romans must trust the God who both quickened Abraham's "dead" body and raised Jesus from the dead for their justification (4:23–25).[17]

Romans 5:6

In Rom 5:6 we find Christians referred to as "weak" at the beginning of the carefully-structured paragraph (5:6–8) that describes the nature of the divine love to which v. 5 referred. The reference comes as the initial member of a series of descriptive terms for the pre-conversion state of the Christian. After stating how God, through the agency of the Holy Spirit, has revealed

---

14. Cf. the OT parallels where God is the "healer" of the unfruitfulness of women: Gen 16:2; 20:18; 1 Sam 1:9–20.

15. Schlatter, *Glaube*, 307.

16. See Mundle, *Glaubensbegriff*, 97. Cf. also Gal 3:6–8, where the descendents of Abraham are described as *hoi ek pisteōs*.

17. Commenting on Romans 4:13–25, Jewett (*Romans*, 343) notes, "Whether one's declaration of war against God had occurred as a Jew or a Gentile, it was exposed and overcome by the cross of Christ. Christ's shameful death on behalf of the shamed conveyed in a new way the divine 'grace' that Paul had identified as the key to Abraham's promise (4:16b)."

his love to the faithful, thereby engendering hope in the fulfillment of his promises, the apostle declares: "For while we were still weak [*ontōn hēmōn asthenōn*], at the right time Christ died for the ungodly."[18]

A comparison of the structure of vv. 6–8 strongly suggests the likelihood that Paul is employing the familiar rabbinic argument *a minori ad maius* (which is even more apparent in vv. 9–11) to emphasize that it was for *sinners* that Christ died, for men and women who were neither righteous nor good (v. 7)[19] and, therefore, were totally unworthy of God's love. Thus these verses essentially refer to the hostile attitude of humans to God. But they also refer to the relationship in which God sees people; indeed, the point of Paul's message is the paradox that while—or in spite of the fact that—God sees people as unworthy objects of his love, he forgives them and reconciles them to himself.[20] Paul uses three words in vv. 6–8 to describe those whom God loves and for whom Christ died: weak, ungodly, and sinners. All three expressions refer to humans in their preconversion situation and therefore cannot easily be differentiated from each other. While *asthenēs* usually refers to the Christian in Paul, it is used here to indicate the impotency of unregenerate people to justify themselves and is best rendered "powerless" (cf. NIV; NEB). The expression *ontōn hēmōn asthenōn* is then explained and expanded by the following expression in v. 6, *hyper asebōn*: Because people are *astheneis* and therefore unable to produce their own right standing before a holy Being, at the time appointed by God (*kata kairon*) "Christ died for the ungodly [*hyper asebōn*]."

These *asebeis* (cf. 4:5 where the term is used to describe Abraham) cannot in every respect be distinguished from the *astheneis*; yet the idea is strengthened and carried a step further when Paul adds *asebeis* here and *hamartōloi* in v. 8. Christ died at "the proper time" in the sense that our helplessness under the law had been exposed and our inability to save ourselves had become apparent. But in that his death accomplished the

18. In place of *eti gar* at the opening of the verse, B reads *ei ge*, and Db G it vg read *eis ti gar*. External authority preponderates in favor of the reading *eti gar*, and it is much easier to understand how it could be changed in order to avoid the repetition of *eti*. The variant *eti* after *asthenōn* probably should also be retained in the text, although in an English translation both occurrences of *eti* can hardly be reproduced. Cranfield suggests that the word was repeated after the genitive absolute for the sake of clarity (*Romans*, 1.263).

19. All commentators acknowledge the difficulty of establishing the distinction Paul makes between *dikaios* and *agathos* in 5:7, but this is no reason to consider the verse a gloss, as does Fuchs, *Freiheit*, 16.

20. Taylor, *Forgiveness*, 75.

atonement for *sin*, Christ is said to have "died" for the *ungodly* men and *sinners*. In other words, it was not merely our helplessness, but our godlessness and sinfulness, that required the sacrifice of Christ on our behalf. The term *astheneis* must then emphasize the saving *power* of Christ, while the words *asebeis* and *hamartōloi* underscore the *redemptive efficacy* of his atoning death. Nevertheless, the difference between what we cannot do (since we are weak) and what we are (ungodly and sinners) is not great, because the ungodly and sinful are by definition without strength to help themselves. When we assesses our ungodliness and then discover our own powerlessness to do anything about it, each of us becomes—as Paul states in 4:5 with reference to Abraham—a "person who does not work but trusts [God] who justifies *ton asebē*." Apart from Christ we remain both weak and godless; in Christ we can no longer be described as godless but we do retain our fundamental ontological weakness (*permanens infirmitas*), as Paul makes clear in other places (cf. 6:19; 8:26; 1 Cor 1:27; 15:43). It follows, therefore, that no fundamental identification can be made between the term "weak" and the terms "ungodly" and "sinners."[21] Paul does not speak of sin when he refers to weakness, and Rom 5:6 does not appear to be an exception to this. Our weakness is not sin, but the inability to save ourselves that the power of God's justifying act in Christ has overcome. What Paul is concerned to bring out with the adjective *asthenōn* is only the fact of our helplessness: "[Christ] did not wait for us to start helping ourselves, but died for us when we were altogether helpless."[22]

Romans 6:19

In this pericope (6:15-23) Paul is contrasting freedom and slavery, and in so doing he openly admits in v. 19a that he is speaking "after the manner of men" (*anthrōpinon legō* = *kata anthrōpon legō*, cf. Rom 3:5; Gal 3:15).[23] This

---

21. See Kuß, *Römerbrief*, 1.208; also Wolter, *Heil*, 170. Schlier, however, interprets the expression "while we were still weak" to mean "zu der Zeit der Krankheit unserer Sünde" (*Grundzüge*, 135).

22. Cranfield, *Romans*, 1.264.

23. This statement in 19a occurs between two major sections of Paul's argument in 6:15-18 and 19-23. Since it has no connective it is difficult to determine whether it relates to what precedes or what follows. Because "es wird nicht ganz leicht sein, einen *fortlaufenden Gedankengang* in Röm 6 festzustellen" (Michel, *Römer*, 213n.), the question cannot be answered with finality. Bruce Kaye's suggestion that 6:19a relates to *both* the preceding and following material is perhaps the most satisfactory conclusion *(Thought*

rabbinic expression is a technical term in Paul's letters, constituting "an apology for a statement which, but for the apology, would be too bold, almost blasphemous."[24] The apostle is clearly aware of the fact that the figure of slavery is inadequate to describe the Christian life; it implies bondage, whereas in reality the Christian state is true liberty. Yet he does not intend to disabuse himself of the metaphor, for as awkward as it is to compare the Christian's obedience to Christ with the yoke of slavery, the comparison is unavoidable.

Paul gives as his reason for speaking according to human experience and, consequently, in human expressions, "because of the weakness of your flesh" (*dia tēn astheneian tēs sarkos hymōn*). The apostle does not explain the nature of the weakness he has in mind—whether it relates to comprehension or to moral fiber is difficult to decide.[25] Hodge is typical of those who prefer the latter meaning: "He used this illustration, he says, *on account of the weakness of their flesh*; not intellectual weakness, but such as arose from the *sarx*, their nature as corrupt. It was their lack of spirituality which rendered such illustrations necessary."[26] Contextual considerations, however, may be said to favor the first alternative, namely, that "weakness of the flesh" refers to the difficulties and limitations of human language. Michel[27] is undoubtedly correct in making *hymōn* dependent not only upon *sarkos* but upon the entire expression *tēn astheneian tēs sarkos*. What is in question is therefore not the moral frailty of human nature *per se* (*sarx*), but human weakness in general, and in this context specifically the dullness of human understanding that necessitates that truth be taught in metaphors drawn from everyday experience and knowledge. Figures of service, bondage, the slave mart, etc., are perhaps unworthy of the subject of which Paul speaks, but the imperfect spiritual comprehension of his readers makes it necessary for the apostle to accommodate his language to their infirmity. As Murray states: "The dullness of our understanding makes it necessary

---

Structure, 26).

24. Daube, *Rabbinic Judaism*, 396.

25. But not impossible, as Sand seems to think: "Eine genaue Bestimmung der *astheneia* bei Paulus ist nicht möglich, auch dort nicht, wo sie mit dem 'Fleisch' in Verbindung gebracht wird" (*"Fleisch,"* 140).

26. Hodge, *Romans*, 209. Similarly Käsemann (*Römer*, 174) explains *astheneia* as "die Anfechtung des Christen durch die Regungen des Fleisches."

27. *Römer*, 213n.

that we be taught the truth in figures drawn from the sphere of our human relations."²⁸

We must therefore not be misled into thinking that *astheneia tēs sarkos* means anything other than the sphere of human weakness in which the individual participates. The extension of *astheneia* to denote moral weakness (i.e., sinfulness) is not made by Paul. Reicke correctly observes: "Sin is not traced back to sarx, but has an independent position in the universe. It only works through the weakness of sarx in the individual and lives in the sarx of the latter (Rom vii. 14, 17f.)."²⁹ Paul apologizes for the way in which he expresses himself, not because of the sinfulness of his readers but because the figure of slavery, humiliating and degrading though it is, ironically can best express the obligations of being under grace despite the *Menschlichkeit* even of Christians.

Romans 8:3

Romans 8 is concerned with the Christian's present and future existence in which the dominant agent is the Spirit, who is given to the believer by God. With reference to our helpless situation apart from the grace of Christ, Paul speaks of the invasion of God's son into the world with the purpose of imparting life (8:3-4).³⁰ God effected liberation from sin and death "by sending his own son in the likeness of sinful flesh and for sin; [thereby] he condemned sin in the flesh" (8:3b). This mission of the son was necessary because of the "incapacity of the law" (*to . . . adynaton tou nomou*).³¹ The

---

28. Murray, *Romans*, 233.

29. Reicke, "Body and Soul," 203; cf. Sand: "Diese Unvollkommenheit und Schwachheit aber besagt nicht, dass *sarx* hier den alten, sündigen Menschen bedeute" ("*Fleisch*," 140n.). In Pauline thought, *sarx* is at best neutral; it is only when it becomes the norm and primary sphere of living that it becomes positively sinful.

30. Rom 8:3-4 are connected with v. 2 by *gar* and indicate the basis upon which the internal operation of the Spirit is grounded: the Christ event. This reference to the historical event of the sending of the son recalls the traditional form: "God sent his son" (Gal 4:4). Paulsen (*Röm 8*, 182) considers 8:3-4 to be a relatively fixed piece of formal tradition (a "teleologisches Schluss aus einer kerygmatischen Formulierung"), whereas Lyonnet considers 8:3 to be more "una presentazione polemica" (*Nuovo Testamento*, 132).

31. The expression *to adynaton* is problematical: it may be taken either as nominative or accusative and in either an active or passive sense. The accusative case is preferred by Sanday and Headlam, *Romans*, 191, who place it in apposition to the principal clause, "God . . . condemned sin in the flesh." Cranfield (*Romans*, 1.378) agrees and argues on

powerlessness of the law consists in its inability to solve the problem of sin in the flesh.[32] The law makes demands and condemns when its demands go unfulfilled, but it cannot make us right before God, nor can it break the power of sin or overcome the flesh. The law should make alive, for that was its intention (7:10), but it cannot bring life because "we" are not able to fulfill its demands: *en hō ēsthenei dia tēs sarkos*. This weakness of the law was not in itself, but in the *sarx*, i.e., not *extra nos* but *in nobis* (cf. Rom 2:14-15). It thereby became *ho nomos tēs hamartias kai tou thanatou* (8:2), even though its origin was God and its nature was holy, righteous, and good (7:12). Hence the law was necessarily weakened, for its sphere of operation was the flesh that cannot be subject to the law of God (8:7).[33]

The logic of Paul's argument concerning the law in the broader context of Romans 7 and 8 is well summarized by Lohse: the *nomos tou theou* is resisted by *heteros nomos* operating in the *nomos tou noos mou*, and holds me captive *en nomō hamartias* that finds its (sinful) expression in *tois melesin mou*. However, a new possibility is opened to me by the dispensation of "the life-giving Spirit in Christ Jesus" who liberates me from the state of slavery to the flesh.[34] While the *sarx* is not in itself evil or sinful, it is "weak" and therefore can be easily deceived (7:11), requiring only the "occasion" (*aphormēn*) for sin. It is, as Robinson[35] puts it, the *fomes peccati*, the tinder that requires only the flame. The whole process is succinctly summarized in 7:11: "For sin, taking hold of the opportunity afforded by the commandment, deceived me, and through the commandment put me to death." Therefore, we can try to serve the law of God with our mind, but we will fail since our *sarx* follows the law of sin (7:25). In the thinking of Paul these two laws are one and the same. The law contains the will of God and so is the *nomos theou*. Because, however, it leads to a bond between itself and sin, the law becomes a *nomos hamartias*. But in Christ the law of sin

---

that basis that *adynaton* has a passive sense (378-79). There is certainly no basis, however, for Pallis's suggestion that the text should read *ton gar antidikon mou* (*Romans*, 98), nor is there textual support for O'Neill's argument that the words *dia tēs sarkos* (8:3b) were added to the original text by a later commentator (*Romans*, 137-38).

32. Among the discussions of law in this section of Romans, that by Limbeck stands out for its perceptiveness: *Ohnmacht des Rechts*, 84-91.

33. In agreement is Schreiner (*Romans*, 401): "The inadequacy of the law is not due to its context (cf. 7:12); the weakness of the law is located in the flesh, the unregenerate nature of human beings."

34. Lohse, "*nomos tou pneumatos*," 286.

35. *The Body*, 37.

and death is once and for all abolished, thereby setting free from the law believers in Jesus Christ (8:2) and fulfilling the righteous requirements of God in them (8:4). Thus, sin is condemned in the very sphere where it was most plainly manifested—"in the flesh."

"What the law demanded" (*to dikaiōma tou nomou*) is precisely what the law could not perform, weakened as it was through the flesh.[36] By sending his son God effected what the law could not do, so that in Christ believers die to their sinful state and no longer face condemnation (*katakrima*). Henceforth believers can experience new life by living according to the Spirit rather than according to the flesh. This power resides in the Spirit, not in the one whom the Spirit indwells. Paul therefore speaks of the law as being fulfilled *in* believers, not *by* them (*plērōthē en hēmin*, 8:4).

This association of the law's incapacity with the idea that the new regime effects what the law could not is a further indication that the antithetical relationship between *asthenein* and *dynatoun* is a standard and fundamental Pauline formula. Those who are "in the flesh" reveal one aspect of their humanity by their persistent inability to obey the law (8:8). Only as they live *en pneumati*—"in" or "by the Spirit"—that is, by the Spirit's regenerating and renewing power, are they able to carry out the purposes of God.[37] Thus it is understandable that the apostle uses the expressions *adynatos* and *asthenein* to complete and define each other. Both expressions have a common meaning, namely, "das Unvermögen, die Kraftlosigkeit, Unfähigkeit, Ohnmacht, Schwäche des Gesetzes."[38] The powerlessness of the law that is due to the weakness of our human nature has been overcome and its righteous requirement fully met in the saving work of Christ. Now, through the liberation from sin and death by the agency of "the law of the Spirit of life," Christians can experience the vivifying power of God that is now active in those believers who yield themselves to it. Paul is therefore perfectly consistent with what he has written earlier about being "strengthened in faith" by resting on the promises of God (4:19), although now he is viewing the same truth from a slightly different perspective by describing the same revivifying force to be that of the indwelling Spirit. The law can

---

36. "Das Gesetz offenbart den Willen Gottes. Aber es kann nicht selbst die Erfüllung bewirken—es ist 'schwach' (Röm 8, 3)" (Conzelmann, *Grundriss*, 249). Similarly Hubner says the law was "depraved" by the *sarx* (*Gesetz*, 127).

37. Feuillet considers this antithesis between the law and the Spirit to be "la donnée fondamentale des chapitres 7 et 8 de l'Épître aux Romains." See his essay, "Les attaches bibliques," 340.

38. Dülmen, *Theologie des Gesetzes*, 121n.

neither give us the ability to do God's will nor prevent us from disobeying it; but the new interior Guest gives us life and enables us to live according to "the law of the Spirit of life in Christ Jesus" (8:2).

Romans 8:26

The subsection of Romans 8 that has the "prayer-problem" of Christians as subject (8:26-27) presents a variety of interpretative problems that are extremely difficult to resolve. Anyone who attempts an explanation of this passage would be compelled to agree with Niederwimmer that these verses belong "zu den erstaunlichsten Abschnitten des Neuen Testaments."[39] For instance, why does Paul choose the example of prayer to illustrate the *astheneia* to which the aid of the Spirit must be addressed? Possibly it is because prayer is one of the most elementary religious responsibilities devolving upon the Christian. The context, however, would seem to indicate that Paul is more specifically concerned to continue the "groaning" motif of the earlier sections (cf. *hōsautōs de kai* at the beginning of v. 26): Christians are dependent upon Christ for final redemption, and their deep (and deepening) consciousness of adoptive sonship finds its corresponding expression in the dynamic of their prayers. Therefore, Paul is saying that the tension between the present suffering and the future glory is being experienced not only by the creation (vv. 18-22) but also by believers as they await the salvation of their bodies (vv. 23-25). Since suffering is an indispensable prelude to glorification, the present situation of Christians is characterized by a state of "weakness," a time of tribulation as well as hope, though Paul is quick to add that the present suffering cannot compare with the future glories of the coming age (v. 18).[40] Hence not only does the creation sigh for the time of redemption (8:22), but "we" sigh also, that is, the *entire* creation, including Christians (8:23).

One aspect of this sighing is the groaning of the Spirit on behalf of Christians whose "weakness" prevents them from knowing how to pray (8:26). The statement *hōsautōs de kai to pneuma sunantilambanetai tē*

---

39. Niederwimmer, "Gebet," 252. On the participation of the Holy Spirit in the prayer-life of the believer see, in addition to Niederwimmer (252-65) and the articles cited in the following notes, Dietzel, "Beten im Geist," 12-32; Fuchs, "Anteil des Geistes," 293-302; Mitchell, "Intercessory Ministry," 230-42; Meyer, "The Holy Spirit," 3-18; Paulsen, *Überlieferung und Auslegung*, 107-32; and Osten-Sacken, *Römer 8*, 85-86, 93-95.

40. See Gager, "Functional Diversity," 325-37, esp. 328.

astheneia hēmōn suggests that the idea of "weakness" should be understood in a comprehensive sense as covering the whole range of weakness that is characteristic of the present life.[41] The "prayer-problem" of the Christian is but one aspect of the infirmity in view, though in Paul's mind (according to the next sentence) it uniquely exemplifies the Christian's helplessness and total dependence upon God. This particular aspect of the Spirit's activity in behalf of the believer not only illustrates the range of the Christian's weakness—extending even to one's prayer-life—but also is a reminder that apart from the agency and instrumentality of the Spirit of God, there would be no Christian existence in the first place (8:9–11). As believers, they are the dwelling-place of "the Spirit of life" (8:2), who regenerates and renews them and who expresses in their life the presence and fullness of Christ. As the Christian's hope in ultimate redemption is engendered by the Spirit, so also the believer's "prayer-infirmity" is overcome by the Holy Spirit.

Here Paul links the "assistance" (*sunantilambanetai*) of the Spirit with the work of intercession done on the behalf of the faithful. The language recalls 2 Cor 12:7–10, where the apostle related his weakness to the compensating factor of the power of God to overcome his "thorn in the flesh," which, despite intensive petitioning, was allowed to continue to buffet him. This illustrates how Paul's complete dependence upon the power of the risen Christ found its natural expression in his prayers. Likewise, Rom 8:26–27 is an indication that Paul viewed prayer as the paradoxical meeting of God's power with human weakness. In content this passage is clearly related to that in 2 Corinthians, although here the characteristic "boasting" and "apostleship" references, for example, are lacking. The "weakness" motif is, however, present in the expression *tē astheneia hēmōn* as well as in the admission of ignorance (*ouk oidamen*), if not also implicit throughout the chapter. Thus Stendahl observes that "the whole chapter is a theological reflection at the heart of Paul's life of prayer, full of exuberant language, mingled with hard-learned realism as to weakness and trust in God in the midst of weakness."[42] In this way the present subsection (vv. 26–27) has reference not only to prayer-*astheneia* in general but also in a more specific sense to the prayer-life of the apostle Paul. The verses describe, as Cullmann has noted, the most profound aspect of the Pauline understanding of prayer, namely that prayer must be the work of the Holy Spirit himself

---

41. This would follow even if one adopts the reading *tais astheneiais* (K L P *Byz*) in place of the singular.

42. Stendahl, "Paul at Prayer," 244. This point is also made by Stanley, *Boasting*, 46.

because of the inability of the believer.⁴³ God's mighty works are thus being manifested not only in the work and witness of the apostle but also in his prayers. Because no believer is exempt from "groaning," however, Paul stresses here the *communal*, not the private, aspect of prayer (cf. "*we* do not know. . ."; "*our* weakness").

It is proper, therefore, to speak of prayer as part of the Christian's ministry for Christ that can be accomplished, like other acts of service, only with the aid and suprapersonal power of the indwelling Spirit. If other ministries depend upon the enablement of God, how much more does this activity that de Quervain⁴⁴ can describe as "den rechten, höchsten und köstlichen Gottesdienst" lay bare the Christian's need of divine succor? No other activity speaks more eloquently of the contemporaneity of God's working in the life of the believer by the Holy Spirit, whose outpouring is indeed a manifestation of the Messianic Age, yet whose work the Christian is already enjoying as the pledge of the completion of the process of salvation (8:23). This activity of the Spirit on the behalf of Christians in their prayer life suggests that for Paul prayer is the ultimate showplace of the power of God revealed in human weakness, since it takes place at the most fundamental level of the believer's relationship with God. Only when Christians confess their prayer-*astheneia* can that weakness be overcome by the Holy Spirit and prayer become not merely a possibility but a reality.⁴⁵ Thus in Pauline thought prayer takes on a special significance to the degree that it is effected by the Spirit, who intercedes with wordless groans for those unable to pray.

On this understanding, the passage comprising vv. 26–27 must be considered, as suggested above, as a continuation of the contrast between the present life that is characterized by the Spirit's activity in the midst of weakness and suffering and the future glorious existence of the believer. In the present, Christians have received the Holy Spirit who stamps them with the mark of sonship and bestows upon them the full rights of adopted children of God (8:23). This right of inheritance is qualified, however, first by the fact that the final inheritance has yet to be received, and second by the fact that this sonship is attained through suffering, which is characteristic of the generic sphere of human weakness and frailty (8:18).⁴⁶ Although they are already saved, freed from sin and the law, and in possession of the

---

43. Cullmann, "La prière," 95. See also Rickards, "Romans 8:26," 247–48.
44. Quervain, "Vom Gebet," 192.
45. Bieder, "Gebetswirklichkeit," 31.
46. Cf. Gager, "Functional Diversity," 327.

Holy Spirit, Christians still long for final redemption, the glory of which has not yet been openly revealed. Their own groans (8:23), as well as those of the Spirit within them (8:26), are cries for the final, public manifestation of adoption and for ultimate liberation from the *astheneia*, *phthora*, and *atimia* to which they have been subjected (cf. 1 Cor 15:42–43).

According to Paul (other authors are silent here), our present weakness is uniquely exemplified by our life of prayer. The precise problem is that we do not know how to pray as we ought: *to gar ti proseuxōmetha kathodei ouk oidamen*. The wording (esp. *ti proseuxōmetha*) indicates that it is not our ignorance of the right method of prayer that is the problem, but our ignorance of the proper content of prayer, i.e., what to pray for. To pray as we ought, we must pray according to the will of God (*kata theon*, v. 27), but this we are unable to do: precisely that is our "prayer-problem."[47] Therefore, what Christians cannot do God undertakes to perform by his Spirit, who "helps" (*sunantilambanetai*) believers by "interceding" (*hyperentynchanei*) for them with wordless sighing. The verbs that Paul uses for the Spirit's activity suggest that the apostle has in mind a progression from a situation in which the Spirit merely comes to our aid to a situation in which the Spirit actually prays "for us."[48] Neither here nor in the larger context is anything said about *our* prayer, the only exception being the cry "Abba, Father" which, as a token of their adoption, believers can express only when the address is effected by the Spirit (8:15).[49] This does not mean that the believer is resolved of any responsibility in prayer; the Christian's personal involvement *in actu orationis* is suggested not only at 8:15 but also by the reference to "our hearts" (*tas kardias*) in 8:27, where the place of intercession in the praying community is specified. Unmistakably, however, the emphasis is upon the part played by the Holy Spirit of God in prayer, which overshadows—indeed, because of the Christian's *astheneia*, overcomes— the activity of the believer. Whatever other part Christians may play, it is

---

47. See Cranfield, *Romans*, 421, who correctly notes the parallel between *katho dei* and *kata theon* in v. 27. See also Michel, *Römer*, 272; Hodge, *Romans*, 278; Murray, *Romans*, 311; MacRae, "Romans 8:26–27," 227–30.

48. This is clearly Paul's meaning even if the words *hyper hēmōn* (C K P *Byz* it vg) after *hyperentynchanei* are considered a secondary addition.

49. Taking (at least) the second *pneuma* in v. 15 to refer to the Holy (not human) Spirit, as would seem demanded by the reference to adoption. See Cranfield, *Romans*, 396–97; Michel, *Römer*, 260; and Barrett, *Romans*, 163–64. Regarding the address "Abba, Father," Jeremias notes that it was the most important element in the Lord's own prayer-life: "In diesem *einen* Wort Vater liegt das hochheilige Geheimnis seines Lebens—und seines Gebets" ("Gebets-Leben," 140).

the Spirit who makes intercession in, through, and for them. This efficacious work of the Holy Spirit in the Christian's stead is well summarized by Schweizer: "Das erste und wichtigste Geschenk ist also gerade nicht eine Kraft, die uns zu neuen Leistungen befähigt, sondern das Beten, in dem wir Gott machen lassen, in dem wir auch einmal schwach sein und uns das Starkwerden von ganz anderswoher schenken lassen dürfen."[50] Therefore, "nicht einmal das Beten ist also unsere Leistung,"[51] because, as Cullmann[52] also affirms, prayer is not merely a human act but a gift of God. In the situation of human *astheneia* the Spirit intercedes for us and prays in us to God, who understands and accepts this prayer because it was made according to God's will on behalf of the faithful. Prayer is consequently in a real sense God speaking with himself (in the believer) by an "inner-trinitarian process"[53] in which the Holy Spirit is the "principe actif de notre prière filial."[54] True prayer exceeds what we are able to think or say; this very poverty, however, is what turns our human speech by the Spirit into "groans too deep for words," which, although they have no expressive power, are accepted and understood by the God "who sees in secret."

This fact that prayer takes place in "the heart," where only God can understand what transpires, argues against understanding the "groanings" of the Spirit as a reference to the phenomenon of glossalalia in the early church.[55] As Cranfield[56] asserts, these utterances are the Spirit's *own* groanings, so that it is improbable that they intend to indicate the audible ecstatic utterances of certain specially-gifted Christians: they are uttered at a level too deep for human comprehension, where *ho eraunōn tas kardias* (i.e., God the Father) alone has access. Moreover, whereas tongues-speaking was considered a special charismatic gift possessed by some members of the church, this passage is clearly referring to the prayer-life of all believers. Glossalalia is, furthermore, primarily an act of praise and not intercession. Michel rightly concludes, "Es leigt nicht nahe, an Glossolalie oder Gemeindegebet zu denken, weil irdische Vorgange nicht ohne weiteres Ab-

50. Schweizer, *Heiliger Geist*, 119.

51. Ibid.

52. "Prière," 100.

53. The term is used by Niederwimmer, "Gebet," 252.

54. Marchel, *Abba*, 238. The entire section of Marchel's dissertation dealing with "La prière 'Abba' et l'action du Saint-Esprit" (232–46) is well worth reading.

55. See Käsemann, *Perspektiven*, 211–36, for a presentation of this view.

56. *Romans*, 423.

bild eines himmlischen Vorgangs sein mussen. Es geht hier vielmehr um einen *himmlischen, apokalyptischen Vorgang*."[57] Thus, while the content of the Spirit's *stenagmoi alalētoi* is unknown, its character is sure: intercession, being intelligible to God.

Because the activity of the Spirit on the Christian's behalf has overcome the problem of prayer—which could not be mitigated, relieved, or resolved with human solutions—Paul can joyfully write in 8:28 that the Spirit is now working for the elect in every situation for their good.[58] Those who love God face no obstacle that will be able to check the redemptive work of Christ or to cause the "groaning" to go unheard. The Spirit, says Paul, not only pleads for the saints according to the will of God (v. 27), but also causes the sufferings of the present time (*panta*)[59] to contribute to their eternal well-being. Thus the groaning of the Spirit may be said to have as its final object the attaining of ultimate salvation based on God's faithfulness to his plan. Whereas prayer reveals, not our power, but our *astheneia*, the Spirit of God, acting in and through human weakness, is at work to impart to us the confidence that in every circumstance of life, in concert with the divine will, the purposes of God are being attained. To aid and effect this process the Spirit intercedes for us, aids in our weakness, and works all things for good to those who love God and are called by him (8:26–28).

Romans 14:1, 2; 15:1

In Romans 14:1—15:13 Paul deals with the question of "weak" and "strong" Christians. The danger that by their conduct the strong will cause the weak to stumble is real, as is the corresponding danger that the weak will pass judgment upon the strong (14:2). Paul's exhortations are preponderantly directed toward the strong, since they evidently had more room to maneuver

---

57. Michel, *Römer*, 273. In agreement is J. Schneider, "*stenazō, ktl.*," *TWNT* 7:602.

58. Taking *pneuma* as the understood subject of *synergei*, as suggested by, e.g., Black, "Romans viii 28," 166–72, and adopted by the NEB. The reading *ho theos* (p46 A B) is probably an early attempt by an Alexandrian editor to clear up the ambiguity regarding the subject of *synergei*, though Ross, "Rom. VIII. 28," 82–85, thinks *ho theos* is original. Since we view v. 28 as rounding off vv. 26–27, the Spirit may be implied as subject *ad sensum*. For a thorough discussion of all the alternatives, see Cranfield, *Romans*, 425–29, who, however, with the majority of commentators and translators, prefers *panta* as the subject of *synergei*.

59. According to 8:18, 37, *panta* here must refer to the sufferings and adversities of the present life.

than the weak (cf. 14:1; 15:1). Nevertheless, Paul regards both the strong and the weak as ultimately responsible for the unity of the church, for *all* must stand before the judgment seat of God to be judged for their own actions and attitudes (14:10).[60]

Paul's concern with ethical behavior here is a feature of the righteousness of God that is Paul's great theme in Romans. Paul could (and did) compress the entire OT system of commandments into one sentence: "you shall love your neighbor as yourself" (Rom 13:9 = Lev 19:18), thus making it applicable to saints of every age.[61] As regards responsible Christian conduct, love is the greatest means by which the Christian fulfills the will of God (cf. 13:8). For the believer, Christ himself is the norm for ethics, since ethics is based on the crucifixion of Christ, which demonstrates the radical love of God for humanity. Nothing in the church exposes the violation of this principle more than the flagrant discrimination against which Paul directs his entreaty in these verses, for nothing contradicts the attitude of the Savior more than Christians disdaining or condemning each other.

Paul therefore begins his discussion in 14:1 by commanding the strong to "accept the one who is weak in faith" (*ton . . . asthenounta tē pistei proslambanesthe*). That the weak individual here is not *physically* ill is clear from the addition of *tē pistei*. Paul's meaning is that these individuals' *faith* is weak, that is, their faith is not strong enough to enable them to grasp the full liberty they have in Christ, the consequence of which is an overscrupulous observance of formal rules. They are not bothered by doctrinal questions *per se*, but rather plagued by an anxious uncertainty as to whether it is proper to do certain things. In v. 23 Paul can describe the weak person as *ho diakrinomenos*, for the weak are paralyzed as it were by inhibitions rooted deep in their subconsciousness; they cannot, therefore, help but hesitate or doubt the propriety of their actions, i.e., whether or not they are *ek pisteōs* (v. 23).[62]

This specialized use of *pistis* becomes perfectly clear in v. 2, where Paul states that the weak confine their diet to vegetables (*ho de asthenōn lachana esthiei*). They lack the inner liberty of other Christians (here, obviously the

---

60. Roetzel, *Judgement*, 104–05. On this section in general, see Rauer, "*Schwachen*," 76–184, esp. 94–107.

61. See Baird, "Reading Romans," 55.

62. Not that these "doubters" felt they were "weak" in any way: "In ihren Augen ist es natürlich *keine* Schwäche, sondern vielmehr eine Vollkommenheit, wenn sie sich verpflichtet fühlen, die Vorschriften und Auflagen des Christusglaubens zu ergänzen . . ." (Rauer, "*Schwachen*," 93).

"strong" must be in view) to make no distinction between various foods. Paul does not indicate the specific reason that the weak Christians advance for their position, since their motives are evidently a purely personal matter. The closest NT parallel is perhaps to be found in Colossians, where mention is made of those who practice various forms of abstinence (2:16, 21–22) and who participate in religious festivals and celebrations (2:16). However, the Colossian situation is a parallel only if one assumes that the weak in Rome do indeed refrain from wine (vv. 12, 21) and observe special days (vv. 5–6).[63] Even so, one cannot be certain of the exact motivations for the action of the weak; and it is a pity since great importance attaches to the apostle's estimation of them (being, in his opinion, "neutral"). The important matter to observe, however, is that sharp differences of opinion in these matters—as they undoubtedly existed in the Roman church—are not to be excluded in the church, for they are not evil in and of themselves. What *is* wrong lies in the reaction of the strong by "looking down" on the weak and by arguing acrimoniously and divisively over their actions (v. 3).[64] That attitude in turn compels the weak to retaliate by condemning their omnivorous brothers and sisters. Both practices are unacceptable: the one because the weak act out of conviction; the other because the strong are received into God's household (v. 3). Paul states further in v. 6 that Christians who eat meat do so to the Lord (*kyriō*) by giving thanks over it to God. Likewise, Christians who decide to abstain from eating meat offer to God a prayer of thanksgiving over their meal of vegetables. As O'Brien writes, "Both recognize that what they eat are the gifts of God to be enjoyed, and they express their gratitude by their prayers of thanksgiving."[65] In the end it is therefore irrelevant what the meals consist of since they are eaten with thanksgiving as unto the Lord and not merely as secular repasts. Therefore,

---

63. At first (14:2) Paul speaks only of *eating*, not of drinking or celebrations; it remains uncertain, therefore, whether or not the weak in Rome also drank no wine and honored certain days; cf. Rauer, "*Schwachen*," 97ff.; Schmithals, *Römerbrief*, 97. At any rate, the weak in Rome were unquestionably much more "Christian" (and less gnostic) than the heretics at Colosse (cf. Barrett, *Romans*, 257–58). In this connection, Goppelt notes that, whereas the prohibition of meat and wine is not in the OT, it was practiced in the Diaspora because of the fear that these items might have been used in sacrificial ceremonies and therefore were *koina*. The observance of special days also may refer to the practice of dispersed Jews out of reverence for the feast days, and especially for the Sabbaths (*Christentum und Judentum*, 96–97).

64. This would suggest that the terms "strong" and "weak" are borrowed from the language of the strong. Paul uses them in a similar, but much less derisive, sense.

65. O'Brien, "Thanksgiving," 58.

Paul calls upon all the members to examine their own convictions and to exercise love with regard to those who do not share them.

Since the weaker members of the community demand the greatest care and attention, Paul in 15:1 exhorts the strong (*hoi dynatoi*) to bear the weaknesses (*ta asthenēmata*) of those who are unable (*hoi adynatoi*[66]) to do so themselves.[67] This is *their* moral obligation (cf. *opheilomen*), arising from the fact that it is always the special duty of the strong to carry the burden of the weak, and not the other way around. To make this point crystal clear Paul uses for the first time the expression *hoi dynatoi* to refer to the strong, thus making the antithesis between "strong-weak" more fully explicit. As "strong" individuals, their very strength makes them debtors to those without strength (the "not-strong"); therefore, to the strong belongs the responsibility of making the initial move toward reconciliation. Paul, himself one of the strong, knows from recent experience (in Corinth) just how difficult—yet how important—is bearing the weaknesses and failings of weaker Christians.

The verb used by Paul to describe the support rendered by the strong is *bastazein*, which does not merely mean "endure,"[68] but rather to undertake the charge of; it speaks not of an attitude of resignation, but of a spirit of love and caring.[69] Paul employed the same word when he enjoined the Galatians to "bear each other's burdens, and thus fulfill the law of Christ" (Gal 6:2). The burden of caring for the weak is an obligation that God himself lays upon the strong; it involves, besides caring, a readiness to try to "please"

---

66. *hoi adynatoi* = *hoi asthenountes*. *Asthenēmata* is a hapax in the NT.

67. We have intentionally passed over the variant in 14:21, inasmuch as *asthenei* does not appear in modern editions of the Greek NT. In most MSS. *proskopei* is followed by the words *ē skandalizetai ē asthenei* (ℵc B D G 33 *Byz* vg), and if the latter words are original, the text would then read, "It is good not to eat meat or to drink wine, or to do anything whereby your brother or sister stumbles, or is offended, or is made weak." The two expressions *skandalizetai* and *asthenei* may then be considered as consequences of a slightly lesser degree than *proskoptei*: Christians should abstain from actions that may be injurious to others by causing them either to stumble, to be offended, or to be weak, i.e., injured to even the slightest degree (cf. Hodge, *Romans*, 426, who quotes Calvin to this effect). Metzger regards the longer reading as "a Western expansion" and suggests that "the original text was modified or expanded by copyists who recollected I Cor 8.11-13" (*Textual Commentary*, 532). On the whole, however, the weight of external evidence appears to favor the longer reading.

68. E.g., Barrett, *Romans*, 269.

69. See Büchsel, "*bastazō*," *TWNT* 1:597; Michel, *Römer*, 443n.; Käsemann, *Römer*, 368; Murray, *Romans*, 197.

(*areskein*)⁷⁰ the weak (v. 2). As Hodge remarks, what is called for here is not merely "a weak compliance with the wishes of others . . . but to the exercise of an enlightened benevolence; to such compliances that have the design and tendency to promote the spiritual welfare of our neighbor."⁷¹ The language is strongly reminiscent of Paul's statement in 1 Cor 9:19–23 that he became all things to all people, although, as previously demonstrated, the principle "to the weak I became weak that I may win the weak" can refer to Christians only by application, not interpretation. Nevertheless, the basic design is the same: by employing the principle of self-accommodation, stronger Christians are to adjust their actions to whatever will contribute to the spiritual good and edification of others. This course of action is the only proper imitation of Christ, who "did not please himself" (v. 3) and thereby has shown how the true servant of God lives. As God in Christ has received every member of the Church into fellowship with himself, so the Roman Christians must receive each other without any inner reservations due to differences in religious practice (which are indeed *adiaphora* to God and, therefore, of no consequence).⁷²

Whether 14:1—15:13 is to be understood as a theoretical and abstract treatment of a general problem or as referring to actual circumstances in Rome is difficult to decide. The basic problem is the paucity of evidence from which one can derive a picture of life in the Roman church. Not even this passage, despite its length, has sufficient detail to give a completely satisfactory explanation of the identity of the "weak" and "strong" groups. Therefore, even Rauer's unsurpassed study of the problem must be treated with caution because of its hypothetical nature. The events themselves that led Paul to address the conflict between the weak and the strong lie so deeply concealed that it is most difficult—if not impossible—to know exactly what they were.

There are, however, several indications that Paul is not merely writing out of his experience with the Corinthian church (1 Corinthians 8–10). For example, there is no mention in Romans of idols or idol-meats that were behind the problem in Corinth. Furthermore, terms such as *gnōsis* and *syneidēsis*, which play an important part in Paul's discussion in 1 Corinthians, are absent from our text, where the word *pistis* occupies the central position. On the other hand, several features appear in Romans that are

---

70. The *mē heautois areskein* theme is an important one in Romans; see 12:2; 14:7–8; and 14:18.

71. Hodge, *Romans*, 432–33.

72. Cf. Rauer, "*Schwachen*," 95–96.

absent from 1 Corinthians. We read in Romans, for instance, that the weak are vegetarians and that they (possibly) also refrain from wine and insist on the observance of certain days, in contrast to the strong who value all days equally. Moreover, Paul's treatment of the topic in Romans is briefer and of a much more general (and much less polemical) nature. These numerous differences between the accounts in Romans and 1 Corinthians call for some other explanation than the suggestion that Paul's paraenesis here merely "is adapted and generalized especially from Paul's discussion in 1 Cor 8–10 and is addressed to a problem that may arise in any community."[73] In this connection Rauer himself warns: "Wir haben keinen Anlass, die korinthische Parteienbildung auf die römische Gemeinde zu übertragen."[74]

The context of Romans 14–15 does, however, seem to imply that the weak in Rome were a small group of Christians rather than a faction. As they would not have belonged to any group in particular, they probably are to be considered as a minority comprised of individualistic persons noted for their nomistic tendencies. If, following 15:7–12, we identify the weak more specifically with the circumcised, then Paul would have had Jewish Christians primarily in mind when writing, whose thoroughgoing asceticism included total abstinence from meat and wine as well as the celebration of holy days. To this view, however, it is rightly objected that abstinence from *all* flesh and wine is not prohibited by the Mosaic Law. Furthermore, Paul scarcely would have dealt so mildly with these individuals had they been involved in the Judaizer movement against which he struggled openly in Galatians. The weak do, however, show a legalistic tendency to condemn those who feel free to eat anything, and are consequently not without fault. In view of these factors, the most probable opinion is that the weak were Jewish Christians who were stricter than the ceremonial law required and whose ascetic tendencies led to a condemnation of those who disregarded their scruples. The strong, on the other hand, were probably Gentile Christians robust in faith, especially faith in regard to the lawfulness of all kinds of food, which led them to prejudge and scorn their weaker brethren. Because they were in the majority, Paul's exhortations in this section of the epistle are directed mainly toward them.

---

73. Karris, "Occasion of Romans," 99. Karris's arguments in favor of viewing 14:1—15:13 as "general Pauline paraenesis" (99) are carefully answered by Donfried in his article in the same volume, "False Presuppositions," 120–48. Karris, however, has the last word in his brief rejoinder, "Response to Donfried," 149–51.

74. Rauer, "*Schwachen*," 88.

We conclude, then, that it is very probable that a problem between weak and strong Christians was felt at Rome; but in view of the manner in which Paul discusses the problem, it is clear that he does not write about it solely with the local situation in mind since he has no first-hand knowledge of the developing life of the Roman church. Therefore, it hardly seems possible to relate every passage to some specific problem or opponent in Rome, as, for instance, Minear has attempted to do by claiming to have detected no less than five separate groups in the Roman church from certain statements in chaps. 14–15.[75] While the possibility exists that Paul was addressing a real situation in Rome, the contours of the problem are too vague to allow a specific description of the conflict or its participants. This dimension of the problem is addressed by Donfried: "The summary character of Romans has often been noted and frequently with it, the incorrect assumption that such a writing cannot refer to a concrete, historical situation. Must, in fact, the only alternative be either "summary" or "historical"? In view of these letter-essays is not the more plausible alternative with regard to Romans a "both-and"—both sharing and repeating insights gained in prior situations *and* addressing a real situation?"[76]

Perhaps this is the best answer to the problem, despite its tentative nature. Romans is not like the other Pauline letters because it is a "letter-essay," whose *Sitz im Leben* is found neither in the situation of the addresses nor in the purpose of the author, but in a combination of the two. One can therefore proceed on the initial assumption that Romans was written to deal with an actual situation in Rome, though this assumption must be modified by Paul's somewhat abstract style owing to his incomplete personal knowledge of Rome and the Roman church and his overriding desire to set forth his gospel in systematic fashion.[77]

---

75. Minear, *Obedience of Faith*, 8–16. Cf. the similar complaint by Donfried ("False Presuppositions," 126): "While acknowledging that all of Romans, including the more general sections, deals with a Roman problem, it is perhaps misleading to suggest an almost point by point correlation."

76. Donfried, "False Presuppositions," 146.

77. In an excellent monograph on Romans 14–15, Reasoner argues that these two chapters hold the key to understanding Paul's letter to the Romans. The letter is a thoroughly occasional document. Writes Reasoner (*Strong and Weak*, 225–26):

> Now that I have examined Rom 14.1–15.13, it is appropriate to step back and ask how my study of this part of the letter affects how one reads the whole letter. After all, this is the only Pauline letter in which the practical teaching ("special exhortation") is situated at the conclusion of the letter's body, after what is regarded as more general parenesis. It follows that this material in 14.1–15.13

INTRODUCTION TO PHILIPPIANS

Despite efforts to place the composition of Philippians in Caesarea or Ephesus, the evidence points to Rome as the place of writing.[78] Against Caesarea are (a) the fact that there is no mention of an appeal to Caesar; (b) the fact that Paul is expecting an early decision on his case; and (c) the use of terms like "praetorium" and "Caesar's household" that apply more naturally to Rome than to the provinces. Against Ephesus is the weighty fact that there is no record in Scripture of an Ephesian imprisonment of Paul. These factors lead to a dating of the letter towards the end of Paul's detention in Rome sometime between the years AD 60–62 (Acts 28:16, 30).[79]

The occasion for Philippians was clearly the receipt of a gift that had been delivered by Epaphroditus to the apostle in captivity (2:25–26; 4:14, 18). The letter is Paul's expression of thanks to the Philippian church for their token of love. Concerned both by the recent severe illness of their messenger and by a divisive tendency among several members of the church in Philippi itself, he decides to send Epaphroditus back to Philippi with this letter of thanksgiving, including in it further information of his own circumstances in captivity, practical admonitions relating to Christian harmony, and strong warnings against any Judaizers or libertines who may attempt to subvert his gospel.[80]

In Philippians we find weakness language only twice, both times with reference to Epaphroditus (2:26–27). These occurrences, as well as those in the Pastoral letters, which will be examined shortly, represent the common

> would likely have strong connections back to the rest of the letter, and would serve as an indication of the *topos* of the letter. . . . It seems to indicate that Paul's primary *topos* in Romans is not the righteousness of God. It is rather that Paul and his gospel are not shameful, nor does it bring shame on those who identify with it, but rather allows them to boast in God.

78. Lea and Black, *Background and Message*, 442.

79. See Reicke, "Captivity Epistles," 282–86; cf. idem, *Zeitgeschichte*, 165. The question whether Philippians was written early or late during this period remains unresolved. Probabilities favor a date toward the end of the two-year imprisonment mentioned in Acts 28:30; cf. Guthrie, *Introduction*, 535–36; Hendriksen, *Philippians*, 29–31.

80. Some scholars maintain that Paul's polemic against those troubling the church (chap. 3) is so out of harmony with the warm affection displayed elsewhere that the whole or part of chap. 3 must be an interpolated fragment from another letter of Paul. See Bornkamm, "Philipperbrief," 192–202; Rahtjen, "Three Letters," 167–73; Koester, "Pauline Fragment," 317–32. The unity of the epistle is, however, cogently defended by Pollard, "Integrity," 57–66; Jewett, "Epistolary Thanksgiving," 40–53; Guthrie, *Introduction*, 536–39; and Martin, *Philippians*, 36–39.

usage of *astheneia* and cognate words for bodily illness and thus represent the final stage of the Pauline weakness motif.

EXEGESIS OF THE TEXTS

In the section that comprises 2:25–30, Paul turns from his discussion of future plans (the sending of Timothy) to his present concern to commend his co-laborer Epaphroditus, whom he describes in vv. 26–27 as having been "weak," to the Philippian church.[81] The Epaphroditus in question had been chosen by the believers at Philippi to bring their pecuniary gift to Paul, thus making up what had otherwise been lacking in the Philippians' aid (v. 30). Since the care in prison left much to be desired (this would be true even of house-arrest; Acts 28:16, 23, 30), prisoners were dependent for support on friends and relatives. Paul therefore gladly accepted the gift from the Philippians, with whom he felt a special unity. Then, instead of returning home, Epaphroditus remained with Paul as a devoted aid and minister.

Paul describes Epaphroditus in v. 25 as an *apostolos* and a *leitourgos* (cf. *leitourgia* in v. 30). This picture of Epaphroditus as an authorized representative of a community corresponds exactly with the meaning of the Hebrew *shaliach* as one who is sent to represent the person and cause of another.[82] A precise description of the nature of his task is found in 4:18: "But I have received everything in full, and have an abundance; I am made full, having received from Epaphroditus the things you have sent, a fragrant aroma, an acceptable sacrifice, well-pleasing to God." His name, *Epaphroditus*, was common in the Greek-speaking world, meaning "lovely," "amiable," "charming."[83] This name and its abbreviation *Epaphras* are derived from Aphrodite, the goddess of love (hence the meaning "lovely"). Yet the Epaphroditus spoken of here is not the Epaphras of Colossians (1:7; 4:12), for they belong to different cities: Epaphras to Colosse and Epaphroditus to Philippi.[84]

The value that Paul recognized in Epaphroditus is evident in the glowing terms with which he describes him (v. 25): "my brother and fellow-worker

---

81. Epaphroditus, along with Timothy (2:19–24), are presented as two Christ-like men who live solely for the sake of the gospel. See Black, "Discourse Structure," 38–39.

82. Rengstorf, "*apostellō, ktl.*," *TWNT* 1:421.

83. *IDB* 2.107. *Epaphroditos* is the equivalent of the Latin *Venustus*, deriving from *Venus*, the Roman name for Aphrodite.

84. See Barth, *Philipper*, 53.

and fellow-soldier." Eadie[85] sees in these epithets a rise in intensity: first, a Christian brother, then a colleague in labor, and then a companion in danger and conflict. The *syn*-prefix of the last two expressions emphasizes their camaraderie in labor and hardship for the sake of the gospel, once at Philippi and now in the apostle's present confinement in Rome.

Thus Epaphroditus had been sent to bring a gift (as an *apostolos*) and to minister to Paul as his personal attendant (as a *leitourgos*). These terms, as well as the context of vv. 25-30, indicate that Epaphroditus should be considered as an *official* representative of the Philippian church and that it was the intention of the Philippians that he should stay with Paul indefinitely so as to complete the service of the church to the apostle. Understandably, his appearance again in Philippi would have been a matter of surprise and concern to those by whom he had been so delegated. Paul, however, finds it necessary (*anagkaion*) to send Epaphroditus back to the Philippians. When Paul writes in v. 28 that he *had* sent Epaphroditus (*epempsa auton*), he does not mean that Epaphroditus had already left at the time of writing, since the verb is doubtless an epistolary aorist, the writer putting himself in the timeframe of his readers. We may in fact assume that Epaphroditus himself was the bearer of the letter to the church in Philippi. Therefore Paul is all the more desirous to ensure a good reception for Epaphroditus and to take measures to counteract any criticism that his fellow-believers at Philippi may be tempted to level against him.

The reason why the apostle deems it necessary to send Epaphroditus is given in v. 26: *epeidē epipothōn ēn pantas hymas*, "because he was longing for all of you."[86] The cause (*epeidē*) of Epaphroditus' return lies with the latter's fervent longing for all the saints in Philippi. However, another factor was his distress because the Philippians had heard that he had become ill after arriving in Rome, and they were worried about his condition: *kai adēmōn dioti ēkousate hoti ēsthenēsen*. The verb *ēsthenēsen*, as Müller[87] correctly notes, is an ingressive aorist with the meaning "became ill" (and not "was ill"). The news that Epaphroditus had taken ill became known at Phillippi and was the source of their anxiety. However, he had recovered through God's mercy, and now Paul is desirous to return Epaphroditus to Philippi to comfort those who had been alarmed at the news of his illness.

---

85. Eadie, *Philippians*, 152. Cf. also Friedrich, *Philipper*, 157.

86. ℵ* A C D 33 add *idein* ("to see") in v. 26 after *epipothōn* ("longing") on the analogy of Rom 1:11; 1 Thess 3:6; and 2 Tim 1:4 (cf. Metzger, *Textual Commentary*, 613-14).

87. Müller, *Philippians and to Philemon*, 101n.

Epaphroditus' longing for his native city and concern for his home church are described by two strong Greek expressions: *epipothōn* and *adēmonōn*. The first term was used earlier in 1:8 to describe Paul's own fervent desire to see the Philippians again. The second term, a compound of *a-* and *dēmos* (meaning, "away from people, home," and thus metaphorically, "beside oneself, anxious, distressed"), is used to describe Christ's agony in Gethsemane according to Mark 14:33 and Matt 26:37, and denotes extreme mental and physical anguish. If we connect these expressions—as would seem to be required by the close collocation of *epipothōn ēn* and *adēmonōn*—Epaphroditus' desire to be reunited with the Philippians must be understood as a consequence of his concern to relieve the worry of the community at Philippi over his recent illness. In all probability, he desired to present himself in person in order that all could see that he had recovered fully. Undoubtedly he also wished to express his gratitude for all their prayers on his behalf. Furthermore, the possibility that his yearning for the Philippians was a sign of his desire to help them in their afflictions and struggles against the enemies of the gospel, as is argued most persuasively by Lohmeyer,[88] cannot be excluded even though there is no positive evidence for it. Yet it is certain that Epaphroditus would not have left Paul unless the latter had ordered him to do so.

In writing to the Philippians Paul corroborates in v. 27 the report that Epaphroditus had been ill; indeed, "he was sick unto death" (*ēsthenēsen paraplēsion thanatō*). Paul does not bother to describe in detail the nature of the ailment, but the fact that it caused great anxiety at Philippi and that it had almost cost Epaphroditus his life suggests that it was a grave physical illness. Paul further states in v. 30 that Epaphroditus' illness was directly related to his work for Christ in rendering service to Paul as a prisoner, and in v. 27 that it was a source of great sorrow for Paul himself. From this it may be posited that the sickness of Epaphroditus was a consequence of his co-imprisonment with Paul, arising from its difficulties and rigors. Paul seems to have been prepared to endure the death of his companion and to suffer *lypēn epi lypēn* (v. 27) in addition to the misery of his own imprisonment. The implication is that Epaphroditus' life would not have been endangered had he not "sacrificed himself" for the life of Paul (cf. the *leitourgia* motif in v. 30). Now, in returning Epaphroditus as quickly as possible, Paul desires that the church that sent him may have visible proof that "God had mercy on him" (v. 27) by restoring

---

88. Lohmeyer, *Philipper, Kolosser und Philemon*, 119.

his health. The illness had been grave indeed, but Epaphroditus had been rescued from "death's door" (*paraplēsion thanatō*) by God's tender mercy. Paul also wants his return to Philippi to be one of joy on the part of the believers there. He therefore emphasizes that it was his *own* decision that Epaphroditus should return, anticipating the criticism that their ambassador's early return meant that he had failed in his mission. The Philippians can rejoice, writes Paul, at the homecoming of their envoy, because Epaphroditus gave himself even to the brink of death in his service to the imprisoned apostle (vv. 29-30). Such a man not only must be welcomed "in the Lord," that is, in gratitude towards the Lord and in recognition of the Lord's healing power, but also must be held in high regard for his own sterling character and self-sacrificing work of love. Then Paul's own anxiety will be lightened (v. 28b), knowing that Epaphroditus has arrived safely and has been accepted honorably into the congregation.

The service that Epaphroditus had supplemented and completed as a representative of the church at Philippi, even to the point of gambling[89] with his own life, has now become an example that is to be emulated by others. This exemplary emphasis that Paul gives to this section explains its relative length. Indeed, the entire paragraph comprising vv. 25-30 may be considered a praise of Epaphroditus. Why should his return require such a long explanation? Not only was it because his stay with Paul was interrupted earlier than planned and would have called for some sort of explanation,[90] but because it was only fitting that Paul should have paid an extra amount of thanks to Epaphroditus, who had come so near to death by the serious illness he had contracted while serving the apostle. Most importantly, however, we may surmise that Paul is consciously using Epaphroditus as an example of those who are involved in Christian ministry. His presence in Rome in the capacity of the constant attendant of a prisoner had counted for the progress of the gospel, as had Paul's own imprisonment (cf. 1:12-18). He had nearly died in the service of Christ, as had Paul (cf. 1:18-26). He had lived a life in full accordance with the gospel, and, like the Lord he professed to follow, had become a slave, obedient even to the point of death (cf. 1:27—2:16). Epaphroditus

---

89. The participle *paraboleusamenos* is a rare word meaning "to risk, gamble, be venturesome" (cf. Thayer, *Lexicon*, 479). The verb (found only here) is rendered in the Vulgate "tradens animam suam," which might almost be rendered "betraying his soul." From the Greek root derives the ecclesiastical word *parabolanus* ("risker"), a member of an order devoted to nursing the sick and imprisoned and similar hazardous duties (cf. Moule, *Philippians*, 82; Hendriksen, *Philippians*, 144-45).

90. Cf. Gnilka, *Philipperbrief*, 164.

personally and eminently exemplifies the teaching of Paul earlier in the same chapter that the Christian life is rooted in the event of the cross, which produces a practical obedience characterized by unity and mutual service one to another.[91] Christ is the perfect example of giving *mechri thanatou*, but Epaphroditus is a good example of the same selfless attitude, expressed for instance in 2:4 as "not looking out for your own things, but each the things of the other."[92] Therefore, as Epaphroditus has willingly faced suffering and death for the work of Christ, so must the Philippian church as a persecuted community joyfully accept the providential ordering of their situation and count their present suffering as a mark of obedience to their Lord.

INTRODUCTION TO 1 AND 2 TIMOTHY

Because the letters addressed to Timothy and Titus differ from the generally acknowledged Pauline epistles in literary style and vocabulary, as well as in certain doctrinal emphases, most scholars believe they were written by an amanuensis who had great freedom in their composition or by a devoted follower of Paul who utilized some fragmentary letters of the apostle that otherwise would have been lost.[93] We do not propose here to discuss the authenticity of the Pastoral letters, but merely to see what happened to the *astheneia* word-group at the farthest limit of the Pauline corpus. Terms for weakness occur in the Pastorals only at 1 Tim 5:23 and at 2 Tim 4:20, each time with the common Synoptic meaning of sickness.

EXEGESIS OF THE TEXTS

1 Timothy 5:23

The single occurrence of weakness language in 1 Timothy is in Paul's personal note to the addressee in 5:23, advising him to use a little wine for the sake of his frail health (*dia ton stomachon kai tas pyknas sou astheneias*).

---

91. Cf. Reicke, "Unité," 203-12, who writes (212): "L'avis de Paul est que la diaconie mutuelle des croyants doit con firmer leur unité. Il n'insiste pas sur une forme particulière de confession ou d'organisation. L'essentiel, comme le fait voir le Christ lui-même, c'est le sacrifice et le service." See also Kamlah, "Leiden," 220.

92. See Black, "Formal Analysis," 299-308.

93. Metzger, *Background and Content*, 213-14. For history and contours of the problem of authorship, see Kümmel, *Einleitung*, 326-39; Guthrie, *Introduction*, 584-662; Lea and Black, *Background and Message*, 464-71.

Such an "aside" as this bears witness to the authenticity of the letter, since personal instructions of this nature would not have been particularly useful in promoting a Paulinist's ecclesiastical directives to Christians of his own generation.[94] It appears that this thought came to Paul when he wrote in the preceding verse, *seauton hagnon tērei*, "keep yourself pure."[95] The implication is that Timothy was inclined towards asceticism and was therefore refraining from any use of the common beverage lest he might be thought of as a *paroinos* (3:3).[96] The verse is also an indication of Timothy's delicate health and the apostle Paul's sympathy with him.

The statement *mēketi hydropotei* does not mean that Timothy is to abstain from consuming water altogether, but that he is to cease from doing so exclusively.[97] Because wine was commonly used as a healing agent for many ailments, Paul urges Timothy for the sake of his physical health, and eventually of his entire ministry, to avail himself of its medicinal purpose. It is impossible to judge from the context what Timothy's "frequent ailments" were. Perhaps the mention of *stomachos* is an indication that contaminated water had contributed to a case of indigestion, but this suggestion in no way excludes a myriad of other possibilities. Apart from this statement in 5:23, there is little indication in the NT that Timothy was constantly troubled by ill health, unless 2 Tim 4:21 ("come before winter") be taken to mean that Timothy's weak physical condition and proneness to illness made travelling under difficult conditions impossible. The more probable understanding of this verse, however, is that Paul is anxious that Timothy should hasten to reach Italy before shipping ceased for the winter months.

---

94. See, e.g., Meinertz, *Pastoralbriefe*, 22-24. Reicke observes: "Es bedeutet einen primitiven Anachronismus, zu behaupten, jemand hätte dreissig, fünfzig oder neunzig Jahre nach dem Tode des Paulus sich die Mühe gegeben, aus der Apostelgeschichte und den Paulusbriefen einige Namen und Daten herauszupicken, um die zeitgenossen mit gefälschten Paulusbriefen an Privatpersonen zu beglücken, ohne sich über derartige Antiquitäten hinaus um eine überzeugende Imitation der paulinischen Ausdrucksweise und Begriffswelt zu kümmern" ("Chronologie," 83).

95. Dibelius, *Pastoralbriefe*, 63; Kent, *Pastoral Epistles*, 187; Guthrie, *Pastoral Epistles*, 108 (who, however, leans towards viewing v. 23 as a parenthetical statement).

96. Cf. Meredith, "Asceticism," 313. Krause notes that the most important and common beverage in the world in the first century AD was grape wine, although there were more than 195 different known drinks, without even counting the various types of wine (*Griechen*, 79).

97. Spicq observes that *hydropotein* (hapax in the NT) refers to a constant practice, as opposed to *hydōr pinein* (*Saint Paul*, 180).

As Timothy had weighty ecclesiastical responsibilities on his hands, it may be inferred that Paul's command applies to Timothy not only as an individual but also as his representation to the church. Timothy must realize that if he is to be able to admonish the elders to a virtuous life, he himself must be a good example of Christian maturity. The Pauline ethic that Timothy is to model is neither absolute libertarianism nor radical asceticism.[98] Therefore, when his health requires it, it may become necessary for him to drink some wine. The obligations placed on Timothy are heavy and evidently are beginning to take their toll on his health. He cannot expect to enjoy a special immunity from the laws governing health just because he has a responsible position at Ephesus. Indeed, *because* he exercises great responsibility in the congregation, he must, along with others, take every normal means to maintain physical fitness.[99]

It almost goes without saying that there is nothing in this verse to justify the use of heavy drinking. Excessive intake of wine is expressly forbidden by Paul in Eph 5:18, an understandable prohibition in view of the widespread influence of the Dionysian cult centered in Ephesus.[100] The quantity advocated in Timothy's situation is small and its reason clearly stated. Otherwise, the apostle must place restrictions on its use in view of the widespread abuse of wine in the early church. The overseer must not "linger beside his wine" (*mē paroinon*, 1 Tim 3:3); deacons must not be "addicted to much wine" (*mē oinō pollō prosechontas*, 1 Tim 3:8); and older women must not be "enslaved to much wine" (*mēde oinō pollō dedoulōmenas*, Tit 2:3).While Paul clearly does not prohibit the *use* of wine, he emphatically forbids its *abuse* because wine is so often associated with unrestrained living and dissolute behavior (cf. Tit 1:6; 1 Pet 4:4). No doubt it was this very danger that made Timothy hesitant to partake of the beverage in the first place.

2 Timothy 4:20

Here Paul tells Timothy that despite the presence of a doctor and an apostle in the company, he had of necessity left Trophimus ill at Miletus as he journeyed to Rome for the final time (*Trophimon de apelipon en Milētō asthenounta*). Once again, *asthenein* means simply "to be sick"; the illness in question was evidently too serious for Luke to treat, and apparently Paul

---

98. Niederwimmer, " Problem der Ethik," 92.
99. Cf. Holtz, *Pastoralbriefe*, 130.
100. See Rogers, "Dionysian Background," 249–57.

did not attempt to practice divine healing. Trophimus was the disciple who along with Timothy and several others had accompanied the apostle on the last leg of his third missionary journey (Acts 20:4). He is described as an Asian (Acts 20:4) and an Ephesian (Acts 21:29), and had provided the occasion for the riot in the Temple at Jerusalem (Acts 21:29).

The fact that, according to Acts 22:4, Trophimus was with Paul when he journeyed to Miletus does not necessarily contradict Luke's statement in Acts 21:29 that he was with Paul in Jerusalem at the end of the third journey. The present statement that Paul left him ill at Miletus can easily refer to a subsequent visit *after* the apostle's release from his first Roman imprisonment. Guthrie's[101] suggestion that on Paul's subsequent and final journey from Asia to Rome, Trophimus was left at Miletus because he was ill, is adequate to correlate all the facts and best explains how Timothy could have been unaware of the situation.

Special note on Acts 20:35

According to Luke, Paul's address to the elders of Ephesus (Acts 20:17–35) included a reference to "the weak": "In all that I did, I showed you that by so laboring [we] must help the weak [*dei antilambanesthai tōn asthenountōn*] and remember the words of the Lord Jesus: 'It is more blessed to give than to receive'" (v. 35). Three things are striking about this reference to weakness: (a) it is found in the only Pauline speech delivered *to Christians* recorded by Luke in Acts; (b) it is remarkably parallel to the usage of *astheneia*, etc., in the Pauline epistles; and (c) Paul here explicitly states what is otherwise implicit in his letters, namely, that his own treatment of the weak must (*dei*) be imitated by other Christians (the idea is, however, present in 1 Cor 9:22; 12:22; and esp. Rom 15:1, where *opheilein* is used). The context (cf. vv. 31–34) indicates that Paul has poverty, or "economic weakness" primarily in mind, not sickness.[102]

CONCLUSION

Whereas in Philippians and the Pastoral letters the words denote weakness in the purely physical sense, in Paul's letter to the Christians at Rome the

---

101. *Pastoral Epistles*, 178–79.
102. Contra Bruce, *Acts*, 418.

weakness terms retain much of the theological significance they had in the Corinthian letters. The concept of "weakness" is for Paul in the first place the denotation of the human in its frailty, transitoriness, and mortality (5:6; 6:19; 8:26). While sin is not to be inferred from humanness as such, it is of importance to Paul to stress the relationship between our humanity and our propensity to disobey the commandments of God. On the one hand, Paul views "flesh" as a neutral mode of existence, signifying humankind in its weakness, dependence upon God, and perishableness; on the other hand, "flesh" in its pregnant meaning can denote humankind in its sin (7:14–25). There is no indication, however, that flesh denotes human sinfulness *per se*, only human limitation and weakness. Thus Paul writes that he must communicate to the Romans in human terms because they are weak in their natural selves (6:19). In this pronouncement, sin and flesh are kept distinct from each other: to be "weak in the flesh" simply means to be human. In the same way we will want to understand the words, "When we were still powerless, Christ died for the ungodly" (5:6). The meaning of this pronouncement, if one takes into consideration the whole context of Romans 5, cannot be in doubt. Paul is referring to the flesh as that which best describes all that we are in our weakness and utter poverty to work out our own salvation. The very attempt to gain acceptance before God on the basis of our own works clearly reveals the impotence of our humanity. Sin is not to be inferred from such humanness. At the same time, however, the weak are also sinners and enemies of God and, therefore, is in need of the saving activity of Christ Jesus (Rom 5:6–8).

Alongside this weakness in the comprehensive sense of the whole person is also a weakness that certain Christians retain in relationship to questions of religious practice. Here "the weak" are expressly declared to be "weak in faith" (14:1; cf. 14:2; 15:1); they have no certainty regarding their judgment or action, lacking the full conviction of their liberty before God in Christ. Paul does not here speak so much of legitimatizing as indeed of accepting the weaknesses of these Christians. While the weak are incapable of making concessions, the strong can and ought to do so, following the self-denying example of Christ. In yielding to the weak, stronger Christians do not relinquish their own liberty, but fulfill it.

Finally, as in Galatians so in Romans does the absolute inadequacy of the law as a means of salvation fully emerge (8:3). Because its requirement is frustrated by the unwilling and impotent flesh (cf. 8:7), the law becomes a means of putting us to death. We are impotent to work out our own righteousness, nor can we live from the strength of the law. Our only hope is the Christ who in due time died for the ungodly (5:6).

5

The Pauline Concept of Weakness in General

INTRODUCTION

IN THE PREVIOUS THREE chapters we examined the various Pauline statements about weakness in relation to their contexts. This chapter will endeavour to summarize the teaching that can be derived from these passages. We recognize that this kind of analysis involves a certain degree of abstraction and that the aspects we delineate may not necessarily be those of the reader. Nevertheless, it is hoped that the following remarks may serve to bring the understanding of this aspect of Pauline thought into clearer focus and may assist the biblical student to gain a fresh appreciation of the dynamic nature of Paul's letters.

THE PAULINE PERSPECTIVE ON WEAKNESS

We begin by noting that in the Pauline letters we are given no complete or fully developed "doctrine" of weakness or description of the circumstances that call it forth. On the one hand, this is certainly due to the intensely personal character of this theme, which does not always admit of being described or represented by means of systematic language. On the other hand, and even more significantly, account must be taken of the character of Paul's letters as occasional writings to meet certain specific situations in particular churches, even if there is disagreement with respect to this character of his writings. The Pauline epistles are principally pastoral in tone and content and, while they presuppose that Paul himself had a fairly well-developed concept of weakness, they give us only sporadic glimpses of its nature and contours. It should not be assumed, therefore, that the apostle's correspondence reveals the whole of his thinking and teaching regarding the subject of this study, nor is one entitled to reconstruct from such incomplete data a *systematic* theology of the apostle's thought concerning *astheneia*. Nonetheless, we hasten to emphasize that sufficient data have been related by Paul to permit us to reconstruct as least the broad outlines of this subject and the events attending it. This means that one *can* speak of a "doctrine of weakness" in Paul if only in a general and fragmentary sense. This fragmentary character, however, necessitates great care when drawing conclusions and when bringing the separate data together.

Paul's teaching regarding weakness and even the paraenesis resulting from it strongly reflect a high level of understanding on the part of the apostle. Even where we cannot be sure of his meaning due to insufficient data, we can elucidate enough of Paul's insight into Christian weakness to permit a fairly clear picture of the subject to be formed. For example, the notorious problem of Paul's "thorn in the flesh"—what he calls one of his "weaknesses" (2 Cor 12:7–10)—has given rise over the centuries to a myriad of suggestions regarding the character of the particular infirmity that had afflicted the apostle. No doubt in years to come speculative minds will advance fresh proposals, and their suggestions will rightly be welcomed. However, for present purposes, Paul's "thorn" does not demand a final conclusion, for by its very lack of definition it is of more benefit to us than would have been the case otherwise. It is enough that we know that Paul "most gladly" and with full eagerness welcomed it, because it had made him all the more aware of his Master's all-sufficient grace and dynamic power in the midst of his own weaknesses.

The same thing can be said with relation to the specific identity and religious conceptions of the so-called "weak" in Corinth and Rome. To a certain extent it is important that we know something of the weak and strong communities in both churches as well as something of Paul's resolution of the controversy between them. But certain matters, such as whether the weak are to be considered individuals or a party; whether their practices stem from a Judaistic, Gnostic, or Hellenistic background; whether they

The Pauline Concept of Weakness in General

indeed abstain from wine and observe ceremonial holidays; and whether they actually (or only hypothetically) exist in Rome, are circumstantial questions that do not directly relate to the fundamental principles that Paul introduces into the discussion. Although these questions are not without significance, they are not the main concern of the apostle, which is to show how an established community can maintain its unity despite sharp differences of opinion. His answer is to indicate by a series of imperatives and arguments that love can tolerate even the most severe disagreements in matters of personal conviction and that such problems should be resolved in the interests of edification. Because Christ Jesus has accepted the weaker members of the church, for whom he died, so too the strong must accept and support them in an attitude of humility and love (cf. 1 Cor 3:9–13; Rom 14:1; 15:1). Our task at this point, therefore, is not to determine with precision the identity of the weak and the strong in Corinth and Rome, but to demonstrate how Paul deals with them. To Paul the issue is not so much the immature view of the weak as it is the spirit of the so-called "strong" who condemn their weaker brothers and sisters. Thus the apostle deals with the problem of the rightness or wrongness of eating meat only as a side issue, seeking to give his full attention to the more serious spiritual problem so that he might lead both groups on to a fuller understanding and expression of their Christian liberty.[1]

When we speak of Paul's "theology" of weakness, we must remember too that the theological is subordinated to the practical purpose to which Paul had devoted his life and labors. Manson wrote of the apostle, "He is a great Christian thinker; but he does not see the gospel as the manifestation in time of some metaphysical principles or values. For Paul Christianity is not a system of ideas, but a series of events."[2] Indeed, in the final analysis Paul is not concerned to defend a doctrine or even to defend himself. "Who is Paul and who is Apollos but ministers through whom you believed?" (1 Cor 3:5). In Paul's mind the truth of the gospel was the important matter to be defended at all costs. Thus he is not interested in developing a theology of weakness, for it is at most only the wrapping of the true gospel. Christ himself is the core of Pauline theology; the concept of "weakness" is used only to defend and to define that core.

In view of this pragmatic approach of Paul, it is hardly surprising that none of his extant letters contains anything like a systematic treatment of

---

1. See Longenecker, *Paul*, 239–43.
2. Manson, "Christian and Theologian," 11.

weakness, his letters being written to answer particular questions and to meet the needs of the Christian communities. The significance of the Pauline weakness vocabulary without exception grows out of those concrete situations to which he addressed his letters. Though everywhere true, this is perhaps most clearly seen in the Corinthian letters, in which Paul finds himself forced to answer the criticisms of his opponents regarding his own weakness. It is not an exaggeration to say that if Paul had never been so viciously attacked by the opposition in Corinth we might forever have gone without his long narrative concerning weakness in 2 Corinthians 10–13. This lengthy passage, so vital to a clear understanding of Paul's concept of weakness, is available to us today, humanly speaking, because of the failures of certain early Christians. Paul develops especially his christological ideas of weakness in direct relationship with the church at Corinth, seeing this as the most effective way to handle the issues undermining his work among his converts. The emphasis upon Paul's personal weakness is also restricted to the Corinthian audience, apparently because the subject was a matter of debate there. The language of weakness thus conveyed a special meaning to Paul's Corinthian readers, a fact that explains why the terms are not employed with frequency in his other writings, both earlier and later.

Therefore, while it can never be positively ascertained exactly from which source Paul took his idea of weakness, it seems most feasible to look for its *Sitz im Leben* as stemming directly from the circumstances in Corinth rather than from other unrelated sources. This does not necessarily mean that the ideas had not been present to Paul's mind at an earlier stage; but it does imply that the circumstances of composition did not call them forth. One thing, however, is certain: whatever Paul may have received from the secular *Wortschatz*, he remolded it into something quite distinctive and independent in the Corinthian correspondence.

Any study of the Pauline weakness motif must, therefore, take into consideration Paul's concern to be relevant to the Christians to whom he writes. Nowhere in his letters does he attempt to systematize his teaching on weakness. The apostle himself seems oblivious to the pattern and principles that we will offer as "Paul's" theology of weakness. On the other hand, the apostle certainly does have his own ideas about weakness; and every attempt to discern the broad outlines of these ideas is appropriate.

The Pauline Concept of Weakness in General

THE THREE MAJOR SUB-THEMES

As we have said, it would be unjust to Paul, and to ourselves, to construct a systematic picture from such disparate material and then see the whole complex as determinative in any particular case. Nevertheless, certain patterns do emerge, not only in those passages where weakness is a comparatively prominent theme, as in portions of 1 and 2 Corinthians, but also in other less salient passages. Broadly conceived, the Pauline weakness motif is composed of three sub-themes: the *anthropological*, the *christological*, and the *ethical*. These are the three inseparably related components of Paul's gospel as well, and understandably so, since the terms for weakness are used primarily to defend and to illuminate the apostle's preaching.[3]

Weakness as a sign of humanity

The Pauline weakness motif is first of all *anthropological* because it presupposes that one's whole being is dependent upon God and that men and women, as *creatures* of God (like Adam), are susceptible to the limitations of all creation. Paul views men and women as members of the present age (*aiōn*) that is characterized by transitoriness, suffering, and evil. In particular, the present age is under the control of Satan and has been infiltrated by sin, which captures, enslaves, and ultimately kills us. Thus, the concept of "weakness" becomes an apt designation for the extent of our participation in the old aeon insofar as we are mortal and subject to the troubles, illnesses, and temptations of the present age.

Closely associated with our weakness, but not strictly identified with it, is our flesh (*sarx*). By definition, *sarx* is the earthly part of our humanity, denoting our physical and temporal existence. It may have "lusts" and "desires" (Eph 2:3), but in and of itself the flesh is not sinful. In Rom 6:19 the apostle refers to "the weakness of the flesh" that necessitates that he speak to the Romans using analogies drawn from the sphere of human relations. This is an accommodation to the weakness of our understanding and to our inability to comprehend spiritual truth apart from a natural medium. Undoubtedly this weakness of understanding is bound up with our sinful

---

3. These three emphases are not dissimilar to those given by Gäckle in the conclusion of his study (*Starken und Schwachen*, 515–18): (1) "Schwachheit als konstitutives Element des Menschseins"; (2) "Schutz und Kritik kultureller Identität im licht des Evangeliums"; (3) "Starke und Schwache als Paradigma der Konfliktlösung."

nature, which is "worldly" and "natural" as opposed to what is "spiritual" and "immaterial" (cf. Rom 15:27; 1 Cor 3:1; 2 Cor 1:12).

Yet Paul does not appear to equate our weakness with sinfulness, even though in another context he can characterize humanity by both concepts (cf. Rom 5:6–8). The point of Paul's linking weakness with the flesh is simply to underscore the earthliness of his readers' faculties of comprehension, which forces him to describe the spiritual relationship between God and the Christian in such crude, human terms (cf. Rom 8:15). The flesh in this sense denotes the human personality as directed toward earthly pursuits rather than the service of God.

This same connotation of weakness as human powerlessness over against God is found in Rom 8:26, where Paul refers to the infirmity of the Christian that requires the help of the Spirit's power, particularly in the matter of prayer. According to Paul, nothing lays bare the helplessness of believers like their "prayer-weakness." This consists in the fact that we do not know what to pray for as we ought, that is, as is suited to the occasion and as our necessities require. It is at this point that the Holy Spirit comes to our aid, praying for us in words that transcend articulated formulation yet which ascend, understood by God, to the very throne of grace. This is one example among many passages in Paul where weakness is made parallel to the antithetical concept of power (usually *dynamis*). The impotence and incapability that characterize the whole range of earthly existence require divine intervention. In turn, our infirmity of understanding and of prayer become the place in which the help and power of God come to expression.

The corresponding concept of humanity's "salvation-weakness" belongs unquestionably to this same category. In its negative aspect, salvation refers to our deliverance from sin and from bondage to the world with its decay and corruption. To execute this judgment upon sin the law is totally impotent, as Paul says, because it is "weakened by the flesh" (Rom 8:3). But what the law was powerless to do is precisely what God did by sending his son in the likeness of sinful flesh and for sin. The law, as it is confronted with sin, reveals its own utter lack of redemptive efficiency, being deprived of its power by reason of the flesh. It has become impotent; therefore, the person who looks to the law, and especially to the works of the law, as the way of salvation and acceptance with God, remains in bondage to sin and its guilt, defilement, and power (Gal 4:9). Law as law, as commandment that demands obedience, does not have any potency or provision for the salvation of sinners, who must therefore rely completely upon the power of

The Pauline Concept of Weakness in General

another to accomplish their justification. The time of our greatest helplessness was, however, the proper and fitting time for God's efficacious work to be wrought by the death of his son (Rom 5:6). The crucifixion of Christ belongs to "the fullness of the time" (Gal 4:4) and to "the consummation of the ages" (Heb 9:26) because it was the time in which Christ subdued sin, thus fulfilling what the law and the flesh were powerless to accomplish.

In another vein, Paul can also use the words in several instances in the specific sense of bodily weakness, i.e., physical illness, thus approximating the fundamental usage common to all literature in antiquity. He clearly uses the root for sickness with reference to Epaphroditus (Phil 2:26, 27), Timothy (1 Tim 5:23), and Trophimus (2 Tim 4:20), his close companions in the gospel ministry. Paul probably uses the root for sickness with reference to himself when he speaks of an "infirmity of the flesh" as the cause for the initial preaching of the gospel among the Galatians (Gal 4:13). If we are correct in concluding that Paul is referring to a *physical* infirmity, we can think of this weakness as a particular disease or ailment, the specific diagnosis of which is, however, a mystery. Cases of illness among Christians in NT times indicate that the apostolic commission to heal (cf. Mark 16:18) could not be effected indiscriminately to heal oneself or one's friends. Normal means of healing were available for Timothy's gastric problem, for instance, and even in the company of Paul Trophimus became too ill to travel any further. The classical Pauline passage on illness (2 Cor 12:7-10) is in this respect most striking of all, in that Paul's "thorn in the flesh" remained with the apostle despite even the most intensive prayer for its removal. Paul states three reasons for its existence: to keep him from becoming proud because of his revelations and visions (v. 7); to enable him to experience the power of Christ (v. 9); and to teach him the true purpose of hardships, persecutions, and personal difficulties (v. 10). Indeed, the entire passage is concerned more with the power and grace of the Lord than with the weakness of the apostle. Physical infirmity is evidence that the body "is sown in weakness" (1 Cor 15:43), and is a cogent reminder of the creature's dependence upon the Creator. In this respect, the case of Paul is remarkably like that of Jacob, who learned to depend totally upon God only after he had been inflicted with a physical injury (Gen 32:24-32). These instances of illness show us that the real issue in the matter of human suffering is our relationship to God rather than our own physical condition, as painful as it may be.

Sometimes there is a link between individual sin and individual suffering, though in the case of disease a direct connection may not be obvious.

From the account of the Lord's Supper in 1 Cor 11:17–34 it is clear that the penalty for unworthy participation at the Eucharist may be sickness or even death (1 Cor 11:30). The Lord himself had caused this judgment to fall upon the Corinthians in order that they might repent. However, if they had "discerned" themselves, they would not have been judged and punished (v. 31). The sin that Paul rebukes is therefore all the more serious, because Christians who eat without respecting the body (of Christ) are in danger of attributing their own physical illness to natural causes, thus ignoring its purpose.

Finally, it is important to realize that the Pauline conception of weakness in the anthropological sense is different from the common Greek conception of the body as something inherently evil. In Paul, human finiteness is emphasized, but never deprecated, in stark contrast to the neo-Platonic concept of the created world as a corruption of the original divine ideal. The Pauline conception is that of the *weakness* yet *nobility* of humanity, for in his thinking the human problem is *sin*, not the infirmity, finiteness, and mortality that characterize all dependent life. The limitations of this physical life will be eradicated in the kingdom; but in the meantime, weakness is a fact of human existence that cannot be evaded. While the new age has already broken into history, the believer still experiences the power of the old age as a member of Adam's humanity. Weakness is therefore not simply the occasional experience of sickness or powerlessness, but a fundamental mark of the individual's worldly existence. This emphasis permeates the whole of Paul's understanding of humanity and rests fundamentally on an anthropological, not a theological, basis.

Weakness as the showplace of God's might

In a second line of thought, Paul speaks of weakness as the platform from which the power of God is exhibited in the world. This aspect of weakness is quite different in character from the preceding anthropological category. In general, weakness as mere humanness is directed toward our participation in the created order, with no further thought in mind and (in secular authors) no consideration of divine intervention. Now, however, weakness takes on a whole new dimension as it is focused and defined by Paul's christology. Through the death and resurrection of Christ God's power becomes operative in our mortal existence, and those who belong to Christ, who are "in" him, participate in his death and life. Now the Spirit of God who raised

The Pauline Concept of Weakness in General

Jesus from the dead also gives life to those whom he indwells (Rom 8:11) so that the believer in Jesus is one who is united *with Christ* in weakness and power. This emphasis upon the believer's participation in the death and resurrection of Christ, seen most clearly in Romans and 2 Corinthians,[4] is of no mean importance as it concerns the significance and meaning of the Pauline weakness motif. When Paul speaks of "weakness" in this sense, he is no longer speaking of generic human weakness, but of weakness "in Christ," the one who "was crucified in weakness" (2 Cor 13:4). From a purely human perspective, the suffering and death of Christ appeared to be powerlessness and foolishness (1 Cor 1:25, 27); but God was at work in Christ's weakness, revealing in it the ultimate display of power by raising him from the dead (2 Cor 13:4). Thus Paul asserts that it is in the sufferings that he experiences as an apostle that divine power is most clearly revealed, having been told by the Lord himself that "power is perfected in weakness" (2 Cor 12:9). This christological aspect of the Pauline weakness motif is disclosed especially in the course of the apostle's arguments against his Corinthian opponents in 2 Corinthians 10–13.

Since the key to Pauline theology is to be found in the apostle's thought regarding Jesus Christ, it is not surprising that Paul relates human weakness to the life of faith that bears the marks of God's redeeming power. His theology of weakness is christocentric because his view of the Christian life is essentially a response to the relationship he enjoys with his crucified, resurrected, and ascended Lord. Paul's doctrine of weakness is thus subservient to his doctrine of Christ, for in Paul's view weakness can be truly understood only in relation to Jesus Christ. While Paul, like the OT writers, relates weakness to our fallen nature in Adam, insisting that by our participation in creation, the world, and the flesh we are weak beings, he does not, however, leave us there, but further asserts that *in Christ* human weakness takes on a whole new significance by becoming the place where divine power is revealed. There are therefore two counterbalancing emphases in Paul's teaching: a solidarity with Adam by which all humanity under the influence of the natural sphere inherit the generic characteristic of weakness; and a solidarity with Christ by which human weakness under the influence of the Holy Spirit is transformed into a showplace of the divine on earth and a badge of honor. Hence from a purely theological point of view, the most distinctive meaning of weakness is detected in the

---

4. See Tannehill, *Dying and Rising*, 7–47 and 84–100 respectively. See also Schweizer, "Die 'Mystik,'" 183–203.

christological character the words acquire when Paul asserts that the power of God is operative in our earthly existence (which is otherwise weak and corruptible). In the very impotence and mortality of the flesh is concealed the resurrection power of God, operative both in the life of the church (cf. Acts 4:7, 33; 6:8) and in the life of every believer (cf. Phil 4:13; Col 1:11).

This aspect of Paul's understanding of weakness is expressed most profoundly in the famous statement of 2 Cor 12:9 that divine power finds its full scope in human weakness. This promise of the Lord, predicated upon his pronouncement "My grace is sufficient for you," is the vantage-point from which the whole of the Pauline weakness motif can be seen in its proper perspective. Paul is well content with weaknesses, not because they are desirable in and of themselves, but because they are the vehicle through which the all-sufficient power of his Lord becomes prominent. Human weakness paradoxically provides the best opportunity for divine power.

It is this principle that makes weakness more meaningful to Paul than to his opponents or even his converts. Whenever he feels himself to be weak—a fragile earthen vessel, persecuted, insulted, beset with afflictions of every kind—he feels Christ's strength. Behind all his doubts, insecurities, and anxieties is the assurance that God is manifesting his son in and through his life. Paul's message, as well as his life, was the revelation of that fact.

Paul's "theology" of weakness, therefore, cannot be understood apart from both the man Paul and his relationship to Christ. Nor can we correctly understand the emphasis he gives the words in 2 Corinthians apart from a recognition of the close connection in Paul's thought between Christ and weakness. The christological orientation of Paul's weakness language is clearer here than in any other of his writings. Here the terms "Christ" and "weakness" are more than just somehow related: they are co-functional. In contrast to the false apostles who boast in their fleshly wisdom and strength, Paul declares that for him all boasting is excluded except in the "weakness" (cross) of Christ, of which the Christian retains a permanent witness. Because the gospel is most clearly presented in human weakness, Paul not only preaches Christ crucified but also gladly bears in his body the death of Jesus as the means to manifest his life. This bearing of the weakness of Christ is the apostle's greatest mark of legitimacy.

Therefore, in marked contrast with his opponents, Paul asserts the positive significance of weakness and suffering inasmuch as such weakness reveals the power of Christ and the true meaning of the gospel. As Fuchs writes,

The Pauline Concept of Weakness in General

> Ce qui autorise l'apôtre, c'est qu'il est appelé par le Christ lui-même à signifier l' évangile dans son existence même. C'est pourquoi, sans paradoxe, l'apôtre peut revendiquer avec force sa faiblesse, parce qu'elle désigne l'honneur qui lui est fait de participer ainsi à l'évangile lui-même.[5]

Thus, Paul views his participation in Christ's weakness not only as a means to experience the power of Christ's resurrection, but also as a means of fulfilling his own ministry of preaching the gospel. In itself, weakness indicates that Paul is still a part of the created order and that he awaits ultimate redemption; but when weakness becomes a means by which the Lord exercises his power, it shows that God's might has indeed manifested itself in the world through the death and resurrection of Christ, thereby overcoming the inability of the law and the flesh (Rom 5:6; 8:3).

Given this emphasis upon the death of the Savior, it may be suggested that the most important contribution Paul makes to the development of the weakness motif is the relation he establishes between the idea of weakness and the cross of Christ. The gospel for Paul is nothing more than the weakness of Christ, who "was crucified in weakness but lives by the power of God" (2 Cor 13:4). Without the cross of Christ he would never have known true weakness or learned its deepest meaning. Likewise, Paul also says there is no power available to the Christian except that of the resurrection. For Paul, both weakness and power are inseparably tied up in the death and resurrection of Christ. Therefore if we desire a formal designation of the Pauline idea of weakness at the height of its evolution, we can hardly do better than to call it the weakness of the cross; for when we ask Paul what weakness is, he points us to the cross of Christ. Nowhere else in the NT can we find a revelation of weakness comparable to this in degree or scope. In the death of Christ is revealed "the weakness of God" (1 Cor 1:25). Consequently, when Paul speaks of weakness he identifies it with the crucifixion of his Master. This is exactly the same conception that finds expression in the doctrines of the Incarnation and Humiliation of Christ (cf. Phil 2:5–11). Yet the weakness revealed in the death of Christ is in no way independent of the apostle's own weakness; it is "in Christ," says Paul, that he is weak (2 Cor 13:4). Thus the apostle does not merely tolerate his weaknesses; he boasts in them and bears with joy the crucifixion of his Lord in his own body as the surest sign of true apostleship. This principle

---

5. Fuchs, "La faiblesse," 253. For further theological implications of this see Lochman, "Die Kraft," 45–61.

finds its most fundamental and impressive expression in the words of 2 Cor 12:9b: "Therefore I will boast all the more gladly about my weaknesses, in order that Christ's power may rest upon me."

Weakness in the Church

In the third and final place, the terms in the group are developed in relationship to their *ethical* significance for the Christian. After all that has been said on "being weak in Christ," experiencing God's "power perfected in human weakness," etc., this significance of weakness as something that must be overcome is maintained with a great degree of consistency, especially in hortatory contexts. Both 1 Corinthians 8 and Romans 14 refer to the weak in the church who lack the full knowledge of faith, expressed in ascetic and legalistic behavior. While Paul's sympathies very clearly lie with the weak, he admits that they are still immature and need to grow in knowledge and faith. Yet Paul is careful to point out that there is a place for weak Christians in the believing community. They must never be condemned by stronger believers; indeed, Paul explains in great detail that the strong have a special responsibility for the weak members of the church. In 1 Corinthians 8 and Romans 14 they are to put aside their differences and live together with the weak in love before their common Lord. In 1 Thess 5:14 they are to stand by their weaker brothers and sisters, tenderly and sympathetically consoling, encouraging, and upholding them. In every instance the strong are to fulfill their special duty toward the weak in a spirit of unity and love lest they lead the weak astray, cause them to fall, and ultimately bring about their spiritual ruin.

It is clear that this ethical aspect of weakness in Paul's writings grows out of the apostle's teaching regarding the reciprocal, mutually edifying love of believers. For Paul, the church is composed of individuals who have been vitally united with Jesus Christ, and thereby inextricably joined to all others confessing the same Lord. As members of the same spiritual family, the "body of Christ," Christians are to live together in a spirit of mutual dependence and unity, serving each other in love (Gal 5:13) and in oneness of soul and purpose (Phil 2:1–2). It is because of this corporate aspect of the church that Paul time and again speaks out against every form of spiritual individualism, particularly the more refined form that crops up in regard to standards of spirituality in the church.[6] The Corinthians, for

6. Cf. Ridderbos, *Paul*, 294–97.

The Pauline Concept of Weakness in General

example, had turned Paul's preaching of freedom into the libertarian axiom "all is permitted to me" (1 Cor 6:12) in order to justify their individualistic application of Christian liberty to the eating of meat offered to idols. Although Paul gives due recognition to Christian liberty on the one hand, he emphatically warns the libertarians against abusing their freedom in Christ by giving the weak an occasion to sin (1 Cor 8:9). If the strong wish to assert their liberty without the restraints of love, they will be sinning against the spiritual Head of the church, that is, against Christ himself (1 Cor 8:12). Paul's teaching is not against the expression of Christian liberty, but that Christians must exercise their liberty before God on the basis of what is good for the entire community and not only for themselves. Similarly, Paul warns the stronger Christians in Rome against the same abuses of liberty, for the liberty wrought by Christ is to be tempered by love, concern, and respect for the "brother and sister for whom Christ died" (Rom 14:15). In all things the strong are to seek after that which is mutually beneficial and edifying (Rom 14:19).

Another example of Paul's ethical teaching regarding weakness is in the same line and directs itself likewise against individualism in the church. It concerns the special *charismata* in the church, i.e., the "spiritual gifts" that the Holy Spirit imparts to each believer. In Corinth, especially, there existed the danger that individualism might interfere with the harmonious and fruitful ministry of believers within the community. From the context of 1 Corinthians 12–14 it can be inferred that those who claimed a "pneumatic" status in Corinth had placed an inordinately high premium on the more spectacular gifts.[7] Especially the gifts of tongues and of ecstatic prophecy were taken to be the most important pneumatica. 1 Cor 13:1 suggests that these Corinthians perhaps thought they could even speak a type of "heavenly dialect" as evidence that they had attained to the highest degree of spiritual awareness. They had forgotten, or perhaps not known, that only those gifts that exalted Christ as Lord were suitable for Christian worship.[8] Although Paul was willing to acknowledge the validity of the more spectacular gifts of the Spirit, he insisted that love was basic to all other gifts (1 Corinthians 13). He taught further that there are many gifts of the Spirit and that *all* are necessary, be they didactic, therapeutic, miraculous, or ecstatic. But Paul also emphasized that no gift in and of itself has any value, no matter how spectacular it may appear, for the essential question is whether

---

7. See Pearson, *Pneumatikos-Psychikos*, 46.
8. Schweizer, "Service of Worship," 337.

or not the gift edifies the church as it is exercised in love. For example, the apostle defends the use of tongues; it was a gift of the Spirit and one that Paul himself possessed and practiced. But because it did little to edify the church, Paul could say that he preferred to speak five words with his mind than thousands in a tongue (1 Cor 14:9). It is not a surprise, in light of this exaltation in Corinth of certain charismatic powers, that the gifts that the Corinthians praised the most are relegated by Paul to the foot of the lists given in 1 Corinthians 8 (12:8–10, 28, 29–30).[9]

Paul teaches that those members who possess the more conspicuous gifts and therefore enjoy greater prominence have a special duty to foster the spiritual unity of the church. In the service of Jesus Christ there is no place for individualism, no matter how great or impressive one's abilities may be. Conversely, Paul must also emphasize that those members of the church who appear to be weaker are just as indispensable as the other members for the proper functioning of the body of Christ. Despite their apparent secondary nature and less glamorous appearance, their presence and functioning are vital in sustaining life. To follow Paul's analogy of the human body, we may think of these weaker members as the sensitive internal organs such as the lungs or the liver that are so susceptible to injury and whose only protection is that which the surrounding members afford. These organs, hidden from view and often taken for granted, must, however, be present and operative or there is no functional body. All other members, including those possessing greater external beauty and recognition, are dependent upon their existence.

For this reason the apostle is emphatic that all members, even "weaker" members, are important, for they are included in the body as a necessary part of the church's development and ministry (1 Cor 12:22). The failure of the strong to be considerate of those who did not possess such a spectacular manifestation was a failure to recognize the mutual dependence of every member and the unity that characterizes Christ's body (1 Cor 12:12–13). For Paul, the Christian life is a life of continual tension, but also one of growth and continual purification until final maturity and victory are experienced at the second coming of Christ.[10] Therefore, those who have not yet reached a full knowledge of the faith and are "weak" have their place in the church as a community of growing saints. The many individual

---

9. On the significance of the order of the charismata, see Smalley, "Spiritual Gifts," 427–33.

10. See Wenham, "Christian Life," 80–94 for a full treatment of this subject.

members of the community, including those who are less mature, are actually demonstrating rather than negating the purposes of Christ within his church. In the final analysis, by virtue of the Christian's intimate, redemptive fellowship with Christ, weakness is never merely human weakness but an opportunity to manifest God's power. That "God chose the weak things of the world to shame the strong" (1 Cor 1:27) explains why Paul constantly refers the Christian acceptance of weak individuals back to their relationship with God. Because weaker members are chosen, stronger members have no basis to reject them. Christ died for the weak in a special sense (1 Cor 8:11) and revealed in his self-surrender that the church's love for its weaker members is the real secret and the clearest expression of its holy purpose on earth.

This leads us to one final feature that is characteristic of the Pauline concept of weakness: its markedly *theocentric* character. God depends neither upon our strength nor our achievements, not even in the church. Instead, he seeks out the weak, ungodly, and hostile to redeem them and to fit them as vessels of his strength. Weakness is—as the Lord had expressed it to Paul—the place where *God's* power is perfected. Christians have nothing to give of themselves; the strength they exhibit is the strength God has infused into them. Thus between Christ and the Christian there is such an intimate identification in weakness that both are said to live "by the power of God" (2 Cor 13:4).

PAUL'S RELEVANCE FOR TODAY

Paul's view of weakness, regardless of how highly developed it may be, is not to be understood only as an abstract doctrine, for it was developed in view of actual conditions. In the first place, weakness impresses upon us the reality of our finiteness and dependence upon God. Human attempts are completely useless to please God; with all of our effort, we can do nothing. It is just this attitude that Paul declares when he says he is weak. He can claim no credit for any of his successes for he knows he has been sustained by God. If he has achieved anything, it is only by God's power working through a weak, yet yielded, vessel. Thus human initiative, human boasting, and human merit have no place in the thought of the apostle Paul.

Likewise, Paul teaches that God's way of exhibiting power is altogether different from our way. We try to overcome our weakness; God is satisfied to *use* weakness for his own special purposes. Too many Christians become disheartened over their infirmities, thinking that only if they were stronger in themselves they could accomplish more for God. But this point of view, despite its popularity, is altogether a fallacy. God's means of working, rightly understood, is not by making us stronger, but by making us weaker and weaker until the divine power alone is clearly manifested in our lives.

Finally, for Paul weakness is the greatest sign of apostleship because it identifies Christians with their crucified Master. By his death Christ proved that God's weakness was stronger than our strength. This same Christ has now become the example that Christians are to follow. By bearing the cross of Christ and dying daily with him, they participate in the weakness of Christ. This identification with their Lord enables them to glory in their weaknesses, not merely endure them.[11]

Therefore, rather than wrestle with God for freedom from their weaknesses and limitations, the faithful see in these the power of another, who promised, "My grace is sufficient for you, for strength is perfected in weakness" (2 Cor 12:9), and of whom it was written, "He is not weak toward you but is powerful in you. For indeed he was crucified because of weakness, yet he lives because of the power of God" (2 Cor 13:4).

CONCLUSIONS TO CHAPTER 5

We have now examined every occurrence of *astheneia* in its context, in its relation to Pauline thought as a whole, and in light of the popular and religious conceptions that underlie it. This has led to several conclusions that may finally be summarized:

1. In the Gospels and in Acts, as well as in the majority of NT epistles, there is no development of the theme of weakness into a broad theological motif such as we can discern in Paul. Scattered instances of a theological usage are the exceptions that prove the rule.

2. Paul's theology of weakness developed in a dynamic fashion in response to the situations facing him, and his particular formulations on weakness are consistently adapted and designed to meet particular issues at hand.

3. The Pauline usage from early to late stages reveals an erratic development when analyzed in strict chronological sequence. Yet a broad developmental pattern emerges. This pattern is distinctively bell-shaped:

---

11. For a fuller development of this theme, see Black, *Jesus Paradigm*.

while the terms are used infrequently in his early and later epistles, a sizable complex of the terms is discernible in the *Hauptbriefe*, which represent Pauline thought during the middle period of the apostle's career.

4. In Paul's latest epistles the words convey little or no theological significance and are used with the common secular Greek meaning of sickness.

5. In the Pauline letters, the terms for weakness figure prominently only in Romans and 1 and 2 Corinthians, which are usually designated to be "doctrinal" in content. However, here they are important terms not only in Paul's theology but also in his ethical teaching.

6. Paul develops the words into a *major* theme only in the Corinthian letters, where weakness plays a significant role in the Pauline apostolic defense. In 2 Corinthians, where the attack against Paul is at its strongest, the largest complex of weakness language in Paul is to be found.

7. The *Sitz im Leben* for the motif is provided, at least partially, in Corinth and the Corinthian correspondence. Especially the argumentative situation of l and 2 Corinthians seems to have been the primary controlling factor in Paul's use of weakness terminology. Here Paul shows a tendency to borrow the terms from his opponents and then to define them in terms of his own theology.

8. Paul can use the terms in a favorable or unfavorable sense, depending upon the context, so that precise determinations of the meaning will always require close attention to the immediate setting. However, the distinctively pejorative use of *astheneia* is represented only in the mouth of Paul's opponents.

9. Although the words have a distinctive place in Paul's theological and ethical vocabulary, they do not constitute the core of his gospel; rather they are used to defend and to illuminate that core.

10. Even in the Corinthian letters, several instances of the terms are used in the ordinary secular Greek sense without any specific "Christian" or "Pauline" connotations; yet, those places where he employs the words without any distinctive meaning are still an important aspect of the Pauline motif.

11. Because weakness directs him away from himself and to God, Paul can, and often does, assert the positive meaning of weakness.

12. Paul's conception of weakness stands in a dynamic relationship with his christology. In Corinthians, it is his focus on *Christ* that binds his various pronouncements together and gives unity to their miscellaneous contents.

13. The central idea in the Pauline weakness motif is that the greatest revelation of divine power has occurred in the person and work of Jesus Christ in the midst of his human and earthly existence.

14. Paul is defensive of his own infirmities only because a misunderstanding of weakness leads to error concerning the nature and acquisition of divine strength. Paul is strong, but only because he is "in Christ."

15. Integrally connected with the understanding of Paul's concept of weakness is the antithetical concept of strength. In some cases this background is brought into focus and the concept of strength is explicitly mentioned, whereas at other times the contrast is only implied. Paul specifically connects weakness with the opposite idea of power in 1 Cor 1:25, 26; 4:10; 15:43; 2 Cor 10:10; 12:5, 9, 10; 13:3, 4, 9; Rom 4:19; 5:6; 8:3; 14:1, 2; 15:1, passages that show the importance of both words in Paul's vocabulary. The emphasis is often upon the fact that the powerful apostle is also the weak and suffering one; *Paulus potens* is at the same time *Paulus infirmus*.

16. In the Pauline ethic, a firm conviction of monotheism is of less importance than the love of one's Christian brothers and sisters. Paul insists that strong Christians should hold their liberty in check in deference to their weaker brothers and sisters. Moreover, the duty of the strong is not only to avoid placing stumbling blocks before the weak, but also to remove them.

17. The translator should recognize that the uses of *astheneia*, etc. in Paul are not homogeneous, and there is no single English root that translates all of them with equal success or precision.

18. Concerning the influence of other writings upon Paul, the apostle's concept of weakness must be finally understood against the broad context of his own message and mission. Paul cannot be said to have borrowed Hellenistic concepts, though Hellenistic influences are discernible in his usage of the root for physical weakness and for powerlessness in general.

19. It is possible to detect some informal and non-literary relationships between the teaching of Paul and the writings of the OT. For example,

the association of *asthenein* with *skandalizein* is strongly reminiscent of the OT prophetic use of *asthenein* to denote the fate of the ungodly. However, OT parallels with Pauline thought do not necessarily indicate direct literary dependence. All we can say with certainty is that OT Greek, while not a source for Paul's thought in that it supplied him with exact modes of expression, did provide Paul with a perspective from which to interpret the nature of human weakness.

20. Although the idea of God's power revealed in weakness is not wholly absent in the OT, the concept of "weakness, the showplace of God's might" as such, is found fully developed only in Paul. Furthermore, the christocentric emphasis that the apostle gives the words distinguishes his point of view from that of the OT. For Paul weakness is rooted in the death of Christ. This may explain why the apostle never quotes the OT *in extenso* when developing a concept regarding weakness.

21. Paul teaches that humanity as a creation of God is weak; yet God desires to reveal his own strength through the infirmities of human existence. He therefore chooses the weak in order to confound the strong. This he accomplishes by what the world considers foolish and feeble, namely, the cross of Christ, which is nonsense to those who perish but the power of God to those being saved. By his death Christ proved that God's weakness was stronger than human strength. Therefore, Christ has become the example that Christians are to follow. By bearing his cross and dying daily with him, they become participants in the weakness of Christ. This identification with their Lord enables them to glory in their weaknesses, not merely endure them.

22. In addition to this positive truth, there is a negative aspect of weakness that is expressed by a weak faith and a weak conscience. Yet there is a place in the church even for weak believers, who must be accepted by stronger Christians on the basis of their election and Christ's love for them.

23. For Paul, weakness is the greatest sign of apostleship because it identifies him in a plain way with his crucified Master. Through weakness the power of the resurrection finds its fullest expression in the apostle, in his apostolic mission, and in the communities he founded. Christ's power is present with Paul in his weaknesses and with all those whom the Spirit of Christ indwells.

Bibliography

Aejmelaeus, Lars. "'Christ is Weak in Paul': The Opposition to Paul in Corinth." In *Nordic Paul*, 117-31. New York: T. & T. Clark, 2008.
Akin, Daniel. "Triumphalism, Suffering, and Spiritual Maturity: An Exposition of 2 Corinthians 12:1-10 in its Literary, Theological, and Historical Context." *CTR* 4 (1989) 119-44.
Andrews, Scott B. "Too Weak Not to Lead: The Form and Function of 2 Cor 11:23b-33." *NTS* 41 (1995) 263-76.
Arnold, Clinton E. "Returning to the Domain of the Powers: *Stoichea* as Evil Spirits in Galatians 4:3, 9." *NovT* 36 (1996) 55-76.
Baird, William. "On Reading Romans in the Church Today." *Int* 34 (1980) 45-58.
———. "Visions, Revelation, and Ministry: Reflections on 2 Cor 12:1-5 and Gal 1:11-17." *JBL* 104 (1985) 651-62.
Baltensweiler, H. "Erwägungen zu I Thess. 4, 3-8." *TZ* 19 (1963) 1-13.
Bammel, Ernst. "*Ptochos, ktl.*" In *TWNT* 6:885-915. Edited by G. Kittel and G. Friedrich. Stuttgart, 1959.
Bandstra, A. J. *The Law and the Elements of the World. An Exegetical Study in Aspects of Paul's Teaching*. Kampen: Kok, 1964.
Barr, James. *The Semantics of Biblical Language*. Oxford: Oxford University Press, 1961.
Barré, M. L. "Paul as 'Eschatological Person': A New Look at 2 Cor. 11:29." *CBQ* 37 (1975) 509-14.
———. "Qumran and the 'Weakness' of Paul." *CBQ* 42 (1980) 216-27.
Barrett, C. K. *A Commentary on the Epistle to the Romans*. New York: Harper & Brothers, 1957.
———. *A Commentary on the First Epistle to the Corinthians*. HNTC. New York/Evanston: Harper & Row, 1968. HNTC NT Commentaries. New York: Harper & Row, 1973.
———. "Things Sacrificed to Idols." *NTS* 11 (1965) 138-53.
Barrier, Jeremy W. "Visions of Weakness: Apocalyptic Genre and the Identification of Paul's Opponents in 2 Corinthians 12:1-6." *ResQ* 47 (2005) 33-42.
Bartchy, Scott S. "'When I'm Weak, I'm Strong': A Pauline Paradox in Cultural Context." In *Kontexte der Schrift Band 2, Kultur, Politik, Religion, Sprache-Text*, 49-60. Stuttgart: W. Kohlhammer, 2005.
Barth, Gerhard. *Der Brief an die Philipper*. Zürcher Bibelkommentare NT 9. Zürich: Theologischer Verlag, 1979.
Barth, Markus. "The Kerygma of Galatians." *Int* 21 (1967) 131-46.
Bates, W. H. "The Integrity of II Corinthians." *NTS* 12 (1965) 56-69.

Bibliography

Bauer, Karl-Adolf. *Leiblichkeit, das Ende aller Werk Gottes.* SNT 4. Gütersloh, Mohn, 1971.
Behm, J. "*Noeō, ktl.*" In *TWNT* 4:1013–16. Edited by G. Kittel and G. Friedrich. Stuttgart, 1942.
Best, Ernest. *A Commentary on the First and Second Epistles to the Thessalonians.* BNTC. London: Black, 1972.
Betz, Hans Dieter. *Der Apostel Paulus und die sokratische Tradition: Eine exegetische Untersuchung zu seiner "Apologie" 2 Korinther 10–13.* BHT 45. Tübingen: Mohr, 1972.
———. *A Commentary on Paul's Letter to the Churches in Galatia.* Hermeneia. Philadelphia: Fortress, 1979.
Binder, Hermann. "Die angebliche Krankheit des Paulus." *TZ* 32 (1976) 1–13.
Black, Matthew. "The Interpretation of Romans viii 28." In *Neotestamentica et Patristica: Eine Freundsgabe, Herrn Professor Dr. Oscar Cullmann zu seinem 60 Geburtstag überreicht*, 166–72. Edited by W. C. van Unnik. Supplements to Novum Testamentum 6. Leiden: Brill, 1962.
Black, David. "The Peculiarities of Ephesians and the Ephesian Address." *GTJ* 2 (1981) 59–73.
———. "Paul and Christian Unity: A Formal Analysis of Philippians 2:1–4." *JETS* 28 (1985) 299–308.
———. "The Discourse Structure of Philippians: A Study in Textlinguistics." *NovT* 37 (1995) 16–49.
———. *The Jesus Paradigm.* Gonzalez, FL: Energion, 2009.
Blackman, E. C. "The Task of Exegesis." In *The Background of the New Testament and its Eschatology: Studies in Honour of C. H. Dodd*, edited by W. D. Davies and David Daube, 3–26. Cambridge: Cambridge University Press, 1956.
Boice, J. M. *Galatians.* In Vol. 10 of *The Expositor's Bible Commentary* (Romans—Galatians). Grand Rapids: Zondervan, 1976.
Bornkamm, Günther. "Herrenmahl und Kirche bei Paulus." *ZTK* 53 (1956) 312–49.
———. "Der Philipperbrief als paulinische Briefsammlung." In *Neotestamentica et Patristica: Eine Freundsgabe, Herrn Professor Dr. Oscar Cullmann zu seinem 60 Geburtstag überreicht*, edited by W. C. van Unnik, 192–202. Supplements to Novum Testamentum 6. Leiden: Brill, 1962.
Bouttier, Michel. *La Condition Chrétienne selon Saint Paul.* Geneve: Labor et Fides, 1964.
Bring, R. *Der Brief des Paulus an die Galater.* Berlin: Lutherisches Verlagshaus, 1968.
Bruce, F. F. *The Acts of the Apostles.* London: Tyndale, 1953.
———. "'All Things to All Men': Diversity in Unity and Other Pauline Tensions." In *Unity and Diversity in New Testament Theology: Essays in Honor of George E. Ladd*, edited by Robert A. Guelich, 82–99. Grand Rapid: Eerdmans, 1978.
———. "St. Paul in Macedonia: The Thessalonian Correspondence." *BJRL* 62 (1980) 328–45.
Büchsel, Friedrich. "*Bastazō*." In *TWNT* 1:596–97. Edited by G. Kittel and G. Friedrich. Stuttgart, 1933.
Buck, C. D. *A Dictionary of Selected Synonyms in the Principle Indo-European Languages.* Chicago: University Press, 1949.
Bultmann, Rudolph. "Allgemeine Wahrheiten und christliche Verkündigung." *ZTK* 54 (1957) 244–54.
———. *Theologie des Neuen Testaments.* 5th ed. Tübingen: Mohr, 1965.

Bibliography

Burdick, Donald W. "*Oida* and *Ginōskō* in the Pauline Epistles." *New Dimensions in New Testament Study.* Edited by Richard N. Longenecker and Merrill C. Tenney. Grand Rapids: Zondervan, 1974.

Burton, E. *The Epistle to the Galatians.* ICC. Edinburgh: T. & T. Clark, 1950.

Buttrick, George A., ed. *The Interpreter's Dictionary of the Bible.* 4 vols. New York: Abingdon, 1962.

Byrne, Brendan. *"Sons of God"—"Seed of Abraham": A Study of the Idea of the Sonship of God of all Christians in Paul against the Jewish Background.* AnBib 83. Rome: Biblical Institute, 1979.

Cambier, J. "Le critère paulinien de l'apostolat en 2 Co 12, 6s." *Bib* 43 (1962) 481–518.

Campbell, W. S. "Romans III as a Key to the Situation and Thought of the Letter." *NovT* 23 (1981) 22–40.

Chantraine, P. *Dictionnaire Etymologique de la Langue Greque.* Paris: Klincksleck, 1968.

Chow, John K. *Patronage and Power: A Study of Social Networks in Corinth.* JSNTSup 75. Sheffield: Sheffield Academic, 1992.

Clavier, H. "Brèves remarques sur la notion de *sōma pneumatikon.*" In *The Background of the New Testament and its Eschatology: Studies in Honour of C. H. Dodd,* 342–62. Edited by W. D. Davies and David Daube. Cambridge: Cambridge University Press, 1956.

Collange, J. -F. *Énigmes de la Deuxième Épître de Paul aux Corinthiens: Étude Exegetique de 2 Cor. 2:14–7:4.* Cambridge: Cambridge University Press, 1972.

Conzelmann, Hans. *Der erste Brief an die Korinther.* KEK 5. 12th ed. Göttingen: Vandenhoeck & Ruprecht, 1981.

———. *Grundriss der Theologie des Neuen Testaments.* München: Kaiser, 1976.

Cranfield, C. E. B. *A Critical and Exegetical Commentary on the Epistle to the Romans.* ICC. 2 vols. Edinburgh: T. & T. Clark, 1975.

Cullmann, Oscar. "La prière selon les Épîtres pauliniennes." *TZ* 35 (1979) 90–101.

———. "The Proleptic Deliverance of the Body According to the New Testament." *The Early Church.* London: SCM, 1956.

Dahl, M. E. *The Resurrection of the Body: A Study of 1 Corinthians 15.* London: SCM, 1962.

Dahl, Nils A. "The Particularity of the Pauline Epistles as a Problem in the Ancient Church." In *Neotestamentica et Patristica: Eine Freundsgabe, Herrn Professor Dr. Oscar Cullmann zu seinem 60 Geburtstag überreicht,* edited by W. C. van Unnik, 261–71. Supplements to Novum Testamentum 6. Leiden: Brill, 1962.

Danker, Frederick William. *A Greek-English Lexicon of the New Testament and Other Early Christian Literature: Based on Walter Bauer's Wörterbuch.* 3rd ed. Translated and revised by William F. Arndt and F. Wilbur Gingrich. Chicago: University of Chicago Press, 2000.

Daube, David. *The New Testament and Rabbinic Judaism.* London: Athlone, 1956.

Delling, Gerhard. "*Skolops.*" In *TWNT* 7:411–15. Edited by G. Kittel and G. Friedrich. Stuttgart, 1964.

———. "*Stoicheō, ktl.*" In *TWNT* 7:670–82. Edited by G. Kittel and G. Friedrich. Stuttgart, 1964.

———. "*Tassō, ktl.*" In *TWNT* 8:27–49. Edited by G. Kittel and G. Friedrich. Stuttgart, 1969.

Dibelius, Martin. *Die Pastoralbriefe.* Handbuch zum Neuen Testament 13. Tübingen: Mohr, 1955.

Dietzel, Armin. "Beten im Geist." *TZ* 13 (1957) 12–32.

Bibliography

Dihle, Albert. "*Oligopsychos.*" In *TWNT* 9:666-67. Edited by G. Kittel and G. Friedrich. Stuttgart, 1973.

Dobschütz, E. von. *Die Thessalonicher Briefe: Bearbeitet von Ernst von Dobschütz mit einem Literaturverzeichnis von Otto Merk herausgegeben von Ferdinand Hahn.* KEK 10. Göttingen: Vandenhoeck & Ruprecht, 1974.

Dodd, C. H. "*Ennomos Christou.*" In *More New Testament Studies*, 7-10. Manchester: Manchester University Press, 1968.

Donfried, Karl Paul. "False Presuppositions in the Study of Romans." In *The Romans Debate*, edited by Karl Paul Donfried, 120-51. Minneapolis: Augsburg, 1977.

―――. "A Short Note on Romans 16." In *The Romans Debate*, edited by Karl Paul Donfried, 50-60. Minneapolis: Augsburg, 1977.

Drane, John W. "Why Did Paul Write Romans?" In *Pauline Studies: Essays Presented to F. F. Bruce on his 70th Birthday*, edited by Donald Hagner and Murray Harris, 208-27. Grand Rapids: Eerdmans, 1980.

Dülmen, Andrea van. *Die Theologie des Gesetzes bei Paulus*. Stuttgarter biblische Monographien 5. Stuttgart: Katholisches Bibelwerk, 1968.

Eadie, John. *A Commentary on the Greek Text of the Epistle of Paul to the Galatians*. Reprint. Grand Rapids: Baker, 1979.

―――. *A Commentary on the Greek Text of the Epistle of Paul to the Philippians*. Reprint. Minneapolis: James and Klock, 1977.

―――. *A Commentary on the Greek Text of the Epistles of Paul to the Thessalonians*. London: Macmillan, 1877.

Ellis, E. Earle. "Paul and His Co-Workers." *NTS* 17 (1970-71) 437-52.

―――. "'Weisheit' und 'Erkenntnis' im 1. Korintherbrief." In *Jesus and Paulus. Festschrift für Werner Georg Kümmel zum 70. Geburtstag*, edited by E. Earle Ellis and Erich Grässer, 108-29. Göttingen: Vandenhoeck & Ruprecht, 1975.

Epp, Eldon J. "Paul's Diverse Imageries of the Human Situation and His Unifying Theme of Freedom." In *Unity and Diversity in New Testament Theology*, 100-16. Edited by Robert A. Guelich. Grand Rapids: Eerdmans, 1978.

Fee, Gordon. "*Eidōlathuta* Once Again: I Corinthians 8-10." *Bib* 61 (1980) 172-97.

Feine, P., J. Behm, and W. G. Kümmel. *Einleitung in das Neue Testament*. 20th ed. Heidelberg: Quelle & Meyer, 1980.

Feuillet, A. "Les attaches bibliques des antithèse pauliniennes dans la primière partie de l' Épître aux Romains (1-8)." In *Mélanges Biblique*, edited by A. Descamps and André de Halleux, 70-94. Gembloux: Duculot, 1970.

Fisher, Fred. *Commentary on 1 and 2 Corinthians*. Waco, TX: Word, 1975.

Fitzmyer, Joseph A. *First Corinthians*. AB 32. New Haven: Yale University Press, 2008.

Frame, J. E. *A Critical and Exegetical Commentary on the Epistles of St. Paul to the Thessalonians*. ICC. Edinburgh: T. & T. Clark, 1912.

Friedrich, Gerhard. *Der Brief an die Philipper*. Das Neue Testament Deutsch 8. 14th ed. Göttingen: Vandenhoeck & Ruprecht, 1976.

―――. "Die Briefe an die Thessalonicher." In *Die Briefe an die Galater, Epheser, Philipper, Kolosser, Thessalonicher und Philemon*. Das Neue Testament Deutsch 8. Göttingen: Vandenhoeck & Ruprecht, 1976.

―――. "Freiheit und Liebe im ersten Korintherbrief." *TZ* 26 (1970) 81-98.

Frisk, H. *Griechisches Etymologisches Wörterbuch*. 3 Vols. Heidelberg: Winter, 1970.

Fuchs, Eric. "La faiblesse, gloire de l'apostolat selon Paul (Étude sur 2 Co 10-13)." *Études théologiques et religieuses* 2 (1980) 231-53.

Bibliography

Fuchs, Ernst. "Der Anteil des Geistes am Glauben bei Paulus. Ein Beitrag zum Verständnis von Römer 8." *ZTK* 72 (1975) 293–302.

———. *Die Freiheit des Glaubens: Römer 5–8 Ausgelegt.* München: Kaiser, 1949.

Furnish, Victor Paul. *The Love Command in the New Testament.* New York: Abingdon, 1972.

———. *Theology and Ethics in Paul.* Nashville: Abingdon, 1968.

———. *II Corinthians.* AB 32A. New York: Doubleday, 1984.

Gäckle, Volker. *Die Starken und die Schwachen in Korinth und Rom.* WUNT 200. Tübingen: Mohr/Siebeck, 2004.

Gager, John G. "Functional Diversity in Paul's Use of End-Time Language." *JBL* 89 (1970) 325–37.

Gamble, Harry Jr. *The Textual History of the Letter to the Romans.* Studies and Documents. Grand Rapids: Eerdmans, 1977.

Garland, David E. *1 Corinthians.* BEC. Grand Rapids: Baker, 2003.

———. "The Dispute over Food Sacrificed to Idols (1 Cor 8:1–11:1)." *Perspectives in Religious Studies* 30 (2003) 173–97.

Gaventa, Beverly Roberts. *First and Second Thessalonians.* Louisville: John Knox, 1998.

Georgi, D. *Die Gegner des Paulus im 2. Korintherbrief.* WMANT 11. Neukirche: Neukirchener Verlag, 1964.

Gnilka, Joachim. *Der Philipperbrief.* HTKNT 10. Freiburg: Herder, 1968.

Goddard, A. J., and S. A. Cummins. "Ill or Ill-Treated? Conflict and Persecution as the Context of Paul's Original Ministry in Galatia (Galatians 4:12–20)." *JSNT* 52 (1993) 93–126.

Goppelt, L. *Christentum und Judentum im ersten und zweiten Jahrhundert.* Beiträge zur Förderung christlicher Theologie 55. Gütersloh: Bertelsmann, 1954.

Grant, F. C. "The Economic Background of the New Testament." In *The Background of the New Testament and its Eschatology: Studies in Honour of C. H. Dodd*, edited by W. D. Davies and David Daube, 96–114. Cambridge: Cambridge University Press, 1956.

Grosheide, F. W. *The First Epistle to the Corinthians.* NICNT. Grand Rapids: Eerdmans, 1953.

Güttgemanns, Erhardt. *Der leidende Apostel und sein Herr.* Forschung zur Religion und Literatur des Alten und Neuen Testaments 90. Göttingen: Vandenhoeck & Ruprecht, 1966.

Guthrie, Donald. *New Testament Introduction.* Downers Grove: InterVarsity, 1971.

———. *The Pastoral Epistles.* Tyndale. Grand Rapids: Eerdmans, 1957.

Hainz, Joseph. *Ekklesia.* Strukturen paulinischer Gemeinde-Theologie und Gemeinde-Ordnung. Münchener Universitäts-schriften 9. Regensburg: Pustet, 1972.

Hanse, Hermann. "*Echō, ktl.*" In *TWNT* 2:816–32. Edited by G. Kittel and G. Friedrich. Stuttgart, 1935.

Harris, Murray. *2 Corinthians.* In vol. 10 of *The Expositor's Bible Commentary (Romans-Galatians).* Grand Rapids: Zondervan, 1976.

———. *The Second Epistle to the Corinthians.* Grand Rapids: Eerdmans, 2005.

Harrison, Everett F. *Introduction to the New Testament.* Grand Rapids: Eerdmans, 1971.

Hays, Richard B. *First Corinthians.* Louisville: John Knox, 1997.

Heading, John. *The Second Epistle to the Corinthians.* Kilmarnock: Ritchie, 1966.

Heckel, Ulrich. *Kraft in Schwachheit: Untersuchungen zu 2 Kor 10–13.* Tübingen: Mohr, 1993.

Bibliography

———. "Der Dorn im Fleisch: Die Krankheit des Paulus in 2 Kor 12,7 und Gal 4,13f." *ZNW* 84 (1993) 65-92.

Hendriksen, William. *Exposition of Galatians*. New Testament Commentary. Grand Rapids: Baker, 1968.

———. *Exposition of Philippians*. New Testament Commentary. Grand Rapids: Baker, 1962.

———. *Exposition of I and II Thessalonians*. New Testament Commentary. Grand Rapids: Baker, 1955.

Hengel, Martin. "MORS TURPISSIMA CRUCIS. Die Kreuzigung in der antiken Welt und die 'Torheit' des 'Wortes vom Kreuz.'" In *Rechtfertigung. Festschrift für Ernst Käsemann zum 70. Geburtstag*, edited by Johannes Friedrich et al., 125-84. Tübingen: Mohr, 1976.

Heinrichs, Albert. Review of *Der Apostel Paulus und die sokratische Tradition* by H. D. Betz. *JBL* 94 (1975) 310-14.

Hiebert, D. Edmond. *The Pauline Epistles*. Vol. 2 of *An Introduction to the New Testament*. Chicago: Moody, 1977.

Higgens, A. J. B. *The Lord's Supper in the New Testament*. London: SCM Press, 1956.

Hill, David. *Greek Words and Hebrew Meanings*. Cambridge: Cambridge University Press, 1967.

Hodge, Charles. *Commentary on the Epistle to the Romans*. Reprint. Grand Rapids: Eerdmans, 1972.

———. *An Exposition of the Second Epistle to the Corinthians*. New York: Robert Carter & Brothers, 1860.

Holtz, Gottfried. *Die Pastoralbriefe*. THNT 13. Berlin: Evangelische Verlagsanstalt, 1965.

Hubner, Hans. *Das Gesetz bei Paulus*. Forschungen zur Religion und Literatur des Alten und Neuen Testaments 119. Göttingen: Vandenhoeck & Ruprecht, 1978.

Hughes, Philip E. *Paul's Second Epistle to the Corinthians*. NICNT. Grand Rapids: Eerdmans, 1962.

Jegher-Bucher, Verena. "'The Thorn in the Flesh'/ 'Der Pfahl im Fleisch': Considerations about 2 Corinthians 12:7-10 in Connection with 12:1-13." In *Rhetorical Analysis of Scripture*, 338-97. Sheffield: Sheffield Academic Press, 1997.

Jeremias, J. "Das Gebetsleben Jesu." *ZNW* 25 (1926) 123-40.

Jewett, Robert. "The Epistolary Thanksgiving and the Integrity of Philippians." *NovT* 12 (1970) 40-53.

———. *Paul's Anthropological Terms. A Study of Their Use in Conflict Settings*. Arbeiten zur Geschichte des antiken Judentums und des Urchristentum 10. Leiden: Brill, 1971.

———. *Romans*. Minneapolis: Fortress, 2007.

Kamlah, E. "Wie beurteilt Paulus sein Leiden?" *ZNW* 54 (1963) 217-32.

Karris, Robert J. "The Occasion of Romans: A Response to Professor Donfried." *CBQ* 36 (1974) 356-58.

———. "Romans 14:1-15:13 and the Occasion of Romans." In *The Romans Debate*, edited by Karl Paul Donfried, 75-99. Minneapolis: Augsburg, 1977.

Käsemann, Ernst. "Der gottesdienstliche Schrei nach der Freiheit." In *Paulinische Perspektiven*, 211-36. Tübingen: Mohr, 1969.

———. *Die Legitimität des Apostels: Eine Untersuchung zu II Korinther 10-13*. Darmstadt: Wissenschaftliche Buchgesellschaft, 1956.

Bibliography

———. *An die Römer*. Handbuch zum Neuen Testament 8a. 4th ed. Tübingen: Mohr, 1973.

Kaye, Bruce. *The Thought Structure of Romans with Special Reference to Chapter 6*. Austin, TX: Schola, 1979.

Kent, Homer A. *The Pastoral Epistles*. Chicago: Moody, 1958.

Kitzberger, I. "Die 'Starken' und 'Schwachen' in Rom und Korinth: Eine Darstellung des Konfliktes und des paulinischen Lösungsversuches." Diplom-Arbeit, University of Salzburg, 1977.

Köster, H. "The Purpose of the Polemic of a Pauline Fragment (Phil. III)." *NTS* 8 (1961-62) 317-32.

Krause, Wilhelm. *Die Griechen*. Wien: Deuticke, 1969.

Krug, Johannes. *Die Kraft des Schwachen: Ein Beitrag zur paulinischen Apostolatstheologie*. Tübingen: Francke, 2001.

———. "Der Dorn im Fleisch: Die Krankheit des Paulus in 2 Kor 12,7 und Gal 4:13f." *ZNW* 84 (1993) 65-92.

———. "Jer 9,22f. als Schlüssel für 2 Kor 10-13: Ein Beispiel für die methodischen Probleme in der gegenwärtigen Diskussion über den Schriftgebrauch bei Paulus." In *Schriftauslegung im antiken Judentum und im Urchristentum*, 206-25. Tübingen: Mohr, 1994.

Kurapati, C. J. "Spiritual Bondage and Christian Freedom according to Paul: An Exegetical and Theological Exposition of the Epistle to the Galatians." PhD diss., Princeton, 1976.

Kuss, Otto. *Der Römerbrief*. 2 vols. Regensburg: Pustet, 1957.

Lagrange, M. J. *Saint Paul: Épître aux Galates*. Echter Bibel. Paris: Lecoffre, 1950.

Lambrecht, Jan. "Zwakheid en Kracht (2 Korintiers 12, 1-13) Kritische Beschouwingen bij de Nieuwe Bijbelvertalling." *Bijdragen* 66 (2005) 326-40.

———. "The Fool's Speech and its Context: Paul's Particular Way of Arguing in 2 Cor 10-13." *Bib* 82 (2001) 305-24.

———. "Dangerous Boasting: Paul's Self-Commendation in 2 Corinthians 10-13." In *The Corinthian Correspondence*, 325-46. Louvain : Leuven University Press, 1996.

Lea, Thomas D., and David Alan Black. *The New Testament: Its Background and Message*. 2nd ed. Nashville: Broadman & Holman, 2003.

Leivestad, Ragnar. *Christ the Conqueror: Ideas of Conflict and Victory in the New Testament*. London: SPCK, 1954.

Lenski, R. C. H. *The Interpretation of St. Paul's First and Second Epistle to the Corinthians*. Columbus, Ohio: Wartburg, 1946.

———.*The Interpretation of St. Paul's First and Second Epistle to the Corinthians*. Minneapolis, MN: Augsburg, 1963.

Lietzmann, Hans. *An die Korinther I/II*. Handbuch zum Neuen Testament 9. 5th ed. Tübingen: Mohr, 1969.

Lightfoot, J. B. *Saint Paul's Epistle to the Galatians*. London: Macmillan, 1892.

Limbeck, M. *Von der Ohnmacht des Rechts. Untersuchungen zur Gesetzeskritik des Neuen Testaments*. Düsseldorf: Patmos, 1972.

Lincoln, A. T. "'Paul the Visionary': The Setting and Significance of the Rapture to Paradise in II Corinthians xii. 1-10." *NTS* 25 (1979) 204-20.

Link, H. -G. "Schwachheit." *TBNT* 2 (1971) 1101-05.

Lochman, J. M. "Dein ist die Kraft: Die Macht Gottes und die Welt der Mächte." *TZ* 37 (1981) 45-61.

Bibliography

Lohmeyer, Ernst. *Die Briefe an die Philipper, an die Kolosser und an Philemon*. KEK. Göttingen: Vandenhoeck & Ruprecht, 1953.

Lohse, Eduard. *Die Entstehung des Neuen Testaments*. 3d ed. Stuttgart: Kohlhammer, 1979.

———. *Grundriss der neutestamentliche Theologie*. Theologische Wissenschaft 5. 2d ed. Stuttgart: Kohlhammer, 1979.

———. "*Ho nomos tou pneumatos tēs zōēs*: Exegetische Anmerkungen zu Röm 8,2." In *Neues Testament und christliche Existenz*, 279-87. Edited by H. D. Betz and L. Schattroff. FS Herbert Braun. Tübingen: Mohr, 1973.

Longenecker, Richard N. *Galatians*. WBC 41. Dallas: Word, 1990.

———. *Paul, Apostle of Liberty*. New York: Harper & Row, 1964.

———. "The Pedagogical Nature of the Law in Galatians 3:19-4:7." *JETS* 25 (1982) 53-61.

Loubser, Johannes A. "Paul and the Politics of Apocalyptic Mysticism: An Exploration of 2 Cor 11:30-12:10." *Neot* 34 (2000) 191-206.

Lührmann, Dieter. *Glaube im frühen Christentum*. Gütersloh: Mohn, 1976.

Lyonnet, Stanislas. *Il Nuovo Testamento alla Luce del' Antico*. Studies of Brescia Paideia 3. Brescia: Paideia, 1972.

MacGorman, J. W. "The Law as Paidagogos: A Study in Pauline Analogy." In *New Testament Studies: Essays in Honor of Ray Summers*, edited by Huber L. Drumright and Curtis Vaughan, 99-111. Waco: Markham, 1975.

MacRae, G. W. "A Note on Romans 8:26-27." *HTR* 73 (1980) 227-30.

Manson, T. W. "Paul the Christian and Theologian." *On John and Paul: Some Selected Theological Themes*. Edited by Matthew Black. London: SCM, 1967.

———. *Studies in the Gospels and Epistles*. Edited by Matthew Black. Manchester: University Press, 1962.

Marchel, W. *Abba, Père! La prière du Christ et des chretienes*. AnBib 19. Rome: Biblical Institute, 1963.

Martin, Ralph P. *The Epistle of Paul to the Philippians*. Tyndale. Grand Rapids: Eerdmans, 1969.

———. *2 Corinthians*. WBC 40. Waco: Word, 1986.

Martin, Troy W. "Whose Flesh? What Temptation? (Galatians 4:13-14)." *JSNT* 74 (1999) 65-91.

Martyn, J. Louis. *Galatians*. AB 33A. New York: Doubleday, 1997.

Marxsen, Willi. "Auslegung von 1 Thess 4, 13-18." *ZTK* 66 (1969) 22-37.

———. *Einleitung in das Neue Testament*. 3d ed. Gütersloh: Mohn, 1964.

Masson, Charles. *Les Deux Épîtres de Saint Paul aux Thessaloniciens*. Commentaire du Nouveau Testament 11a. Neuchatel: Delachaux & Niestlé, 1957.

Maurer, Christian. "Glaubensbindung und Gewissensfreiheit im Neuen Testament." *TZ* 17 (1961) 107-17.

———. "*Synoida, syneidēsis*." In *TWNT* 7:897-918. Edited by G. Kittel and G. Friedrich. Stuttgart, 1964.

McCant, Jerry W. "Paul's Thorn of Rejected Apostleship." *NTS* 34 (1988) 550-72.

McDonald, J. I. H. "Was Romans XVI a Separate Letter?" *NovT* 16 (1970) 369-72.

Mearns, C. L. "Early Eschatological Development in Paul: The Evidence of I and II Thessalonians." *NTS* 27 (1981) 137-57.

Meinertz, M. *Die Pastoralbriefe des Heiligen Paulus*. 4th ed. Bonn: Hanstein, 1931.

Meredith, Anthony. "Asceticism—Christian and Greek." *Journal of Theological Studies* 27 (1976) 313-32.

Bibliography

Metzger, Bruce. *The New Testament, Its Background, Growth, and Content*. New York: Abingdon, 1965.
———. *A Textual Commentary on the Greek New Testament*. New York: United Bible Societies, 1971.
Meyer, Paul W. "The Holy Spirit in the Pauline Letters." *Int* 33 (1979) 3-18.
Michel, Otto. *Der Brief an die Römer*. KEK 4. 5th ed. Göttingen: Vandenhoeck & Ruprecht, 1978.
Milligan, George. *St. Paul's Epistles to the Thessalonians*. Reprinted. Minneapolis: Klock & Klock, 1980.
Minear, P. S. *The Obedience of Faith: The Purposes of Paul in the Epistle to the Romans*. Studies in Biblical Theology 19. London: SCM, 1971.
Minn, H. R. *The Thorn That Remained, or St. Paul's Thorn in the Flesh*. Auckland: Institute Press, 1972.
Mitchell, Curtis. "The Holy Spirit's Intercessory Ministry." *BSac* 139 (1982) 230-42.
Moore, A. L. *The Parousia in the New Testament*. Novum Testamentum Supplement 13. Leiden: Brill, 1966.
Morgenthaler, Robert. *Statistik des neutestamentlichen Wortschatzes*. Zürich: Gotthelf, 1958.
Morray-Jones, C. R. A. "Paradise Revisited (2 Cor 12:1-12): The Jewish Mystical Background of Paul's Apostolate." *HTR* 86 (1993) 265-92.
Morris, Leon. *The First and Second Epistles to the Thessalonians*. NICNT. Grand Rapids: Eerdmans, 1959.
———. *The Gospel of John*. NICNT. Grand Rapids: Eerdmans, 1971.
———. "The Theme of Romans." In *Apostolic History and the Gospel: Biblical and Historical Essays Presented to F. F. Bruce on His 60th Birthday*, edited by W. Ward Gasque and Ralph P. Martin, 249-63. Grand Rapids: Eerdmans, 1970.
Moule, C. F. D. "The Judgment Theme in the Sacraments." In *The Background of the New Testament and its Eschatology: Studies in Honour of C. H. Dodd*, edited by W. D. Davies and David Daube, 464-81. Cambridge: Cambridge University Press, 1956.
Moule, H. C. G. *The Epistle to the Philippians*. Cambridge Bible. Cambridge: Cambridge University Press, 1893.
Muller, Jac J. *The Epistles of Paul to the Philippians and to Philemon*. NICNT. Grand Rapids: Eerdmans, 1955.
Mullins, Terence Y. "Paul's Thorn in the Flesh." *JBL* 76 (1957) 299-303.
Mundle, Wilhelm. *Der Glaubensbegriff des Paulus*. Darmstadt: Wissenschaftliche Buchgesellschaft, 1977.
Murray, John. *The Epistle to the Romans*. NICNT. Grand Rapids: Eerdmans, 1968.
Mussner, F. *Der Galaterbrief*. HTKNT. Freiburg: Herder, 1974.
Niederwimmer, Kurt. "Das Gebet des Geistes, Röm. 8, 26f." *TZ* 20 (1964) 252-65.
———. "Das Problem der Ethik bei Paulus." *TZ* 24 (1968) 81-92.
Nielsen, H. K. "Paulus' Verwendung des Begriffes *Dynamis*: Eine Replik zur Kreuzestheologie." *Die Paulinische Literatur und Theologie*. Edited by S. Pedersen. Göttingen: Vandenhoeck & Ruprecht, 1980.
O'Brien, Peter T. "Thanksgiving within the Structure of Pauline Theology." In *Pauline Studies: Essays Presented to F. F. Bruce on His 70th Birthday*, edited by Donald Hagner and Murray Harris, 50-66. Grand Rapids: Eerdmans, 1980.
O'Donnell, Hugh. *Education in Wisdom*. Rome: Gregorian University Press, 1969.

Bibliography

Oepke, A. *Der Brief des Paulus an die Galater.* THNT 9. 2nd ed. Berlin: Evangelische Verlagsanstalt, 1957.
Olson, S. N. "Confidence Expressions in Paul: Epistolary Conventions and the Purpose of 2 Corinthians." PhD diss., Yale, 1976.
O'Neill, J. C. *Paul's Letter to the Romans.* London: Cox & Wyman, 1975.
———. *The Recovery of Paul's Letter to the Galatians.* London: SPCK, 1972.
Oostendorp, D. W. *Another Jesus: A Gospel of Jewish-Christian Superiority in II Corinthians.* Kampen: Kok, 1967.
Osten-Sacken, Peter von der. *Römer 8 als Beispiel paulinischer Theologie.* Forschungen zur Religion und Literature des Alten und Neuen Testaments 112. Göttingen: Vandenhoeck & Ruprecht, 1975.
Pallis, A. *To the Romans.* Liverpool: Liverpool Booksellers, 1920.
Palmer, W. W. "To Die is Gain (Phil 1:21)." *NovT* 17 (1975) 203–18.
Paulsen, H. *Überlieferung und Auslegung in Römer 8.* WMANT 43. Neukirche: Neukirchener Verlag, 1974.
Pearson, Birger. *The Pneumatikos-Psychikos Terminology in I Corinthians.* SBLDS 12. Missoula, MT: University of Montana, 1973.
Pickett, Raymond. *The Cross in Corinth: The Social Significance of the Death of Jesus.* JSNTSup 143. Sheffield: Sheffield Academic Press, 1997.
Pierce, C. A. *Conscience in the New Testament.* Studies in Biblical Theology 15. Chicago: Allenson, 1955.
Polaski, Sandra Hack. "2 Corinthians 12:1–10: Paul's Trauma." *RevExp* 105 (2008) 279–84.
Pollard, T. E. "The Integrity of Philippians." *NTS* 13 (1966) 57–66.
Powers, Janet Everts. "A 'Thorn in the Flesh': The Appropriation of Textual Meaning." *Journal of Pentecostal Theology* 18 (2001) 85–99.
Prast, Franz. *Presbyter und Evangelium in nachapostolischer Zeit.* Forschung zur Bibel 29. Stuttgart: Katholisches Bibelwerk, 1979.
Quervain, Alfred de. "Vom Gebet als dem rechten Gottesdienst und dem eigentlichen Werk des Christen." *TZ* 2 (1946) 192–204.
Rahtjen, B. D. "The Three Letters of Paul to the Philippians." *NTS* 6 (1959–60) 167–73.
Rauer, Max. *Die "Schwachen" in Korinth und Rom.* Biblische Studien (Freiburg, 1895) 21. Freiburg: Herder, 1923.
Reasoner, Mark. *The Strong and the Weak: Romans 14.1–15.13 in Context.* Cambridge: Cambridge University Press, 1999.
Reicke, Bo. "Body and Soul in the New Testament." *ST* 19 (1965) 200–12.
———. "Caesarea, Rome, and the Captivity Epistles." In *Apostolic History and the Gospel: Biblical and Historical Essays Presented to F. F. Bruce on His 60th Birthday,* 277–86. Edited by W. Ward Gasque and Ralph P. Martin. Grand Rapids: Eerdmans, 1970.
———. "Chronologie der Pastoralbriefe." *Theologische Literaturzeitung* 101 (1976) 82–94.
———. *The Disobedient Spirits and Christian Baptism.* Copenhaven: Munksgaard, 1946.
———. "The Law and the World according to Paul." *JBL* 70 (1951) 259–76.
———. *Neutestamentliche Zeitgeschichte.* 2d ed. Berlin: Walter de Gruyter & Co., 1968.
———. "*Proistēmi.*" In *TWNT* 6:700–03. Edited by G. Kittel and G. Friedrich. Stuttgart, 1969.
———. "Syneidesis in Röm. 2, 15." *TZ* 12 (1956) 157–61.
———. "Unité chréttiene et diaconie, Phil. ii 1–11." In *Neotestamentica et Patristica: Eine Freundsgabe, Herrn Professor Dr. Oscar Cullmann zu seinem 60 Geburtstag überreicht,*

edited by W. C. van Unnik, 203-12. Supplements to Novum Testamentum 6. Leiden: Brill, 1962.

Rengstorf, K. H. "*Apostellō, ktl.*" In *TWNT* 1:397-447. Edited by G. Kittel and G. Friedrich. Stuttgart, 1933.

Rickards, Raymond R. "The Translation of *tē astheneia* in Romans 8:26." *BT* 28 (1977) 247-48.

Ridderbos, H. *The Epistle of Paul to the Churches of Galatia*. NICNT. Grand Rapids: Eerdmans, 1953.

―――. *Paul, an Outline of His Theology*. Translated by John de Witt. Grand Rapids: Eerdmans, 1975.

Rigaux, B. *Saint Paul: Les Épîtres aux Thessaloniciens*. EB. Paris: Lecoffre, 1956.

Rissi, M. "Die Menschlichkeit Jesu nach Hebr. 5, 7-8." *TZ* 11 (1955) 28-45.

Robertson, A. T. *A Grammar of the Greek New Testament in the Light of Historical Research*. Nashville: Broadman, 1934.

Robinson, John A. T. *The Body*. SBT 5. London: SCM, 1957.

Roetzel, Calvin J. *Judgement in the Community. A Study of the Relationship between Eschatology and Ecclesiology in Paul*. Leiden: Brill, 1972.

―――. *The Letters of Paul: Conversations in Context*. Atlanta: John Knox, 1975.

―――. "The Language of War (2 Cor. 10:1-6) and the Language of Weakness (2 Cor. 11:21b-13:10)." *BibInt* 17 (2009) 77-99.

Rogers, Cleon. "The Dionesian Background of Ephesians 5:18." *BSac* 136 (1979) 249-57.

Ross, J. M. "Pánta synergeî, Rom. VIII. 28." *TZ* 34 (1978) 82-85.

Ruef, John. *Paul's First Letter to Corinth*. Philadelphia: Westminster, 1977.

Ruiz, Guillermo. "Ma Puissance se déploie dans la faiblesse (II Cor, 12, 9) une interprétation d'Irénée de Lyon." In *Recherches et tradition*, 259-69. Paris: Beauchesne, 1992.

Saake, Helmut. "Paulus als Ekstatiker." *NovT* 15 (1973) 153-60.

Salis, Pierre. "L'écharde dans la Chair: Un Signe visible de la présence de Dieu? La dimension dramatique de la Vie: Perspectives à partir de II Corinthiens 12,1-10." *Revue de théologie et de philosophie* 127 (1995) 27-41.

Sand, Alexander. *Der Begriff "Fleisch" in den paulinischen Hauptbriefen*. Biblische Untersuchungen 2. Regensburg: Pustet, 1967.

Sanday, W., and A. Headlam. *A Critical and Exegetical Commentary on the Epistle to the Romans*. ICC. Edinburgh: T. & T. Clark, 1902.

Sandelin, Karl-Gustav. *Die Auseinandersetzung mit der Weisheit in 1 Korinther 15*. Abo: Abo Akademi, 1976.

Schlatter, Adolph. *Der Glaube im Neuen Testament*. Leiden: Brill, 1885.

Schlier, Heinrich. *Der Brief an die Galater*. KEK. 14th ed. Göttingen: Vandenhoeck & Ruprecht, 1971.

―――. *Grundzüge einer paulinischen Theologie*. Freiburg: Herder, 1978.

―――. "*Kerdos, kerdainō.*" In *TWNT* 3:671-72. Edited by G. Kittel and G. Friedrich. Stuttgart, 1938.

Schmidt, H. -G., ed. *In der Schwäche ist Kraft: Behinderte Menschen im Alten und Neuen Testament*. Hamburg: Wittig, 1979.

Schmidt, K. L. "*Kolaphizō.*" In *TWNT* 3:818-21. Edited by G. Kittel and G. Friedrich. Stuttgart, 1938.

Schmithals, Walter. *Die Gnosis in Korinth: Eine Untersuchung zu den Korintherbriefen*. SNT 9. Gütersloh: Mohn, 1975.

―――. *Der Römerbrief als historisches Problem*. SNT 9. Gütersloh: Mohn, 1975.

Bibliography

Schneider, J. "*Stenazō, ktl.*" In *TWNT* 7:600–03. Edited by G. Kittel and G. Friedrich. Stuttgart, 1964.

Schneider, Sebastian. "Glaubensmängel in Korinth: Eine neue Deutung der 'Schwachen, Kranken, Schlafenden' in 1 Kor 11,30. " *FNeot* 9 (1996) 3–19.

Schrage, Wolfgang. *Die konkreten Einzelgebote in der paulinischen Paränese.* Gütersloh: Mohn, 1961.

Schreiber, Alfred. *Die Gemeinde in Korinth. Versuch einer gruppendynamischen Betrachtung der Entwicklung der Gemeinde von Korinth auf der Basis des ersten Korinther-briefes.* Neutestamentliche Abhandlungen 12. Münster: Aschendorff, 1977.

Schreiner, Thomas R. *Romans.* BECNT. Grand Rapids: Baker, 1998.

Schütz, J. H. *Paul and the Anatomy of Apostolic Authority.* SNTSMS 26. Cambridge: Cambridge University Press, 1975.

Schweizer, Eduard. *Heiliger Geist.* Stuttgart: Kreuz, 1978.

———. "Die 'Mystik' des Sterbens und Auferstehens mit Christus bei Paulus." *Neutestamentliche Aufsätze* (1955–1970). Zürich: Zwingli, 1970.

———. "*Sarx, ktl.*" In *TWNT* 7:118–51. Edited by G. Kittel and G. Friedrich. Stuttgart, 1964.

———. "The Service of Worship. An Exposition of I Corinthians 14." *Neot.* Zürich: Zwingli, 1963.

Sieffert, F. *Der Brief an die Galater.* KEK 7. 7th ed. Göttingen: Vandenhoeck & Ruprecht, 1880.

Smalley, Stephen S. "Spiritual Gifts and 1 Corinthians 12–16." *JBL* 87 (1968) 427–33.

Smith, Charles R. "Errant Aorist Interpreters." *GTJ* 2 (1981) 205–26.

Snoeberger, Mark A. "Weakness or Wisdom? Fundamentalists and Romans 14.1—15.13." *Detroit Baptist Seminary Journal* 12 (2007) 29–49.

Spicq, C. *Notes de Lexicographie Néo-Testamentaire.* 2 vols. Göttingen: Vandenhoeck & Ruprecht, 1978.

———. *Saint Paul: Les Épîtres Pastorales.* EB. 4th ed. Paris: Lecoffre, 1969.

Stählin, Gustav. "*Asthenēs, ktl.*" In *TWNT* 1:118–51. Edited by G. Kittel and G. Friedrich. Stuttgart, 1933.

Stanley, David. *Boasting in the Lord: The Phenomenon of Prayer in Saint Paul.* New York: Paulist, 1973.

Stendahl, Krister. "The Apostle Paul and the Introspective Conscience of the West." *HTR* 56 (1963) 199–215.

———. "Paul at Prayer." *Int* 34 (1980) 240–49.

Stephenson, A. M. G. "A Defense of the Integrity of 2 Corinthians." *The Authority and Integrity of the New Testament.* Theological Collections 4. London: SPCK, 1965.

Tannehill, Robert. *Dying and Rising With Christ.* BZNW 32. Berlin: Töpelmann, 1967.

Tasker, R. V. G. *The Second Epistle of Paul to the Corinthians.* TNTC. Grand Rapids: Eerdmans, 1971.

Taylor, T. M. "The Place of Origin of Romans." *JBL* 67 (1948) 281–95.

Thayer, Joseph. *A Greek-English Lexicon of the New Testament.* 4th ed. Edinburgh: T. & T. Clark, 1955.

Theissen, Gerd. "Die Starken und Schwachen in Korinth." *Evangelische Theologie* 35 (1975) 155–72.

Thierry, J. J. "Der Dorn im Fleische (2 Kor xii 7–9)." *NovT* 5 (1962) 301–10.

Turner, Nigel. *Style.* Vol. 4 of *A Grammar of New Testament Greek*, by J. H. Moulton. Edinburgh: T. & T. Clark, 1976.

Tyson, Joseph B. "'Works of Law' in Galatians." *JBL* 92 (1973) 423-31.
Viard, André. *Saint Paul: Épître aux Galates*. Paris: Lecoffre, 1964.
Vincent, M. R. *Word Studies in the New Testament*. 4 vols. Grand Rapids: Eerdmans, 1946.
Vos, G. "Alleged Development in Paul's Teaching on the Resurrection." *Princeton Theological Review* 27 (1929) 193-226.
Wan, Sze-Kar. *Power in Weakness*. Harrisburg, PA: Trinity, 2000.
Wanamaker, Charles A. *The Epistle to the Thessalonians*. NIGTC. Grand Rapids: Eerdmans, 1990.
Ward, Roy Bowen. "The Works of Abraham." *HTR* 61 (1968) 283-90.
Wendland, H.-D. *Die Briefe an die Korinther*. Das Neue Testament Deutsch 7. 15th ed. Göttingen: Vandenhoeck & Ruprecht, 1980.
Wenham, David. "The Christian Life: A Consideration of the Nature of Christian Experience in Paul." In *Pauline Studies: Essays Presented to F. F. Bruce on His 70th Birthday*, edited by Donald Hagner and Murray Harris, 80-94. Grand Rapids: Eerdmans, 1980.
Whitely, D. E. H. *The Theology of St. Paul*. Oxford: Blackwell, 1964.
Wilckens, U. *Weisheit und Torheit. Eine exegetisch-religionsgeschichtliche Untersuchung zu I Kor. 1 und 2*. BHT 26. Tübingen: Mohr, 1959.
Williams, S. K. "The 'Righteousness of God' in Romans." *JBL* 99 (1980) 241-90.
Willis, Wendell. "1 Corinthians 8-10: A Retrospective after Twenty-Five Years." *Restoration Quarterly* (2007) 103-12.
Wohlenberg, G. *Der erste und zweite Thessalonicherbrief*. KNT 12. Leipzig: Deichert, 1903.
Wolter, Michael. *Rechtfertigung und zukünftiges Heil. Untersuchungen zu Röm 5, 1-11*. BZNW 43. Berlin: de Gruyter, 1978.
Woyke, Johannes. "Nochmals zu den 'Schwachen und unfähigen Elementen' (Gal 4.9) Paulus, Philo und die *stoicheia tou kosmou*." *NTS* 54 (2008) 221-34.
Yamauchi, Edwin. "Some Alleged Evidences for Pre-Christian Gnosticism." In *New Dimensions in New Testament Study*, edited by Richard N. Longenecker and Merrill C. Tenney, 46-70. Grand Rapids: Zondervan, 1974.
Zahn, Theodor. *Der Brief des Paulus an die Galater*. Leipzig: Deichert, 1905.
Zmijewski, Josef. *Der Stil der paulinischen "Narrenrede." Analyse der Sprachgestaltung in 2 Kor. 11, 1-12, 10 als Beitrag zur Methodik von Stiluntersuchungen neutestamentlicher Texte*. Bonner Biblische Beiträge 52. Köln-Bonn: Hanstein, 1978.
Zuck, Roy B. "The Doctrine of the Conscience." *BSac* 126 (1969) 329-40.

Author Index

Akin, Daniel. 88

Baird, William. 131
Baltensweiler, H. 26
Bammel, Ernst. 40
Bandstra, A. J. 34, 35, 36, 38
Barr, James. xvii
Barré, M. L. 4, 100
Barrett, C. K. 63, 64, 69, 75, 76, 96, 97, 128, 132, 133
Barth, Gerhard. 138
Bates, W. H. 57
Bauer, Karl-Adolf. 83
Behm, J. 17, 55
Best, Ernest. 14, 18, 24
Betz, Hans Dieter. 35, 36, 45, 47, 85
Binder, Hermann. 46, 47
Black, Matthew. 130
Black, David. ix, 68, 74, 137, 138, 142, 162
Blackman, E. C. xvii
Boice, J. M. 34, 36, 41, 45
Bornkamm, Gunther. 80, 137
Bouttier, Michel. 107
Bring, R. 48
Bruce, F. F. 13, 16, 76, 120
Buchsel, Friedrich. 133
Buck, C. D. 2, 80
Bultmann, Rudolph. 14, 65
Burdick, Donald W. 36
Burton, E. 34, 35, 43
Byrne, Brendan. 37

Cambier, J. xvii, 103

Chantraine, P. 1, 2, 3
Clavier, H. 83
Collange, J. -F. 57
Conzelmann, Hans. 59, 63, 64, 71, 76, 124
Cranfield, C. E. B. 117, 119, 120, 122, 128, 130
Cullmann, Oscar. 83, 126, 127

Dahl, Nils A. 113
Delling, Gerhard. 22, 34, 35, 40, 100
Dietzel, Armin. 125
Dihle, Albert. 23
Dobschutz, E. von. 25
Dodd, C. H. 76
Donfried, Karl Paul. 112, 135, 136
Drane, John W. 113

Eadie, John. 22, 35, 45, 47, 48, 49
Ellis, E. Earle. 61, 73
Epp, Eldon J. 51

Fee, Gordon. 69
Feine, P. 55
Fisher, Fred. 64, 67, 76, 89
Fitzmyer, Joseph A. 80
Frame, J. E. 11, 17, 25, 57
Friedrich, Gerhard. 21, 25, 28, 74, 139
Fuchs, Eric. xvii, 110, 156–57
Fuchs, Ernst. 119, 125

Gäckle, Volker. 151
Gager, John G. 125, 127
Gamble, Harry Jr. 112, 113

Author Index

Garland, David E. 74
Gaventa, Beverly Roberts. 25
Georgi, D. 54
Gnilka, Joachim. 141
Goppelt, L. 132
Grant, F. C. 109
Grosheide, F. W. 61, 64, 67
Güttgemanns, Erhardt. xvii, 45
Guthrie, Donald. 10, 13, 55, 112, 114, 137, 142, 143

Hainz, Joseph. 91
Hanse, Hermann. 26
Harris, Murray. 54, 58, 89, 94, 99
Harrison, Everett F. 10, 112, 113
Hays, Richard B. 74
Heading, John. 89
Headlam, A. 122
Heckel, Ulrich. 87, 98
Hendriksen, William. 16, 35, 47, 137, 141
Hengel, Martin. 61
Hiebert, D. Edmond. 10–11
Higgens, A. J. B. 79
Hill, David. xvii, 5
Hodge, Charles. 99, 121, 128, 133, 134
Holtz, Gottfried. 144
Hubner, Hans. 124
Hughes, Philip E. 55, 58, 59, 89, 95, 98, 99–100

Jeremias, J. 101, 128
Jewett, Robert. 47, 118, 137

Kamlah, E. 91, 142
Kasemann, Ernst. xvii, 96, 117, 121, 129, 133
Kaye, Bruce. 120
Kent, Homer A. 143
Kitzberger, I. xvii
Krause, Wilhelm. 143
Kurapati, C. J. 34
Kümmel, W. G. 55, 112, 114, 142

Lagrange, M. J. 42–43, 44
Lea, Thomas D. 142
Leivestad, Ragnar. 50
Lenski, R. C. H. 63, 73, 76

Lietzmann, Hans. 65, 67, 76, 83, 89, 99
Lightfoot, J. B. 48, 49
Limbeck, M. 123
Lincoln, A. T. 97
Link, H. –G. xvi
Lochman, J. M. 157
Lohmeyer, Ernst. 140
Lohse, Eduard. 13, 55, 59, 112, 123
Longenecker, Richard N. 38, 149
Lührmann, Dieter. 117
Lyonnet, Stanislas. 122

MacGorman, J. W. 38
MacRae, G. W. 128
Manson, T. W. 22, 31, 149
Marchel, W. 129
Martin, Ralph P. 93, 137
Martyn, J. Louis. 41
Marxsen, Willi. 13
Masson, Charles. 21, 25
Maurer, Christian. 71, 75
McDonald, J. I. H. 112
Mearns, C. L. 23, 24
Meinertz, M. 143
Meredith, Anthony. 143
Metzger, Bruce. 44, 70, 133, 139, 142
Meyer, Paul W. 125
Michel, Otto. 112, 120, 128, 129, 130, 133
Milligan, George. 22
Minear, P. S. 136
Minn, H. R. 99
Mitchell, Curtis. 125
Moore, A. L. 24
Morgenthaler, Robert. 7
Morris, Leon. 5, 17, 20, 113
Moule, C. F. D. 80
Moule, H. C. G. 141
Muller, Jac J. 139
Mullins, Terence Y. 99
Mundle, Wilhelm. 118
Murray, John. 121–22, 128, 133
Mussner, F. 34, 43, 45, 52
Niederwimmer, Kurt. 125, 129

Nielsen, H. K. 105
O'Brien, Peter T. 132
O'Donnell, Hugh. 60

Author Index

Oepke, A. 43, 45, 47
Olson, S. N. 85
O'Neill, J. C. 42
Oostendorp, D. W. 54
Osten-Sacken, Peter von der. 125

Palmer, W. W. 110
Paulsen, H. 122, 125
Pearson, Birger. 159
Pickett, Raymond. 68
Pierce, C. A. 74
Pollard, T. E. 137
Powers, Janet Everts. 98
Prast, Franz. 17

Quervain, Alfred de. 127

Rahtjen, B. D. 137
Rauer, Max. xvii, 69, 109, 110, 131, 132, 134, 135
Reasoner, Mark. 136–37
Reicke, Bo. 17, 31, 34, 40, 47, 71, 122, 137, 142, 143
Rengstorf, K. H. 138
Rickards, Raymond R. 127
Ridderbos, H. 36, 45, 49, 158
Rigaux, B. 25
Rissi, M. 101
Robertson, A. T. 43, 100
Robinson, John A. T. 47, 116
Roetzel, Calvin J. 13, 78, 131
Rogers, Cleon. 144
Ross, J. M. 130
Ruef, John. 70, 75, 82

Saake, Helmut. 96
Sand, Alexander. 121, 122
Sanday, W. 122
Sandelin, Karl-Gustav. 82
Schlatter, Adolph. 118
Schlier, Heinrich. 41, 44, 45, 47, 77, 120
Schmidt, H. -G., ed. xvii
Schmidt, K. L. 48
Schmithals, Walter. 132
Schneider, J. 130
Schneider, Sebastian. 80
Schrage, Wolfgang. 39
Schreiber, Alfred. 109

Schreiner, Thomas R. 123
Schütz, J. H. 65, 107
Schweizer, Eduard. 47, 129, 155
Smalley, Stephen S. 160
Smith, Charles R. 44
Spicq, C. 22
Stählin, Gustav. xvi, 24
Stanley, David. 126
Stendahl, Krister. 71, 126
Stephenson, A. M. G. 57

Tannehill, Robert. 110, 155
Tasker, R. V. G. 58, 89, 100
Taylor, T. M. 112
Thayer, Joseph. 26, 49, 63, 64, 77, 79, 141
Theissen, Gerd. xvii, 69, 109
Tyson, Joseph B. 39

Vincent, M. R. 26, 63
Vos, G. 83

Wan, Sze-Kar. 86
Wanamaker, Charles A. 11, 17, 24
Ward, Roy Bowen. 116
Wendland, H.-D. 62, 63, 64, 76, 97, 99
Wenham, David. 160
Wilckens, U. 54, 88
Williams, S. K. 115
Wohlenberg, G. 24
Wolter, Michael. 120

Yamauchi, Edwin. 54

Zahn, Theodor. 45, 47
Zmijewski, Josef. 85, 102
Zuck, Roy B. 71,

Scripture Index

Genesis
15:5	116
16:2	118
17:13	116
17:17	116
18:11	116
20:18	118
29:17	4
32:24–32	153

Exodus
40:34	102
15:2	116

Leviticus
19:18	39, 131

Judges
16:17	4

1 Samuel
1:9–20	118

2 Samuel
3:1	4

2 Kings
19:26	4

Job
2:1–5	99, 100

Psalms
6:3	4

Proverbs
24:16	4

Isaiah
29:14	59
53:4	5

Jeremiah
6:21	4
18:15	4

Ezekiel
16:26	116
17:14	4
23:20	116
34:4	4

Scripture Index

Daniel

11:14	4
11:19	4
11:33	4
11:35	4

Zephaniah

1:3	4

Matthew

5:5	68
5:10	68
5:11	102
5:12	102
10:8	5
26:37	140
26:41	5

Mark

8:34	92
9:42	92
9:50	18
14:33	140
14:36	101
14:38	5
16:18	153

Luke

8:2	6
9:2	5
10:9	5 (2x), 6
13:11	6
13:12	6
22:43	101

John

2:23	5
3:16	72
4:46–54	6
4:46	6
5:3–7	6
6:2	5 (2x)
6:14	5
11:1–6	6
11:4	5

Acts

4:7	156
4:9	6
4:33	156
5:1–11	24
5:15	6
5:16	6
6:8	156
9:37	6 (2x)
11:26	96
13:50	48
14:19	48
14:23	16
15:20	54
15:29	54
16:3	75
18:18	63
19:12	6 (2x)
20:4	145 (2x)
20:17–35	145
20:31–34	145
20:35	6, 145
21:29	145 (3x)
22:4	145
28:9	6 (2x)
28:16	137, 138
28:23	138
28:30	137

Romans

1:1–17	115
1:7	113
1:11	139
1:15	113
1:16	68, 114
1:17	115
1:18—8:39	115
1:18—4:25	115
2:1—3:20	115
2:14–15	123
2:14	75
2:28	116

Scripture Index

3:5	120	8:8	124
3:25	45	8:9–11	126
3:27–31	115	8:11	155
4:1–25	113, 116	8:15	128 (3x), 152
4:3	115	8:18–22	125
4:5	119, 120	8:18	125, 127, 130
4:11	45	8:20	45
4:13–25	118	8:22	125
4:15	38	8:23–25	125
4:16	116 (3x), 118	8:23	125, 127 (2x), 128
4:17	116, 117	8:26–28	130
4:18	116, 118	8:26–27	125, 126 (2x), 127, 130
4:19–21	116 (2x)	8:26	120, 125 (2x), 128, 146, 152
4:19	6, 118, 124, 164	8:27	128 (3x), 130
4:20	117 (2x)	8:28	101, 130
4:21	118	8:37	111, 130
4:23–25	118	9:1—11:36	115
5:1	115	12:1—15:13	114, 115
5:5	118	12:2	134
5:6–8	118, 119 (2x), 146, 152	12:3–13	114
5:6	76, 118, 119, 120, 146 (3x), 153, 157, 164	12:9–13	14 (2x)
5:7	119	13:1–7	114
5:8	119	13:8	131
5:9–11	119	13:9	131
5:10	107	14:1—15:13	114, 130, 134, 136 (2x)
5:20	38	14:1—15:6	24
6:3	107	14:1	25, 114, 131 (2x), 146, 149, 164
6:10	107	14:2	114, 130, 131, 132, 146, 164
6:14	122		
6:15–23	120	14:3	132 (2x)
6:15–18	120	14:5–6	132
6:17	122	14:6	132
6:19–23	120	14:7–8	134
6:19	120 (3x), 146 (2x), 151	14:10	131
7:8	38	14:12	132
7:10	123	14:15	159
7:11	38, 123 (2x)	14:18	134
7:12	51, 123 (2x)	14:19	159
7:14–25	146	14:21	132
7:22	51	14:23	131 (2x)
7:25	123	15:1	2, 114, 131, 133, 145, 146, 149, 164
8:2	122, 123, 124, 125, 126		
8:3–4	122 (2x)	15:2	73, 134
8:3	39, 122 (3x), 123, 124, 146, 152, 157, 164	15:3	134
8:4	124	15:14—16:27	115
8:7	123, 146	15:17–12	135

187

Romans *(continued)*

15:27	152
16:1–23	112
16:3–6	112
16:12	17
16:17–20	115
16:23	63

1 Corinthians

1:4–9	56
1:12	69
1:17	66
1:18—4:21	60
1:18–31	64
1:18–25	60 (2x)
1:18	60, 61, 67
1:19	59 (2x)
1:20–25	59 (2x)
1:20	61, 66
1:21	60, 61
1:22	66
1:23	61 (2x), 66
1:24	60, 61, 63
1:25	59, 60, 61 (3x), 63, 65, 105, 110, 111, 155, 157, 164
1:26–31	59 (2x), 62
1:26	62, 63, 164
1:27–28	63 (2x)
1:27	59 (2x), 63, 72, 81, 105, 109, 120, 155, 161
1:28	63, 64
1:29	64
1:30	60, 63, 64
1:31	62, 63
2:1–5	59 (2x), 64, 89
2:1	66
2:2	65 (2x), 66
2:3–4	89
2:3	59, 65, 66 (2x), 67
2:4	66 (3x), 89, 105
2:5	65, 89
2:8	60
2:16–13	60
3:1	60, 152
3:5	149
3:9–13	149
4:1–21	66
4:1	45, 66
4:5	67
4:6–7	67
4:8–13	67
4:8–9	67
4:8	67
4:9	67 (2x)
4:10–13	67
4:10	67, 68 (2x), 105, 164
4:11–13	68
4:11–12	68
4:11	67
4:12–13	68
4:12	17
4:13	68 (2x)
4:14–15	67
4:21	88
5:1–5	26
5:5	100
5:6–12	26
6:12	159
6:19	26
7:1	22
7:21	62
8:1–13	69, 109
8:1	69
8:4	69
8:7–14	25
8:7–13	70, 71, 76, 81
8:7–12	71
8:7	70, 71 (2x), 72, 74 (2x)
8:8	71
8:9–13	92
8:9	70, 71 (2x), 159
8:10	70, 71, 72 (3x)
8:11–13	133
8:11	70, 72, 73, 161
8:12	70, 71, 73, 74, 159
8:13	70, 77
9:1–8	69
9:9–23	69
9:12	77
9:13	77
9:16	77
9:18	77
9:19–23	75, 77, 134

Reference	Page(s)
9:19	75, 76
9:20–23	75
9:20–22	44
9:20–21	76
9:20	76
9:21	76
9:22	76 (3x), 77, 109, 145
9:23	77 (2x)
9:24–27	69
9:27	77
10:1–13	69
10:14–22	70
10:23—11:1	70, 71
10:24	73
10:25	71
10:27	71
10:28	71
10:29	71
11:2–16	77
11:17–34	77, 78 (2x), 154
11:17–22	77
11:17	78
11:20	78
11:21	78
11:23–26	77
11:23	78
11:26	78
11:27–34	63, 77, 78
11:27	78
11:28–29	80
11:28	78
11:29	78 (2x)
11:30	78, 79, 100, 108, 154
11:31	78, 154
11:32	78 (2x), 79
12:1–31	81
12:1	77, 78
12:4–11	105
12:8–10	160
12:12–13	160
12:13	62
12:14–26	81 (2x)
12:14	81 (2x)
12:22	81 (2x), 109, 145, 160
12:24	81
12:28	160
12:29–30	160
13:1–13	81
13:1	159
13:13	74
14:1–25	81
14:9	160
15:1–58	58
15:1–3	82
15:3–7	82
15:10	17
15:12	82
15:18	79
15:30–32	68
15:35–39	82
15:35	82
15:36–41	82
15:42–49	82
15:42–44	82
15:42–43	128
15:43	82, 108, 120, 153, 164
15:44	83
15:47	83
15:56	38
16:5–9	57
16:8	58
16:16	17
16:18	18

2 Corinthians

Reference	Page(s)
1:1	86
1:9	103 (2x)
1:10	103
1:12	55, 152
1:15–18	55
1:23	57
2:1	104
2:3	57
2:4	45, 56 (2x)
2:5–11	56
2:14—7:4	56
2:17	55
3:1	55, 57, 90
3:4–11	55
4:3	55
4:5	45
4:7–12	84
4:7	52
4:8–11	68
4:10	92, 107 (2x), 110

Scripture Index

2 Corinthians *(continued)*

Reference	Pages
4:11	107
4:14	45
4:16	83
5:11–13	55
5:12	57 (2x)
5:13	55
5:14–15	45
5:14	102
5:15	102
5:16	55, 57
5:18—6:2	65
5:18	107
5:19	107
5:21	107
6:2	55
6:3–10	55
6:3	55
6:4–5	68
6:4	103
6:7	68
6:14—7:1	55, 56
7:8	56
7:15	65
8:16–24	59
9:15	56, 57
10:1—13:13	84
10:1–18	86
10:1	55 (2x), 56, 57, 86, 106
10:2	55, 106 (2x)
10:4	111
10:5	54, 55
10:7	55 (2x)
10:9–11	55
10:9–10	87
10:10	55 (3x), 65, 84 (2x), 88, 91, 104, 164
10:11	88
10:12–18	55, 57
10:13–16	55
10:17	57
11:1—12:13	86
11:1	90
11:4	55, 107
11:5	57, 87
11:6	55, 88, 90
11:7–12	55
11:13	54
11:18–29	57
11:18	55, 57, 93
11:20–21	91
11:20	90, 91
11:21—12:10	90
11:21–29	85
11:21	84, 90 (3x), 91, 93 (2x)
11:22–29	57, 91, 93
11:22–28	93
11:22–23	54
11:22	55, 90, 91
11:23–33	46
11:23–29	68, 91, 93, 95
11:23–28	94
11:23	55, 87, 88
11:26–28	103
11:28	92
11:29	84, 90 (2x), 92, 93
11:30—12:10	84 (2x), 85, 90 (2x), 93
11:30–33	94
11:30	93, 97, 102, 110
11:32–33	93, 94
12:1–13	95
12:1–10	94
12:1–7	90
12:1–4	94, 96, 99
12:1	55, 57, 88, 94, 95
12:2–5	96
12:2	95
12:4	96
12:5–10	96
12:5	84 (2x), 85, 97, 100, 102 (2x), 110, 164
12:6	96 (2x), 97
12:7–10	87, 111, 126, 148, 153
12:7–8	93
12:7	48 (2x), 55, 65, 94 (2x), 98, 153
12:9–10	84, 103
12:9	68, 83, 84, 85 (2x), 93, 96, 97, 98 (2x), 100, 102 (2x), 107, 110, 111, 153, 155, 156, 158, 162, 164
12:10	84 (2x), 85, 88, 93, 97, 102, 110, 153, 164
12:12	57, 88, 105
12:14—13:10	87

Scripture Index

12:14	87	3:23–25	38
12:16–19	55	3:23	34
12:19	108	3:24–25	38
13:1–10	104	3:26—4:7	37
13:1–4	59	3:26	33
13:1–3	88	4:1–20	31
13:1	87	4:1–11	33, 43
13:2	57, 89, 104, 111 (2x)	4:1–7	32, 33 (2x)
13:3–5	56	4:1	33
13:3–4	84	4:2	33
13:3	84, 164	4:3–5	37
13:4	68, 84 (2x), 90, 93, 107, 110, 111 (2x), 155 (2x), 157 (2x), 161, 162, 164	4:3	33 (3x), 34 (3x), 35, 40 (2x)
		4:4	51, 120, 153
13:5–6	59	4:5	41
13:9	67, 84, 101, 108 (2x), 164	4:8–11	32 (2x), 33 (2x)
13:10	57, 87 (2x), 89, 108	4:8	34, 35, 36, 37 (2x)
13:11–14	87	4:9	7, 32, 33 (4x), 34, 35, 36 (3x), 37, 40 (2x), 41, 51, 152
13:13	110		
		4:10	35 (2x), 37
## Galatians		4:11	17, 36
1:1	31	4:12–20	32, 40
1:6—2:21	31	4:12	43, 44
1:6–9	36	4:13–15	44
1:6	31	4:13	7, 32, 40 (2x), 42 (4x), 45, 46, 47, 52, 100 (2x), 153
1:7	31	4:14	43, 49, 52, 99
1:9	38	4:15	49 (2x)
1:10	45	4:17	31
1:11	37	4:19	42
1:14	31	5:1–4	38
1:21	95	5:2–4	39
2:4–5	38	5:2–3	37
2:4	31, 75	5:2	36
2:5	75	5:3	36
2:12	31	5:5	39
2:15–21	38	5:6	37, 39
3:1—5:1	31	5:10	31
3:1–6	34	5:11	37
3:1–5	38	5:12	31
3:3	40	5:13–14	39
3:6–9	39	5:13	74, 158
3:6–8	118	5:14	39
3:10	38	5:16–18	39
3:13	40	5:19–26	39
3:15	120	6:1–10	32
3:19–22	37	6:2	76, 133
3:19	34		

Galatians (continued)

6:7–8	38
6:11–18	32
6:11	49
6:12–17	56
6:12–13	38
6:12	37, 116

Ephesians

2:3	151
5:18	144
6:5	65

Philippians

1:3–11	56
1:7	138
1:8	140
1:12–18	141
1:18–26	141
1:27—2:16	141
2:1–2	158
2:4	73, 142
2:5–11	157
2:12	65
2:16	17
2:19–24	138
2:25–30	138, 139, 141
2:25–26	137
2:25	138
2:26–27	137, 138
2:26	46, 47, 100, 139 (2x), 153
2:27	46, 47, 100, 140 (4x)
2:28	139, 141
2:29–30	141
2:30	138 (2x), 140 (2x)
3:2—4:3	56
4:12	138
4:13	67, 84, 98, 156
4:14	137
4:18	137, 138

Colossians

1:11	156
2:8	35
2:16	132 (2x)
2:20	35
2:21–22	132

1 Thessalonians

1:2—3:13	10
1:2–10	56
1:3	12, 28
1:5	12
1:8	12
1:9–10	9
1:9	28
1:10	23
2:3	12
2:6	12
2:9	23
2:10	12
2:12	12
2:13–16	28
2:14–16	10
2:15	12
2:19	12
3:1–5	28
3:2	28
3:5	28
3:6	10, 139
3:10	28
3:13	23, 28
4:1—5:22	10, 21, 26
4:1–12	13
4:1–8	10
4:1	10, 15, 20, 21
4:3–8	10, 25 (3x)
4:5–8	10
4:5	25
4:6–8	26
4:6	25
4:8	25
4:9—5:11	22, 27 (2x)
4:9–12	10, 17, 22 (2x), 25, 27 (2x), 30
4:9–10	15, 22, 23
4:9	22
4:10–12	23
4:10	21, 22
4:11–12	10, 15
4:11	12

Scripture Index

4:12	22
4:13—5:11	26
4:13–18	9, 10, 15, 22, 23, 24, 25, 26, 27 (2x), 30
4:13	21, 22, 23, 28
4:16	12
5:1–11	9, 10, 23, 26 (2x), 27 (2x), 28, 30 (2x)
5:1–3	29
5:1	21, 22, 29
5:3	29
5:4–11	29 (2x)
5:4	29
5:6	29
5:8	12, 28, 29
5:9	29
5:10	29, 30
5:11	21, 30
5:12–22	10, 11 (2x), 12 (4x), 13 (3x), 14 (2x), 15 (3x), 20 (2x)
5:12–15	20
5:12–13	10, 12, 15, 16, 20, 21
5:12	11, 17 (2x), 21 (3x), 24
5:13–22	13
5:14–15	20
5:14	10, 12 (4x), 15 (3x), 17, 18 (2x), 20, 21 (5x), 25, 26, 28, 30, 158
5:16–22	20
5:16–18	11, 12, 19 (2x)
5:16	19
5:18	19
5:19–22	12, 19 (2x)
5:19–20	15
5:23–24	10, 20
5:23	12, 23
5:25–27	10, 20
5:25	21
5:28	10, 20

2 Thessalonians

2:1–2	9
2:5	9
3:1–15	10
3:6–15	23

1 Timothy

1:20	100
3:3	143, 144
3:8	144
5:23	46, 47, 100, 142 (2x), 143, 153
6:6	98

2 Timothy

1:4	139
3:11	49
4:14–18	56
4:14	99 (2x)
4:20	46, 47, 100, 142, 153
4:21	143

Titus

1:6	144
2:3	144

Hebrews

4:15	6 (2x), 93
5:2	6 (2x), 93, 110
5:7	101
7:18	6, 40
7:28	6
9:26	153
11:34	6 (2x)

James

2:12	31
5:14	6

1 Peter

3:1	77
3:7	6
4:4	144

1 John

6:2	5

www.ingramcontent.com/pod-product-compliance
Lightning Source LLC
Chambersburg PA
CBHW070326230426
43663CB00011B/2234

www.ingramcontent.com/pod-product-compliance
Lightning Source LLC
Chambersburg PA
CBHW022007220426
43663CB00007B/998